INTO UEA/CITY London

U14109

Franz Eder | Gerhard Mangott | Martin Senn (eds.)

Transatlantic Discord

Combating Terrorism and Proliferation,
Preventing Crises

Foto: Amerikanische Flagge
Quelle: istockphoto.com

Die Deutsche Bibliothek verzeichnet diese Publikation in
der Deutschen Nationalbibliografie; detaillierte bibliografische
Daten sind im Internet über http://dnb.ddb.de abrufbar.

Die Deutsche Bibliothek lists this publication in the Deutsche
Nationalbibliografie; detailed bibliographic data is available
on the Internet at http://dnb.ddb.de.

ISBN 978-3-8329-2729-5

1. Auflage 2007
© Nomos Verlagsgesellschaft, Baden-Baden 2007. Printed in Germany. Alle
Rechte, auch die des Nachdrucks von Auszügen, der fotomechanischen Wiedergabe und der Übersetzung, vorbehalten. Gedruckt auf alterungsbeständigem
Papier.

This work is subject to copyright. All rights are reserved, whether the whole or
part of the material is concerned, specifically those of translation, reprinting,
re-use of illustrations, broadcasting, reproduction by photocopying machine or
similar means, and storage in data banks. Under § 54 of the German Copyright
Law where copies are made for other than private use a fee is payable to »Verwertungsgesellschaft Wort«, Munich.

Contents

Preface 7

FRANZ EDER, GERHARD MANGOTT, AND MARTIN SENN
Understanding Mars and Venus: A Model for Security
Policy Analysis 9

MATTHIAS DEMBINSKI
Transatlantic Cooperation or Discord: The United States,
the European Union and Nuclear Non-Proliferation 31

DEREK D. SMITH
A Vulnerable Superpower: U.S. Strategy Against Weapons
of Mass Destruction in the 21st Century 63

ANTHONY SEABOYER AND OLIVER THRÄNERT
The EU-3 and the Iranian Nuclear Program 95

DAVID BROWN
The EU and Counter-Terrorism: A Reliable Ally in the
'War on Terror'? 121

JEREMY SHAPIRO AND DANIEL BYMAN
Bridging the Transatlantic Counterterrorism Gap 145

DANIEL S. HAMILTON
Tackling Terror: A Transatlantic Agenda 165

FRASER CAMERON
The European Union and Conflict Prevention 187

REINHARDT RUMMEL
The EU's Preference for Prevention – Burden or Boost for
the Transatlantic Security Partnership? 207

ALICE ACKERMANN
The United States' Perspective on Conflict Prevention 237

About the Authors 249

Preface

After fruitful analyses and debates at the International Conference »Transatlantic Discord«, which we organized as the 2005 Annual Meeting of the Austrian Political Science Association in Vienna, we decided to bring together a set of European and US experts on transatlantic security issues in a follow-up anthology. On the basis of the conference design, these experts analyze structural and conceptual strains in US-European relations and address three major sources of transatlantic tensions in the post-Cold War era: the combat against terrorism, efforts in the non-proliferation of weapons of mass destruction and ballistic missiles as well as the prevention and management of crises. The conceptual framework of both conference and anthology was designed by the editors of this book, all of them specialists in the field of Interational Relations (IR) at the University of Innsbruck.

We express our deep gratitude to our colleague Carola Bielfeldt for her support in the course of the project and especially for her critical remarks on our written work. We would also like to thank the authors of this anthology for their contributions. Last but but not least we would like to thank the US Embassy in Vienna and the Austrian Ministry of Foreign Affairs for their kind financial support of this publication project.

This anthology is the final step of the conference project »Transatlantic Discord« and at the same time the first major step of a new project at the Department of Political Science at the University of Innsbruck. This project is called *International Security Research Group* (ISRG). ISRG is a pool of political scientists who cover the field of international security studies in their research and lectures. The close co-operation of these IR experts is intended to strengthen IR research at the University of Innsbruck, to promote Austrian IR research, and to constantly improve ways and means of teaching IR.

February 2007   *Franz Eder, Gerhard Mangott, and Martin Senn*

Understanding Mars and Venus: A Model for Security Policy Analysis

Franz Eder, Gerhard Mangott, Martin Senn[1]

Introduction

In February 2003, U.S. Secretary of State Colin Powell set out to convince the members of the United Nations Security Council that »the United States knows about Iraq's weapons of mass destruction as well as Iraq's involvement in terrorism«[2]. Against this background, Powell fiercely argued for eventually taking action against the regime of Saddam Hussein. A few days later, U.S. Secretary of Defense Donald Rumsfeld made the same case at the occasion of the Munich Conference on Security Policy:

> It is difficult to believe there could still be any question in the minds of reasonable people open to the facts before them. The threat is there to see for those who will see it. And if the worst were to happen - and we had done nothing to stop it - not one of us here today could honestly say that it was a surprise. It will not be a surprise. We are on notice. Each of our nations. Each of us individually. The only question remaining is: what will we do about it?[3]

On the same day, Germany's Minister of Foreign Affairs Joschka Fischer replied with the words: »Excuse me, I am not convinced.«[4] This rejection of U.S. threat perception and the determination to use force against Iraq expressed the deep skepticism which was shared by a number of European political elites and the majority of European populations.

This brief example illustrates that the transatlantic relationship, which had been held together by the Soviet threat for almost five decades, is char-

---

1 The authors would like to thank Carola Bielfeldt for her valuable support and her constructive criticism of the model.
2 Colin L. Powell. »U.S. Secretary of State Colin Powell Addresses the U.N. Security Council.« United Nations Security Council. February 5, 2003. http://www.whitehouse.gov/news/releases/2003/02/20030205-1.html (accessed December 16, 2006).
3 Donald H. Rumsfeld. »The Global Fight against Terrorism: Status and Perspectives.« Munich Conference on Security Policy. February 8, 2003. http://www.securityconference.de/konferenzen/rede.php?menu_2003=&menu_konferenzen=&menu_2005=&sprache=en&id=102&. (accessed December 16, 2006).
4 Fischer quoted in Petra Spoerle-Strohmenger. »Struggling hard for solutions to the conflict in Iraq.« *39th Munich Conference on Security Policy*, December 16, 2006, 2003. http://www.securityconference.de/konferenzen/2003/index.php?menu_2004=&dir=2005%2FSunday&menu_konferenzen=&menu_2005=&sprache=en&.

acterized by dissent rather than harmony. The actual rift between the USA and Europe was repeatedly highlighted by controversies which evolved around incidents like the unilateral US withdrawal from the ABM Treaty, the decision to deploy a ballistic missile defense system as well as the refusal to ratify the Kyoto Protocol and the Comprehensive Test Ban Treaty. Tensions eventually reached a climax in the above mentioned opposition of a number of European elites to join forces with the coalition of the willing against Saddam Hussein and Donald Rumsfeld's coining of the division between old and new Europe. The degree of disagreement between Washington and Brussels has led Robert Kagan to express their different attitudes as well as the overall politico-strategic distance with the metaphor of Mars and Venus.[5]

Overall, the field of security and defense policy is a predominant, if not the main source of severe and recurring disputes in transatlantic relations. Although the two recent National Security Strategies of the United States (2002 and 2006) and the European Security Strategy (2003) share some common ground regarding the identification of terrorism, the proliferation of weapons of mass destruction and regional destabilization as main threats to their security, there are however profound disagreements about how to avert and combat these threats. Cleavages include the legitimacy of unilateral actions or ad-hoc coalitions versus multilateral actions under the authority of the Security Council, or preventive versus pre-emptive[6] use of force.

This introductory paper establishes a theoretical framework in regard to the perception of threats and the development of countermeasures. It is the aim of the paper to elaborate on two questions: (1) Why do actors – in this particular case the USA and a number of European states – perceive threats differently? (2) Why do actors react differently to perceived threats? Within our framework we distinguish between *risks* and *threats*. The former is defined as a perceived potential constraint in an actor's ability to satisfy its interests, whereas the latter is defined as a perceived manifest constraint.

The framework is developed and tested in two steps. First, we analyze how states perceive and react to risks/threats. In order to do so, we introduce a security policy model and then focus on the process of risk/threat perception. Against this background, we then focus on how states react to these risks/threats. In a second step, we use the model to explain transatlantic discord in regard to the proliferation of weapons of mass destruction (WMD) and their means of delivery.

---

5 See Robert Kagan, *Of Paradise and Power: America and Europe in the New World Order* (New York: Knopf, 2003).
6 The usage of the terms prevention and pre-emption in this paper follows Lawrence Freedman, »Prevention, not Preemption,« *The Washington Quarterly* 26, no. 2 (2003).

How States Perceive Risks/Threats

Introducing the Security Policy Model

The security policy model which we develop in the course of the following pages is neither intended to grasp systemic causes and effects, nor is it designed to analyze the impact of intra-actor processes of preference formation[7] on risk/threat perception and reaction. It rather assumes a (non-)state actor which is characterized by *identities, interests, capabilities,* and *knowledge*. Moreover, the actor employs *strategies* and *tactics*, which in turn have to fulfill the criterion of *sustainability*, to satisfy its interests. Obviously, these elements are subject to constant interaction and change, but for analytical purposes we treat them as given at a certain point of time.

An actor's identity basically means 'who the actor is'. In the framework of this analysis we focus on two types of identities: an actor's *corporate identity* and its *type identities*.[8] According to Alexander Wendt, an actor's corporate identity includes its material shape as well as »a consciousness and memory of Self as a separate locus of thought and activity.«[9] Consequently, an actor can only have a single corporate identity (e.g. as a human being, a state, or a non-state actor). A type identity (e.g. democracy, autocracy) refers to certain characteristics (such as free elections) which are shared among actors.[10] In contrast to its corporate identity, actors can have multiple type identities (e.g. democracy and industrialized state)

An actor's interests are a function of its identities, or as Wendt puts it, »[i]nterests presuppose identities because an actor cannot know what it wants until it knows who it is«[11]. It is necessary to distinguish between *constant* and *changing* interests of actors. Constant interests, or what Wendt refers to as »national interests«[12] in the case of states, derive from a corporate identity and are therefore not subject to change. The most fundamental constant interest is 'survival', which was already mentioned by Kenneth Waltz as the precondition for any other interest of a state.[13] In addition to this fun-

---

7 See, for example, Andrew Moravcsik, »Taking Preferences Seriously: A Liberal Theory of International Politics,« *International Organization* 51, no. 5 (1997).
8 Wendt also discusses role identities and collective identities, which will not be considered in the course of this paper. See Alexander Wendt, *Social Theory of International Politics* (Cambridge: Cambridge University Press, 1999), 224-231.
9 See Wendt, *Social Theory of International Politics,* 225.
10 See James D. Fearon. »What is Identity (As We Now Use the Word).« Stanford, CA. (1999). http://www.stanford.edu/~jfearon/papers/iden1v2.pdf (accessed December 16, 2006), 17.
11 Wendt, *Social Theory of International Politics,* 231.
12 See Wendt, *Social Theory of International Politics,* 233-238.
13 See Kenneth N. Waltz, *Theory of International Politics* (Boston, Mass, et al.: McGraw-Hill, 1979), 91-92.

damental interest, we propose 'territorial integrity', 'political independence', and 'economic well-being' as further constant interests, or preconditions for meeting the interest of survival. While constant interests are unchangeably given as soon as an actor exists or pre-social, changing interests are social in the sense that they *only* derive from interaction within actors (e.g. different parties, trade unions, etc.) and between actors and are therefore in a state of flux. Finally, it is important to mention that both constant and changing interests do not only characterize states but also non-state actors.

An actor's capabilities can be divided into *input* and *output capabilities*. Input capabilities are an actor's potential to gain knowledge about other actors and the environment (e.g. regional or international system) by means of observation, intelligence, or sharing information with other actors. *Knowledge*, which is gathered by the use of input capabilities, can be defined as an actor's information about the external world. The quantity and quality of an actor's knowledge is influenced by its input capabilities, identities, and interest. Output capabilities are an actor's potential to affect other actors and its environment. These capabilities include military and civilian means, diplomacy, economic power as well as soft power defined as »cultural and ideological appeal.«[14]

Strategies are ways or an actor's plan of how to satisfy an interest. *Tactics* are means of pursuing a strategy. A tactic may have a *direct* or *indirect* function in regard to the strategy it is associated with. A direct tactic clearly follows and promotes the ways described by the strategy. An indirect tactic may *seem* to have no connection with a strategy or may even seem to be counter-productive, but after all it is a means of promoting a strategy through veiling or deceiving.

Strategies and tactics have to meet the criterion of *sustainability*. Sustainability means an actor's ability to initiate and keep up a strategy and its associated tactics. This ability is determined by three variables: *compatibility*, *cost-benefit-ratio*, and *legitimacy*. In deciding on a strategy and its associated tactics, an actor has to ensure that it does not impede the actor's ability to satisfy its (other) interests, that it is compatible with other strategies and tactics.[15] Furthermore, strategies and tactics have to follow a cost-benefit ratio, in the sense that the cost of implementing a strategy must not exceed the benefit. Last but not least, an actor also has to consider the internal and external legitimacy of its strategies and tactics. For example, a

---

14 Joseph S. Nye, *The Paradox of American Power: Why the World's Only Superpower Can't Go It Alone* (Oxford; New York: Oxford University Press, 2002), xi.
15 This compatibility has an internal and external dimension. In choosing a certain strategy an actor may also have to be aware of other actor's strategies. For example, a member of an alliance has to take into account the strategies of the alliance and its members when deciding on a strategy.

state actor with a type identity 'democracy' has to ensure that its behavior is supported by a majority of its population. Moreover, any actor has to ensure that its behavior is accepted by other actors and compatible with laws and norms governing the system. Since strategies and tactics of an actor are not always perceived as being legitimate by other actors or (in the case of states actors) by its own population, an actor may employ an indirect tactic of veiling or deceiving in order to create legitimacy.

Figure 1 The Security Policy Model

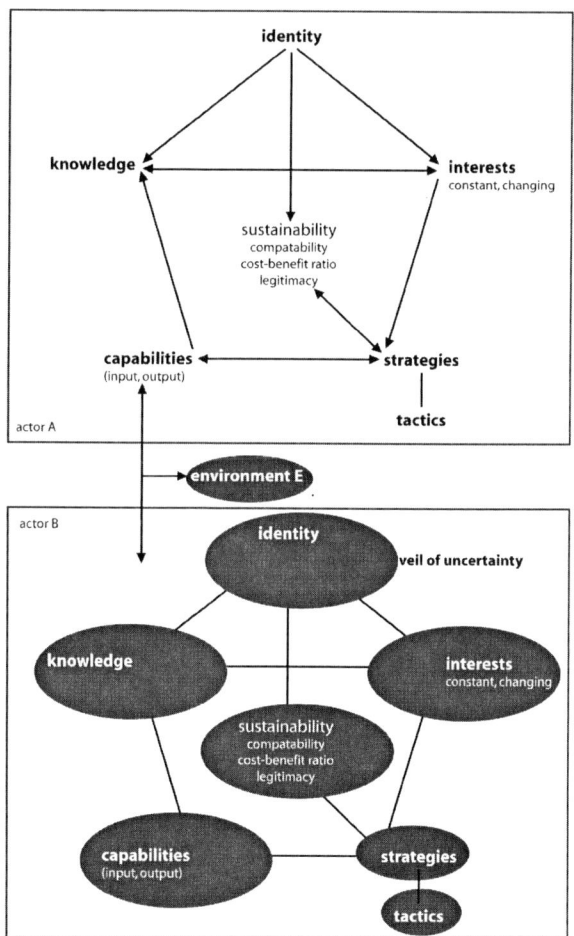

Own illustration

In this context, the »rogue state« concept may serve as an example. Arguing from a liberal perspective[16], Robert Litwak points out that the U.S. emphasis on rogue states is a means of »mobilizing political support both at home and abroad for tough measures against these states.«[17] The characterization of rogue states as irrational and heavily armed actors is therefore intended to create legitimacy for tactics such as sanctions or armed intervention.

The Process of Risk/Threat Perception

After briefly introducing and defining the model's elements, which are summarized in figure 1, we now proceed to the analysis of how actors perceive risk/threats. As we have already mentioned at the beginning of our paper, both risks and threats are perceived constraints in an actor's ability to satisfy its interests. A 'risk' is a potential, future constraint, whereas a 'threat' is a manifest, current constraint. Risks and threats may be perceived as emerging from other (non-)state actors or developments, which neither have identities nor interest, such as the green house effect. For the purpose of illustrating our model, we assume the perception by an actor A of a threat posed by an actor B.

Actor A perceives actor B by means of its input capabilities and is potentially able to gain knowledge about B's identities, interests, capabilities, strategies and tactics, as well as about B's knowledge and the impact of sustainability on its strategies and tactics. In addition to knowledge about B, actor A also collects information about the *environment*[18]. Environment (E) means both the environment of A and the environment of B, which may but need not be identical[19]. So actor A does not only perceive internal factors (identities, interests, etc.) on actor B's behavior but also external, or (sub-) systemic factors. As we will exemplify later, this distinction between internal elements and external »structures [, which] shape and shove«[20], plays an important role in the process of taking action against perceived threat.

16 For different scholarly perspectives on the rogue states concept see Eric Herring, »Rogue Rage: Can We Prevent Mass Destruction?,« *Journal of Strategic Studies* 23, no. 1 (2000).
17 Robert S. Litwak, *Rogue States and U.S. Foreign Policy: Containment after the Cold War* (Washington, D.C. /Baltimore: Johns Hopkins University Press, 2000), 87.
18 See Robert Jervis, *Perception and Misperception in International Politics* (Princeton, N.J.: Princeton University Press, 1976), 35.
19 For example, actor A, which is within regional system X, collects information about actor B and regional system Y of which B is part of. Nevertheless, both actors may in turn be part of a superordinated system Z (e.g. the international system) about which the actors also gain information.
20 Kenneth N. Waltz, »Structural Realism after the Cold War,« *International Security* 25, no. 1 (2000): 24.

In reality, however, A's knowledge about B is neither quantitatively nor qualitatively a full image of the elements constituting B and the environment E. In order to verbalize this 'complication of A's ability to gain information about B and E', we borrow James Buchanan's terminology of the »veil of uncertainty«[21]. Evan B. Montgomery has recently summarized the impact of this veil of uncertainty by stating that »[o]ne of the most significant problems confronted by states in an anarchic environment is the uncertainty over others' intentions and motives that can lead to counterproductive policies and suboptimal outcomes.«[22] As far as the veil of uncertainty is concerned, it is necessary to emphasize that it is not homogenous but that it rather has a varying degree of transparency. Consequently, there are some elements of B which are clearly visible while others are diffuse, only partially visible or entirely invisible. The reasons for this varying degree of transparency are manifold. First, actor A's input capability might provide insufficient knowledge about B and E. Second, and related to the first factor, the degree of transparency depends on actor B's willingness to be transparent. For example, B may be willing to show its environmental policy strategies more openly to A, whereas it may decide to be highly secretive and to pursue clandestine programs in the field of security and defense policy.[23]

Since the veil of uncertainty prevents actor A from gaining complete knowledge about B and E, A »must employ a rough form of the hypothetico-deductive method to ask himself what constellation of forces, beliefs, and goals could explain [B's] behavior.«[24] So actor A re-constructs the elements constituting B (interests, capabilities, etc.) from the information available. As it is shown in figure 2, A eventually assesses – on the basis of the knowledge he assembled about B – whether B currently affects its interests or whether B will do so in future. In a second step, A estimates whether its current/future capabilities will be sufficient and sustainable for safeguarding its interests. Should A conclude that this is not the case, *then B is seen as constituting a risk (potential constraint) or threat (manifest constraint)*.

A potential or manifest constraint in the ability to satisfy the constant interests 'territorial integrity', 'political independence', and 'economic well-

---

21 James Buchanan quoted in Oran R. Young, »The politics of international regime formation: managing natural resources and the environment,« *International Organization* 43, no. 3 (1989): 361-362.
22 Evan Braden Montgomery, »Breaking Out of the Security Dilemma: Realism, Reassurance, and the Problem of Uncertainty,« *International Security* 31, no. 2 (2006): 183.
23 An actor may as well lift the veil of uncertainty as a deliberate act or tactic to assure others of its non-revisionist nature. See Montgomery, »Breaking Out of the Security Dilemma.«
24 Jervis, *Perception and Misperception in International Politics*, 33.

being' can be defined as a 'vital' risk/threat. Vital risks/threats may in turn develop into an 'existential' threat (constraining the actor's ability to survive) depending on their vehemence and duration. So, for example, an attack on an actor's territory may pose a vital threat (constraining its ability to satisfy the constant interest of territorial integrity) but not necessarily an existential threat, since the opponent may only occupy a small piece of territory or may do harm by means of air strikes. But of course the distinction between vital and existential threat is fluent and a matter of perception. For example, North Korea would most likely interpret an air strike against its nuclear capabilities as a first sign of a regime change by force, thus as an existential threat. Overall, it can be argued that there is a tendency – especially in highly competitive systems – to interpret vital risks/threats as existential threats.

Figure 2 *Steps of Risk/Threat Assessment*

Perception	Assessment Interests	
hypothetico-deductive assembling of knowledge about B by A	Does/will B affect A's interests?	**No** threat/risk
		Yes ↓

Assessment Capability	
Does/will A have *sufficient* and *sustainable* capabilities for safeguarding its interests?	**Yes** = no threat/risk
	No = threat/risk
	B is a potential or manifest constraint in A's ability to satisfy a single or multiple interests.

Own illustration

The description of *how* actors perceive risks/threats has already delivered implicit answers to the first central question of this paper, namely *why* actors perceive threats differently. Since actors may have different identities and different interests, different input capabilities and different assessments of the ratio regarding internal and external stimuli of other actors' behaviour, as well as different hypotheses about other actors' interests and strategies, their perception of risks/threats are also likely to be different.

Returning to the assumption that actor A perceives actor B as a threat, it is important to mention that the perception of a threat does not automatically trigger a countering reaction by A. But for the purpose of our analysis we assume that actor A reacts to the threat it perceives as emerging from actor B.

The Process of Reaction to Perceived Risks/Threats

As actor A perceives itself as confronted with a risk/threat[25] by B, it will choose or develop a strategy to avert this risk/threat. The first decision actor A has to make is whether to act on actor B and/or environment E in order to engage the risk/threat. As it was discussed in the previous chapter, this decision depends on the perceived ratio between internal and external factors determining the behavior of actor B.

The strategy of actor A is determined by its current output capabilities and by the strategy's sustainability. Taking these two determinants, it is possible to distinguish between three scenarios, which are illustrated in table 1. The first scenario is that actor A possesses sufficient output capabilities and that the use of these capabilities is assumed to be sustainable. Consequently, actor A makes use (direct tactic) of its capabilities to avert the threat posed by B or E. The second scenario is that actor A does not have sufficient output capabilities. In this case, it will be the direct tactic of A to increase its respective capabilities, or the actor may decide to choose a different tactic, e.g. using other capabilities. Assuming that A was able to increase its capabilities or has already had sufficient capabilities, a third scenario is that actor A has the capabilities but lacks sustainability. At this point, A may decide to abandon the un-sustainable strategy in favor of a new strategy, or he may employ an indirect tactic to deceive its strategy or to ensure sustainability.

The tactics of A may be directed against all elements constituting B. For instance, actor A may decide to terminate the existence (corporate identity) of actor B by means of military intervention. Actor A may also aim at B's interests and capabilities by assuring B of its peaceful intentions or by ridding B of his capabilities (preventive or pre-emptive measures). Actor A may also affect the sustainability of B's strategies by undermining their popular support (e.g. by making use of propaganda campaigns) or by stirring international resistance. Finally, it is also possible for A to block B's strategies and tactics (e.g. by deploying missile defenses to make B's offensive capabilities useless). But the tactics of A may as well be directed primarily against E (or against E and B), depending of A's assessment of the impact of E (external factors) on B. Should A assess that B's behavior is pri-

---

25 The process we describe here is not limited to reactions to perceived threats, since an actor may as well choose strategies and tactics without being confronted with a triggering threat.

marily determined by E, A may attempt to influence E in order to change the behavior of B. Overall, the reaction of an actor depends on:
- its assessment of the threat
- its current capabilities
- its assessment whether a strategy and its associated tactics are sustainable.

As far as the question why actors react differently is concerned, we therefore emphasize that difference in these three factors result in different reactions.

Table 1   Determinants of Strategies and Tactics

Capability	Sustainability	Consequence
+	+	direct tactic (use capability)
-	+	direct tactic (increase capability) or choose different tactic
+	-	indirect tactic (create sustainability)

Testing the Model

In order to test the security policy model, we now apply it on transatlantic perspectives with regard to the proliferation of WMD and ballistic missiles (BM). The model's application is done in two steps: First, we utilize the model to explain *differences in threat perceptions* between the United States and Europe. We then focus on *differences in threat responses*.

Different Perceptions of the WMD Threat

Despite mutual change of course and transatlantic co-operation in the case of the Iranian nuclear program[26], the United States and Europe still have fundamentally different perceptions of risk/threat. For the US the crucial issue is first and foremost *who* has, or is supposed to develop a WMD capa-

---

26   See, for example, Oliver Thränert, »Das große internationale Iran-Puzzle: Teherans Atomprogramm auf der diplomatischen Weltbühne,« *Internationale Politik* 61, no. 8 (2006).

bility.[27] The political nature of the state is the key variable, less so the capabilities themselves. Thus the *type identity* of other actors is the basis of US threat perception. Based on the alleged non-transparent nature of hostile autocratic regimes, or rogue/outlaw regimes as they are referred to in U.S. political rhetoric, the possession of nuclear weapons – even of civilian nuclear programs – creates an incalculable and therefore unbearable risk. To put it in other terms, in case of autocratic regimes, the veil of uncertainty is far more dense than in democracies[28]. So – as it is formulated in the theory of democratic peace – internal characteristics are used as a basis for evaluation of external behavior. An actor's type identity is taken as a basis for assumptions about its interests, strategies, and tactics.

In the case of hostile autocratic regimes the US holds worst-case assessments regarding the interests and both strategies and tactics: these regimes are expected to wage regional aggression (such as Iran supporting Shiite sectarian killings of Sunnis in Iraq, the Lebanon by undermining the elected Siniora government via the Shiite Hezbollah or with financial and military support of Hamas in the Palestinian territory) and long for regional hegemony (like Iran in the region of the Persian Gulf). In addition to regional destabilization rogue regimes are perceived as acquiring a blackmailing capability vis-à-vis the United States and/or its allies. This capability would limit US freedom of action by threatening to unleash armed aggression with unacceptable human costs and even direct attack against United States. In addition to being aggressive and revisionist, rogue regimes are perceived as being irrational. This assumption is both the result of the adversaries' type identity and US knowledge of previous behavior of these regimes (e.g. Iraq's deployment of chemical agents and its invasion of Kuwait or the hostage crisis in Iran)[29]. Based on these variables the US is holding the view

---

27 See Harald Müller, »Nukleare Krisen und transatlantischer Dissens: Amerikanische und europäische Antworten auf aktuelle Probleme der Weiterverbreitung von Kernwaffen,« *HSFK Report*, no. 9/2003: 29.
28 Scott McClellan illustrated this point in a press briefing by stating that the United States is »dealing with outlaw regimes and closed, secretive societies. These are outlaw regimes that go to great lengths to conceal their conduct to deceive and to deny and to hide. And that's why it's important that we make sure that we're doing as good a job as possible to gather the intelligence and be able to confront these threats.« Scott McClellan. »Press Briefing by Scott McClellan.« Washington, D.C. February 2, 2004. http://www.whitehouse.gov/news/releases/2004/02/20040202-9.html (accessed January 20, 2006).
29 For a critical assessment of respective assumptions about Iran see Ted Galen Carpenter, »Iran's Nuclear Program: America's Policy Options,« *CATO Policy Analysis*, no. 578 (2006): 10-12. http://www.cato.org/pub_display.php?pub_id=6690 (accessed December 22, 2006). Likewise, Cha and Kang emphasize that the North Korea is »neither irrational nor undeterrable.« (Victor D. Cha and David C. Kang, *Nuclear North Korea: A Debate on Engagement Strategies* (New York: Columbia University Press, 2003), 4.).

that concepts such as containment or deterrence will not work. Given the incalculable and irrational behavior of rogue adversaries, the US under the George W. Bush administration considers regime change as the ultimate guarantee for security. Eliminating a rogue regime's capabilities is considered insufficient as the risk of rearmament is considered high. Regime change is therefore the only reasonable option left.

The assessment that rogue regimes could pose a serious danger is not unique to the current US administration, but has been a continuous issue of post-Cold War US foreign policy. However, the assessment of the rogue states' capabilities and intentions was less alarming. Based on the assumption that the risk would still require some time to materialize into a threat, the Clinton administration considered medium- and long-term engagement and containment as reasonable policies to contain and decrease the threat potential and to eventually transform the rogue regimes.[30] Thus, the Clinton administration considered long-term evolutionary regime change as best case scenario for threat annulment, but the means employed to achieve this goal were different.

In contrast to the Clinton administration, the George W. Bush administration considers the risk emerging from rogue states to be imminent, thus to be on the brink of materializing into a threat. The respective policies are thus developed against the background of a sense of urgency. This shift is due to both endogenous and exogenous causes. The central endogenous factor is the neo-conservative view on rogue states, which almost entirely focuses on the type identity of these states and is based on a firm conviction that rogue regimes are unchangeably internal and external evildoers[31] which, »if they can get their hands on a weapon, ...will show no hesitation about using it against the United States of America and its cities.«[32] This

---

30 In the case of North Korea, for example, the engagement policy was to some extent based on the widespread assumption that the Stalinist regime was on the brink of collapsing. This policy of engagement and containment was outlined by Anthony Lake in his Foreign Affairs article Confronting Backlash states: »As the sole superpower, the United States has a special responsibility for developing a strategy to neutralize, contain and, through selective pressure, perhaps eventually transform these backlash states into constructive members of the international community.« Anthony Lake, »Confronting Backlash States,« *Foreign Affairs* 73, no. 2 (1994): 46.

31 For example, Condoleezza Rice argues that »[w]e must recognize that truly evil regimes will never be transformed. And we must recognize that such regimes must be confronted, not coddled.« Condoleezza Rice. »Remarks by National Security Advisor Condoleezza Rice on Terrorism and Foreign Policy.« Paul H. Nitze School of Advanced International Studies, Washington, D.C. April 29, 2002. http://www.whitehouse.gov/news/releases/2002/04/20020429-9.html. (accessed January 20, 2007).

32 Ari Fleischer. »Press Briefing by Ari Fleischer.« Washington , D.C. October 12, 2001. http://www.whitehouse.gov/news/releases/2002/04/20020429-9.html. (accessed January 20, 2007).

endogenous factor was further aggravated by an exogenous factor, namely the attacks of 9/11. The terrorist attacks were seen as evidence of the vicious intentions and determination of America's enemies. Since then US security policy is driven by the assumption of a triad of threats: terrorism, hostile autocracies, and WMD.[33] This triad was illustrated in a speech by then National Security Adviser Condoleezza Rice in 2002:

> A ... truth that September 11th underscored was the need to deny terrorists and hostile states the opportunity to acquire weapons of mass destruction. The world's most dangerous people simply cannot be permitted to obtain the world's most dangerous weapons. And it is a stubborn and extremely troubling fact that the list of states that sponsor terror and the lists of states that are seeking to acquire weapons of mass destruction overlap substantially.[34]

So 9/11 resulted in an increased sense of asymmetric vulnerability and contributed to the perception of an immediate, direct and catastrophic risk or even threat. The very fact that continental US territory had been attacked for the very first time caused an immense shock and, in the view of both policymakers and the general public the US, was pushed into an existential struggle.[35] With no time resources left for engagement more imminent and radical actions are considered necessary with regime change being the most important of all.

Summarizing the U.S. position we want to point out that the assessment of rogue state's interests, strategies, tactics and capabilities is primarily based on the perception of the actor's type identity. Regime character is the primary variable defining the US risk/threat assessment.

As far as the European risk/threat assessment is concerned, James Thomson argues that »[f]or the United States, the vector of a possible existential threat has shifted from the USSR to terrorism, the Middle East and Northeast Asia. For Europe, the existential threat has simply disappeared.«[36] We argue that this finding can be explained by the minor importance of other actors' type identity for European threat assessment. Moreover, as Harald Müller points out in the case of Iran, Europeans tend to view autocratic regimes in a more differentiated way than the US.[37] So from the European

---

33 See also Müller, »Nukleare Krisen und transatlantischer Dissens,« 29.
34 Rice. »Remarks by National Security Advisor Condoleezza Rice on Terrorism and Foreign Policy.«
35 See James Thomson, »US Interests and the Fate of the Alliance,« *Survival* 45, no. 4 (2003-04): 212.
36 Thomson, »US Interests and the Fate of the Alliance,« 218. It has been repeatedly argued by U.S. policymakers that the threat posed by hostile autocracies and terrorist organizations exceeds the Soviet threat in terms of quality despite being considerably smaller in terms of quantity. In contrast to the USSR, these new antagonists only have very small chains of command and are (therefore) less calculable and probably not deterrable.
37 See Müller, »Nukleare Krisen und transatlantischer Dissens,« 25.

point of view, regime type does not per se define the very nature of a states interests and strategies. Since autocratic regimes are not regarded as being embodiments of evil and intrinsically threatening, Europe – similar to the Clinton administration – is able to engage with countries the current US administration prefers to treat as pariahs. In the case of Iran, for example, the EU does not hesitate to have diplomatic and close economic relations with an autocratic regime. In the very centre of European threat assessment are a state's capabilities, and not so much the character of the regime possessing them. As the recent statement of French President Chirac[38] and a leaked internal EU document on Iran[39] indicate, European countries could even accept Iran's possession of nuclear weapons. Thus, co-existence with autocratic regimes is perfectly possible. If at all, Europeans thus hope for gradual long-term regime change by evolution. External intervention aiming at regime change is out of question.[40]

Europe also demonstrates a more complex assessment of a state's interests in acquiring a certain capability. Unlike the US, which basically expects a rogue state to acquire threatening capabilities out of an internal desire (for regional hegemony or even irrational attacks against the USA), Europeans rather consider environmental factors contributing to the quest for WMD capabilities.[41] This means that Europeans consider autocratic regimes as capable of rational assessments, decisions and behavior, reacting to external pressures.

Different Reactions to the Proliferation of WMD

As it was already defined earlier, an actor's reaction to a risk/threat depends on the assessment of the risk/threat, the actor's current capabilities, as well as on an assessment of strategies and tactics in regard to their sustainability. As far as the risk/threat assessment of the USA is concerned, it was argued in the previous section that the US focus on the antagonists' type identity and the deduced interests and strategies make the time window for evolution from 'risk' to 'threat' very small. According to the US perspective, to-

---

38 See Elaine Sciliono, »Chirac's Iran Gaffe Reveals a Strategy: Containment,« *New York Times*, February 3, 2007. http://www.nytimes.com/2007/02/03/world/europe/03france.html?ex=1328158800&en=39d2dd4483f96c3c&ei=5088 (accessed February 22, 2007).
39 SeeDaniel Dombey, »EU report on Iran: details and full text,« *Financial Times*, February 13, 2007. http://www.ft.com/cms/s/9222452a-bb66-11db-afe4-0000779e2340.html (accessed February 22, 2007).
40 See Müller, »Nukleare Krisen und transatlantischer Dissens,« 29.
41 See Nicole Gnesotto, »EU, US: visions of the world, visions of the other.,« in *Shift or Rift. Assessing US-EU relations after Iraq*, ed. Gustav Lindstrom, *Transatlantic Book* (Paris: European Union Institute for Strategic Studies, 2003), 25.

day's triad of risks (terrorism, autocracies, WMD) could – with little or no warning – turn into a manifest constraint of the USA's vital interests and even develop into an existential threat. Given this expectation that the risks could suddenly turn into a threat, the George W. Bush administration has primarily focused on *two strategies*: (1) immunizing US and allied territories against attacks with WMD and BM, as well as (2) neutralizing the threat by means of externally enforced or supported regime change.

The strategy of immunization US and allied territories against hostile missile attacks is based on the assumption that the Cold War type of deterrence (by retaliation with overwhelming nuclear force) may not work against enemies willing to sacrifice their populations for irrational ambitions. The immunization strategy is to be pursued by the *direct tactic* of deploying »a multilayered [missile defense] umbrella [which] would not only include the North American continent, but also the entire population (or at least major metropolitan areas) in allied territory in Europe and in Asia.«[42] The multilateralization of missile defense, transforming former national missile defense (NMD) into ballistic missile defense (BMD), is intended to preserve US freedom of action by avoiding blackmail with nuclear attacks on allied countries. In addition to conveying the message to hostile countries that these defensive capabilities render WMD and BM capabilities useless, the tactic of deploying BMD systems is compatible with and even necessary for the second strategy of regime change. In the case of regime change by force, BMD offers protection against WMD attacks by a hostile regime in a terminal struggle. As far as the legitimacy of this tactic is concerned, the George W. Bush administration is sticking to the *indirect tactic* of internally and externally enforcing the deployment of BMD by means of the rogue state concept.[43] The unilateral withdrawal from the ABM treaty was a further tactic enabling the deployment of BMD. The benefit of this treaty withdrawal (i.e. the ability to deploy a nation-wide MD system) was considerably higher than the cost, since the Russian Federation (RF) was – despite contrary announcements – neither willing nor capable of escalating

---

42 Bernd W. Kubbig, »Introduction: The Domestic Politics of Missile Defense,« *Contemporary Security Policy* 26, no. 3 (2005): 390.) This multilateralization of ballistic missile defense was also reflected in the renaming of national missile defense (NMD) into ballistic missile defense (BMD).

43 Nevertheless, skepticisms regarding the necessity and technical feasibility remains in the USA and especially in a number of (allied) countries; see Kubbig, »Introduction: The Domestic Politics of Missile Defense,« 391. For an evaluation of US efforts regarding the development and deployment of a ground-based midcourse defense system, which is intended to protect US territory against hostile missiles, see Bernd W. Kubbig, »America: Escaping the Legacy of the ABM Treaty,« *Contemporary Security Policy* 26, no. 3 (2005): 425-428.

a renewed arms race.[44] In order to ensure the legitimacy of this tactic, the Bush administration relied again on the rogue state concept as well as on emphasizing that the new relationship between the USA and the RF would not require a treaty codifying the Cold War relationship between the two countries.

The second strategy of regime change by force is a product of the narrow US focus on the antagonists' type identity, the assumed interests and strategies, the resulting sense of urgency and the capabilities available to the USA. Accordingly, the preferred tactic of the Bush administration is regime change by means of military force. In the case of the 2003 war against Iraq, internal and external legitimacy was to be achieved by the *indirect tactic* of emphasizing the immediate character of the (WMD and terrorist) threat and the impossibility of influencing the heinous Hussein regime, as well as by convincing the United Nations Security Council of Iraq's failure to disarm. Moreover, the administration used intelligence data as an *indirect tactic* to increase the intervention's legitimacy for the intervention. In this context, Paul Pillar argues as follows:

> The Bush administration deviated from the professional standard not only in using policy to drive intelligence, but also in aggressively using intelligence to win public support for its decision to go to war. This meant selectively adducing data -- »cherry-picking« -- rather than using the intelligence community's own analytic judgments. In fact, key portions of the administration's case explicitly rejected those judgments.[45]

As far as the tactic's cost-benefit ratio is concerned, the cost of attacking Iraq as the weakest member of the »axis of evil« should be outweighed by the benefits. The case of counter-proliferation by regime change was intended to send a clear message to other hostile regimes, namely that the USA would not accept the acquisition of WMD and BM and would not hesitate to use force. To the same extent as Iraq had been »the prototype 'rogue state'«[46], it was intended to be a prototype of US counter-proliferation policy and an illustration of US resolve in dealing with hostile, WMD-armed regimes. Moreover, the intervention for reasons of preventing the (re)emergence of an Iraqi WMD threat and to cease Iraq's alleged support of terrorism was a valuable *indirect tactic* concealing the regime change in Iraq as a tactic contributing to the US strategy of securing a long-term presence in

---

44 See Martin Senn, »A Submissive Nuclear Power? Russia and the United States' National Missile Defense System,« in *Russlands Rückkehr. Außenpolitik unter Vladimir Putin*, ed. Gerhard Mangott, et al. (Baden-Baden: Nomos, 2005), 185.
45 Paul R. Pillar, »Intelligence, Policy, and the War in Iraq,« *Foreign Affairs* 85, no. 2 (2006): 19. See also Stephen Zunes, »The United States: Belligerent Hegemon,« in *The Iraq war: Causes and Consequences*, ed. Rick Fawn and Raymond A. Hinnebusch (Boulder, Colo.: Lynne Rienner Publishers, 2006), 30-31.
46 Robert S. Litwak, »The New Calculus of Preemption,« *Survival* 44, no. 4 (2002): 54.

the Gulf region and Iraq's oil reserves[47] as well as improving the security of Israel.

In the case of the two remaining members of the »axis of evil«, the implementation of the strategy of externally enforced regime is constrained by various factors. First, due to the current engagement of the USA in Iraq and Afghanistan, regime change by force would encounter serious problems due to a lack of US military capability. Second, given the US leadership's lack of credibility after the Iraq intervention and the escalating post-intervention violence in Iraq, a large-scale intervention would definitely lack internal and external legitimacy and it would be rather difficult or even impossible for the administration to mobilize sufficient support. Third, a military intervention in Iran and especially in North Korea could lead to high numbers of victims[48], large-scale devastations and destabilizing flows of refugees. So the costs of a forceful regime change in either Iran or North Korea would definitely outweigh any benefits.

As a consequence of these restraints, the George W. Bush administration was forced to consider other tactics. Since it is not possible to overthrow the Iranian and North Korean regimes for the above mentioned reasons, the US administration had to focus on a near-term tactic of countering the regimes nuclear aspirations by means of multilateral diplomacy (US and EU-3 in the case of Iran, six-party-talks in the case of North Korea) while supporting long-term evolutionary regime change.[49]

Due to its type identity focused risk assessment and the derived focus on regime change, the George W. Bush administration also eschews earlier (»Clintonian«) tactics of dealing with hostile regimes and their (suspected) WMD and BM programs. Even though the Bush administration shares the goal of regime change with Clinton's long-term engagement policy, the latter is incompatible with the current administration's strategy of regime change. As exemplified by the 1994 Agreed Framework, hostile regimes exploit engagement as a means of regime stabilization while remaining secretly determined to build WMD capabilities. So from the George W. Bush administration's point of view, engagement is a tactic which is inapplicable due to the immediate risk emerging from rogue regimes.

---

47 See Zunes, »The United States: Belligerent Hegemon,« 29.
48 Paul French cites an estimate that there could be more than 1 million victims in the course of a full-scale war on the Korean peninsula. See Paul French, *North Korea: The Paranoid Peninsula – A Modern History* (London / New York: Zed Books, 2005), 91.
49 For example, in February 2006 Secretary of State Rice asked Congress for funds to finance Farsi radio programs and other measures which are intended to »support the aspirations of the Iranian people for freedom in their own country.« Condoleezza Rice. »Opening Remarks Before the Senate Foreign Relations Committee.« Washington, D.C. February 15, 2006. http://www.state.gov/secretary/rm/2006/61262.htm. (accessed February 6, 2007).

Moreover, the current administration also rejects its predecessors' approach to multilateral arms control and non-proliferation. Like engagement, multilateral non-proliferation is perceived to entail high costs and low (or no) benefit. As far as the benefits are concerned, the focus on the antagonists' type identity again results in deep skepticism regarding the ability to control their WMD ambitions. This skepticism is expressed by neo-conservative masterminds David Frum and Richard Perle:

> All those non-proliferation treaties in which soft-liners put so much faith are based on the assumption that we can trust the world's least trustworthy regime [Iran] to tell us its deepest secrets. Over the past twenty years, the IAEA has been surprised and surprised and surprised again: by India, by Iraq, by Pakistan, and by North Korea.[50]

So while multilateral arms control and non-proliferation is hardly able to achieve the intended benefits of preventing the spread of sensible technologies to rogue regimes, the resulting restraint in US freedom of action is a considerable cost (e.g. in the case of the Comprehensive Test Ban Treaty).

In contrast to the US perception that rogue states possessing WMD and BM are an immediate and growing risk, Europe sees the consequences of the proliferation of WMD and BM technology as a rather distant risk. Consequently, Europeans do not consider themselves as being under intense time pressure to respond to autocratic regimes allocating WMD. Instead of increasing both defense capabilities and consequence management capacity, Europeans prefer to engage in diplomatic non-proliferation measures. At the center stage of this strategy is an incentive-based approach, which aims at the autocratic regime's engagement by offers of a political, economical, technological and security nature. This is not only considered a viable option due to the perceived lack of time pressure but also as a more reasonable and more successful means of containing the threats by states of concern.

In addition to the more relaxed view on risks, the EU's reaction to WMD is also shaped by its lack of capabilities to address the WMD proliferation threat by means of coercion or (military) force. This apparent lack is most likely to persist as there is no public debate promoting a sense of urgency and necessity to enhance Europe's military defense and counter-proliferation capacities. The lack of public awareness is the result of a lack of political leadership and an enlightened threat and security debate within European states. This sensitivity gap with the US, paired with a lack of leadership on behalf of Europe's political elite, results in a lack of legitimacy for a more emboldened European military effort in counter-proliferation. Moreover, the fact that the social security systems in most European states are in dire straits – not at last due to quickly ageing populations – priority budgetary funding for this sector is viewed as essential for social stability.

---

50 David Frum and Richard Norman Perle, *An End to Evil: How to Win the War on Terror* (New York: Random House, 2003), 109.

The Europeans thus tend to abandon the direct tactic of increasing capabilities.

Given the fact that European societies largely do not subscribe to higher military spending it is not surprising that the use of military force lacks substantial legitimacy among the populations. European states are defined by a post-heroic sentiment, which means that military force is not considered a reasonable, effective and preferred means of conflict resolution. This public sentiment translates into strong elite passivity and reluctance to get engaged in war fighting. Chapter VII mandates therefore are considered an explicit precondition for European decision-makers for any military engagement of its own forces. UN legitimacy is considered a sine qua non for any effort to mobilize public support for military action. However, not only have the Europeans not always stuck to this legal precondition – such as in the Kosovo war of 1999 –, but it is in many cases not so much motivated by the desire to strengthen international law but to contain US unilateralism. Anyway, unlike in the case of the USA, legitimacy is not to be created for fixed tactics but a precondition for any military action; furthermore tactics tend to be developed within the framework of international law.

One more reason for European hesitation to wage wars in counter-proliferation efforts is European economic engagement with many of the states of concern. European countries such as France, Germany and Russia had entertained deep economic co-operation with the Iraqi regime before 2003. All of these countries – including Italy – do have substantial economic interests in Iran. Thus, many European countries do not want to risk economic profits for military counter-proliferation as they do not consider WMD proliferation a threat in the first place.

Concluding Remarks

The model for security policy analysis, which we introduced in the course of this chapter, is intended to offer a systematic approach to the question of whether and how states perceive risks/threats and react to these perceived risks/threats. As it was demonstrated by its application to US and European non-proliferation policies, the model therefore also enables systematic explanations of differing perceptions and reactions. We want to emphasize that the security policy model is still at its early stages. As a consequence, we encourage criticism as an input for its further development.

On the following pages of this anthology, the authors analyze US and European perceptions and policies in the field of nuclear non-proliferation, the combat against terrorism and crisis-prevention. As far as the first field is concerned, the article of Matthias Dembinski offers a fundamental analysis of transatlantic non-proliferation issues and addresses the question whether the respective policies are conflictive or complementary. Derek Smith gives an account of US threat perception as well as of US non- and counter-proliferation policies Oliver Thränert and Anthony Seaboyer eventually focus on Iran's nuclear program as a further test for transatlantic co-operation in the field of nuclear non-proliferation.

In the second field, David Brown argues in favor of 'stable and secure' buttresses on both sides of the Atlantic in order to tackle Islamist threats. Focusing on the European part, Brown describes how the EU's 'counter-terrorist framework has developed', which progresses and changes it experienced and what has to be done in the near future to be successful. Jeremy Shapiro and Daniel Byman focus on transatlantic differences in the perception of and the combat against the terrorist threat. Moreover, the two authors also propose ways and means of possible counter-terrorism co-operation between the USA and Europe. Daniel Hamilton outlines the current state of the transatlantic relationship in the field of counter-terrorism and offers an insight into respective tensions as well as fields of transatlantic collaboration.

Concerning the last field, the prevention and management of crises, Fraser Cameron gives an 'overview and assessment' of the EU's conflict prevention activities. He describes the developments Brussels has enforced since 2001, compares the coherence between the EU's conflict prevention tools and other EU policies and discusses the implications of the delayed generation of an EU Foreign Minister on the EU's conflict prevention capacity. Following Cameron, Reinhard Rummel describes EU's crisis management activities as being in its early stages. According to him, Brussels is still in the 'sphere of learning'. Whereas EU's 'preventive efforts' are internationally accepted, the US, according to Rummel, still does not sufficiently recognize these efforts. Alice Ackermann eventually provides the US perspective on conflict/crisis prevention. In doing so, she first discusses the 'emergence of conflict prevention as a new idea in the international system', then explores US engagement in conflict and crisis management and finally advocates for the 'revitalization of the transatlantic discourse on conflict prevention' as a means of improving transatlantic relations overall.

References

Carpenter, Ted Galen. »Iran's Nuclear Program: America's Policy Options.« *CATO Policy Analysis*, no. 578 (2006). http://www.cato.org/pub_display.php?pub_id=6690 (accessed December 22, 2006).

Cha, Victor D., and David C. Kang. *Nuclear North Korea: A Debate on Engagement Strategies*. New York: Columbia University Press, 2003.

Dombey, Daniel. »EU report on Iran: details and full text.« *Financial Times*, February 13, 2007. http://www.ft.com/cms/s/9222452a-bb66-11db-afe4-0000779e2340.html (accessed February 22, 2007).

Fearon, James D. »What is Identity (As We Now Use the Word).« Stanford, CA. (1999). http://www.stanford.edu/~jfearon/papers/iden1v2.pdf (accessed December 16, 2006).

Fleischer, Ari. »Press Briefing by Ari Fleischer.« Washington, D.C. October 12, 2001. http://www.whitehouse.gov/news/releases/2002/04/20020429-9.html. (accessed January 20, 2007).

Freedman, Lawrence. »Prevention, not Preemption.« *The Washington Quarterly* 26, no. 2 (2003): 105-114.

French, Paul. *North Korea: The Paranoid Peninsula – A Modern History*. London / New York: Zed Books, 2005.

Frum, David, and Richard Norman Perle. *An End to Evil: How to Win the War on Terror*. New York: Random House, 2003.

Gnesotto, Nicole. »EU, US: visions of the world, visions of the other.« In *Shift or Rift. Assessing US-EU relations after Iraq*, edited by Gustav Lindstrom. Paris: European Union Institute for Strategic Studies, 2003, 21-42.

Herring, Eric. »Rogue Rage: Can We Prevent Mass Destruction?« *Journal of Strategic Studies* 23, no. 1 (2000): 184-212.

Jervis, Robert. *Perception and Misperception in International Politics*. Princeton, N.J.: Princeton University Press, 1976.

Kagan, Robert. *Of Paradise and Power: America and Europe in the New World Order*. New York: Knopf, 2003.

Kubbig, Bernd W. »America: Escaping the Legacy of the ABM Treaty.« *Contemporary Security Policy* 26, no. 3 (2005): 410-430.

–. »Introduction: The Domestic Politics of Missile Defense.« *Contemporary Security Policy* 26, no. 3 (2005): 385-409.

Lake, Anthony. »Confronting Backlash States.« *Foreign Affairs* 73, no. 2 (1994): 45-55.

Litwak, Robert S. »The New Calculus of Preemption.« *Survival* 44, no. 4 (2002): 53-80.

–, *Rogue States and U.S. Foreign Policy: Containment after the Cold War*. Washington, D.C. /Baltimore: Johns Hopkins University Press, 2000.

McClellan, Scott. »Press Briefing by Scott McClellan.« Washington, D.C. February 2, 2004. http://www.whitehouse.gov/news/releases/2004/02/20040202-9.html (accessed January 20, 2006).

Montgomery, Evan Braden. »Breaking Out of the Security Dilemma: Realism, Reassurance, and the Problem of Uncertainty.« *International Security* 31, no. 2 (2006): 151-185.

Moravcsik, Andrew. »Taking Preferences Seriously: A Liberal Theory of International Politics.« *International Organization* 51, no. 5 (1997): 513-553.

Müller, Harald. »Nukleare Krisen und transatlantischer Dissens: Amerikanische und europäische Antworten auf aktuelle Probleme der Weiterverbreitung von Kernwaffen.« *HSFK Report*, no. 9/2003.

Nye, Joseph S. *The Paradox of American Power: Why the World's Only Superpower Can't Go It Alone*. Oxford; New York: Oxford University Press, 2002.

Pillar, Paul R. »Intelligence, Policy, and the War in Iraq.« *Foreign Affairs* 85, no. 2 (2006): 15-27.

Powell, Colin L. »U.S. Secretary of State Colin Powell Addresses the U.N. Security Council.« United Nations Security Council. February 5, 2003. http://www.whitehouse.gov/news/releases/2003/02/20030205-1.html (accessed December 16, 2006).

Rice, Condoleezza. »Opening Remarks Before the Senate Foreign Relations Committee.« Washington, D.C. February 15, 2006. http://www.state.gov/secretary/rm/2006/61262.htm. (accessed February 6, 2007).

–. »Remarks by National Security Advisor Condoleezza Rice on Terrorism and Foreign Policy.« Paul H. Nitze School of Advanced International Studies, Washington, D.C. April 29, 2002. http://www.whitehouse.gov/news/releases/2002/04/20020429-9.html. (accessed January 20, 2007).

Rumsfeld, Donald H. »The Global Fight against Terrorism: Status and Perspectives.« Munich Conference on Security Policy. February 8, 2003. http://www.securityconference.de/konferenzen/rede.php?menu_2003=&menu_konferenzen=&menu_2005=&sprache=en&id=102&. (accessed December 16, 2006).

Sciliono, Elaine. »Chirac's Iran Gaffe Reveals a Strategy: Containment.« *New York Times*, February 3, 2007. http://www.nytimes.com/2007/02/03/world/europe/03france.html?ex=1328158800&en=39d2dd4483f96c3c&ei=5088 (accessed February 22, 2007).

Senn, Martin. »A Submissive Nuclear Power? Russia and the United States' National Missile Defense System.« In *Russlands Rückkehr. Außenpolitik unter Vladimir Putin*, edited by Gerhard Mangott, Dmitrij Trenin, Martin Senn and Heinz Timmermann. Baden-Baden: Nomos, 2005, 153-202.

Spoerle-Strohmenger, Petra. »Struggling hard for solutions to the conflict in Iraq.« *39th Munich Conference on Security Policy*, December 16, 2006, 2003. http://www.securityconference.de/konferenzen/2003/index.php?menu_2004=&dir=2005%2FSunday&menu_konferenzen=&menu_2005=&sprache=en&.

Thomson, James. »US Interests and the Fate of the Alliance.« *Survival* 45, no. 4 (2003-04): 207.

Thränert, Oliver. »Das große internationale Iran-Puzzle: Teherans Atomprogramm auf der diplomatischen Weltbühne.« *Internationale Politik* 61, no. 8 (2006): 28-35.

Waltz, Kenneth N. »Structural Realism after the Cold War.« *International Security* 25, no. 1 (2000): 5-41.

–. *Theory of International Politics*. Boston, Mass, et al.: McGraw-Hill, 1979.

Wendt, Alexander. *Social Theory of International Politics*. Cambridge: Cambridge University Press, 1999.

Young, Oran R. »The politics of international regime formation: managing natural resources and the environment.« *International Organization* 43, no. 3 (1989): 355-351.

Zunes, Stephen. »The United States: Belligerent Hegemon.« In *The Iraq war: Causes and Consequences*, edited by Rick Fawn and Raymond A. Hinnebusch. Boulder, Colo.: Lynne Rienner Publishers, 2006, 21-36.

Transatlantic Cooperation or Discord: The United States, the European Union and Nuclear Non-Proliferation

Matthias Dembinski

Introduction

Until recently, the United States and its European allies (plus Canada and Western democracies in Eastern Asia) had been pulling together in the fight against proliferation. Both agreed that the prospect of a further spread of nuclear weapons and its delivery vehicles constitutes one of the gravest threats to security in the post Cold War world; and both agreed *grosso modo* on the proper strategy to combat proliferation. This political unity was reflected in common initiatives as well as in common institutions.

With the war against Iraq, this consensus on strategy crumbled. The emerging differences between the United States and the EU were epitomized in two constitutive planning documents and two specific follow-on documents on non-proliferation policy. The new American strategy was laid out in the National Security Strategy of 2002 and in the National Strategy to Combat Weapons of Mass Destruction.[1] The European response came in the following year with the European Security Strategy and the EU Strategy against Proliferation of Weapons of Mass Destruction.[2] Although the transatlantic dispute has cooled down since then and, starting with the second Bush administration, both sides have been striving towards a transatlantic rapprochement, the events of 2003 have set in motion a process of European self-creation in the area of non-proliferation whose consequences will only be felt in the years to come.

---

1 Cf. The National Security Strategy of the United States of America, Washington, September 2002; National Strategy to Combat Weapons of Mass Destruction, Washington, December 2002.
2 Cf. The Council of the European Union, A Secure Europe in a Better World, Euopean Security Strategy, endorsed on 12. December 2003, available at http://www.consilium.europa.eu/uedocs/cmsUpload/78367.pdf. The Council of the European Union, EU Strategy against proliferation of weapons of mass destruction, endorsed on 12 December 2003, available at http://consilium.europa.eu/uedocs/cmsUpload/st15708.en03.pdf.

These developments raise three sets of questions:
- Is the EU establishing itself as a coherent actor in the area of non-proliferation, able to aggregate the interests of its member states efficiently, demand their loyalty and enable them to speak with one voice and to react collectively to outside challenges?
- To what extent will this emerging European policy be distinct and distinguishable from American approaches? And will this policy complement or contravene American non-proliferation efforts?
- Will the non-proliferation regime suffer or benefit from the emergence of a distinct European non-proliferation policy?

I will discuss these questions in three steps. In a first step, I will describe the era of American and European cooperation on non-proliferation prior to the election of George W. Bush. In a second step, I will try to assess the magnitude of the transatlantic fractures of 2002/03 and the scope of differences between the American and European approaches to non-proliferation. Here, I will discuss changes of the American non-proliferation policy since 2001 as well as European responses. Concerning the latter, I will not restrict myself to an analysis of basic documents but will also evaluate European practices. I will show that the scope of commonalities is still rather broad. Nevertheless, some issues like the relationship between nuclear disarmament and non-proliferation are hotly contested. However, I will argue that concerning those issues the EU, too, has difficulties to act together and speak with one voice. Although there are no clearly shaped ideological differences which put America and Europa as a whole apart, I will argue that a distinct European approach to non-proliferation will nevertheless emerge. In a third step, I will try to assess the implications of this emerging European actorness for the transatlantic relationship and the non-proliferation regime.

Transatlantic and European non-proliferation efforts before 2000.

Transatlantic efforts

Rarely has nuclear nonproliferation been a field where the interests of Western states naturally converge. Although all Western states since the 1960s have been agreeing in principle on the aim to prevent the further spread of nuclear weapons, persisting differences on how to achieve this goal have occasionally hampered cooperation. Nevertheless, before 2000 it would have been grossly inaccurate to speak of a constellation of conflicts or disagreements placing the United States against its European allies. Instead, the transatlantic landscape was characterized by shifting coalitions and changing perceptions. Fault lines ran criss-cross over the transatlantic region between nuclear weapon states and non-nuclear weapon states, between nuclear weapon states within the NPT and France which joint the treaty only in 1992, between states with and without a civilian nuclear industry, between members of NATO and neutrals as well as between disarmament-oriented and pro-active states like Ireland and Canada on the one hand and security-oriented states like, for example, the UK on the other hand. Major differences of opinion pertained to the adequate resolution of the twofold discriminatory character of the non-proliferation regime. On the one hand, the NPT discriminates between nuclear weapon states (NWS) and non-nuclear weapon states (NNWS). Although the commitments of NNWS not to acquire nuclear weapons are balanced by Article VI which requires all states to pursue negotiations on effective disarmament, obligations of NWS and NNWS are unevenly distributed. While the provisions of Articles I to III, prohibiting the acquisition of nuclear weapons by NNWS and establishing a control mechanisms, are precise and strict, Article VI is vague and its concrete meaning open to interpretation. On the other hand, the NPT puts different commitments on the civilian nuclear industry within NNWS and NWS. Article IV guarantees the »inalienable right« to use nuclear energy for peaceful purposes, including reprocessing and enrichment, and encourages member states to exchange technology and nuclear materials. However, while the operation of nuclear industry in NWS is not affected by the treaty, industry in NNWS is obliged to accept safeguards which, depending on their intrusiveness, could reduce its competitiveness.

Before the 1990s, differences of opinion focused on the degree of constrains that should be put on the civilian industry in NNWS whereas differences with regard to the proper interpretation of article VI were suppressed by the purported necessity to deploy American nuclear weapons in Western Europe. After 1990, these differences came to the fore. Since then they have been constituting a major point of contention.

These differences notwithstanding, until 2000 the members of the transatlantic community were recognizable as a unified group of states, bound together by common institutions and sufficiently common perceptions. Regarding institutions, the Western Group (Group of Western European States and Others), one of the tree political groupings within the UN system, functioned as the major locus of coordination among the European and North American democracies on issues of non-proliferation. Within this group the US and the European democracies coordinated their positions at the Conference on Disarmament as well as at the UN 1st Committee and the NPT-Review Conferences. In contrast, after 1990, the Eastern Group as well as the Non-Aligned Group suffered as political organisations due to growing internal division. As non-proliferation grew in importance, other Western institutions like the G-7 and NATO, too, began to develop a non-proliferation agenda.

Despite this complex constellation of attitudes and interests, a certain pattern of intra-Western coordination and collaboration was nevertheless discernable. From the 1960s until the end of the1990s, the United States played a leading role in devising, developing and defending the non-proliferation regime. The US convinced - and sometimes even coerced - its European NATO partners to follow the American lead. Wasington persuaded its partners to join the nascent non-proliferation regime and accept increasingly stringent obligations. In the mid-1970s, Henry Kissinger coerced European supplier countries to abstain from selling critical facilities like enrichment and reprocessing technologies. During the end of the 1970s, President Carter tried to persuade its European partners to abandon the separation of Plutonium for civilian purposes.[3] In the early 1990s, Washington finally succeeded in making full-scope safeguards the accepted prerequisite for trade with nuclear goods and materials.

In contrast, some of the leading European countries took a more dismissive and sceptical stance. Before joining the treaty, France denounced the non-proliferation regime as discriminatory while Germany insisted on less intrusive safeguards that focus on material flows instead of installations, uninhibited civilian nuclear cooperation with states outside the treaty and the right to development of a closed fuel cycle. Britain, although always supportive of the non-proliferation provisions of the treaty, argued that the disarmament provisions should, for the foreseeable future, concern only the two large nuclear weapon states.

This pattern of a pro-active and multilaterally oriented United States and of hesitant and at times reluctant European states survived the first half of the 1990s. During this period, the United States initiated a series of disarmament and non-proliferation measures:

- After the end of the East-West conflict, the United States, together with Russia, embarked on a process of negotiated as well as unilateral reductions of nuclear weapons. Treaties providing for the reduction of strategic weapons were signed in 1991 (START I) and in January 1993 (START II). As a result of this and of reciprocal unilateral reductions of tactical nuclear weapons, the number of deployed American nuclear warheads declined from approximately 27.000 at the beginning of the

---

3 *Nye*, Maintaining a Nonproliferation Regime, in: International Organization, 35:1, 1981, p. 15-38. For a European response see *Kaiser*, The Great Nuclear Debate: American-German Disagreements, in: Foreign Policy, No. 30, 1978, p. 83-110; *Lellouche*, France and the International Nuclear Controversy, in: Orbis, 22:4, 1979, p. 951-965.

1990's to 3.600 at the end of the decade.[4] However, the new Nuclear Posture Review of 1994 rejected further disarmament steps beyond the threshold of START-II. It even alluded to possible new roles of nuclear weapons with regard to the deterrence of 'rogue states'.[5]
- Reacting to the looming danger of a disintegrating nuclear infrastructure in the former Soviet Union, the US pushed for the consolidation of the former Soviet nuclear weapons complex in Russia and launched the Nunn-Lugar initiative aimed at securing nuclear warheads and materials.[6]
- At the insistence of Congress, the US stopped nuclear testing in 1992. In 1995, President Clinton initiated a truly comprehensive test ban treaty.[7] However, when Clinton finally submitted the treaty to the Senate for consultation and ratification in September 1999, the mood in Congress had changed considerably. With 52 to 48 votes in favor, the Comprehensive Test-Ban Treaty (CTBT) clearly missed the necessary 2/3 majority for ratification.
- Additionally, the US proposed a Fissile Material Cut-Off Treaty (FMCT). President George Bush had declared an end to the production of plutonium for military purposes in 1988 – US production of highly-enriched uranium (HEU) had seized in 1964 – but had refused to enter into multilateral negotiations. In September 1993, President Clinton proposed a verifiable cut-off treaty to the UN General Assembly.[8] He later specified that existing stocks of civilian PU and HEU as well as fissile material freed by the dismantlement of nuclear weapons would

---

4 *Dembinski*, Mit START zum Ziel der allgemeinen und vollständigen Abrüstung? HSFK-Report 3, 1993.
5 *Kristensen/Handler*, Changing Targets: Nuclear Doctrine from the Cold War to the Third World, Greenpeace Foundation, 1995.
6 *Allison/Carter/Miller/Zelikow*, Cooperative Denuclearization. From Pledges to Deeds, Havard University, 1993.
7 The White House, Office of the Press Secretary: Statement by the President: Comprehensive Test Ban Treaty, Washington, 11.8.1995. Before this announcement, which echoed a similar declaration by the French President Jacques Chirac the day before (see below), the administration pondered the issue it wanted the comprehensive test ban to be indeed comprehensive or allow small nuclear tests of a few kilograms of TNT.
8 USPIT, 99 (29.9.2003), p. 3-9.

be covered by a FMCT and would hence not be available for military purposes.⁹
- The US proposed the introduction of enhanced verification methods and access rights for the IAEA. These initiatives resulted in the IAEA's 93+2 program and the enhanced safeguards system. This voluntary Additional Protocol of 1997 will, if ratified nationally, provide the IAEA inspectors with the authority to inspect declared as well as undeclared nuclear facilities at no or short notice.
- The United States acknowledged the *principles and objectives of disarmament,* adopted at the 1995 review and extension conference, as well as the *thirteen practical steps* towards disarmament, agreed a the 2000 NPT review conference. Both documents contain concrete disarmament measures which the community of states expects the NWS to undertake in the short and medium-term period. In the logic of the non-proliferation regime both documents constitute the central element of a revised bargain by which the NNWS agree to the unlimited extension of the NPT as well as to more restrictive interpretations of Articles III and IV in return for the agreement of the NWS to concrete steps to implement Article VI.

To sum up, although the Clinton administration's approach to nuclear disarmament and nonproliferation did not mark a radical breach with the past, the adoption of new arms control initiatives nevertheless indicated a change in thinking on the relationship between horizontal and vertical proliferation. With the active support for a CTBT and FMCT outlines of a new American non-proliferation approach became visible. This approach would provide new answers to proliferation challenges by combining non-proliferation and disarmament measures. A test-ban and a fissile material cut-off treaty would, on the one hand, hamper further vertical proliferation and, on the other hand, serve as an additional barrier against horizontal proliferation. Moreover, both instruments would bring the group of undeclared nuclear weapons states within the overall realm of the non-proliferation regime. At the end of the 1990s Israel, India, Pakistan and, with some qualifications, North Korea were widely supposed to possess an undeclared nuclear weapons capability. Although a test-ban and a FMCT would not elim-

---

9 Negotiations in the CD began in 1994. However, although the FMCT had been a long-standing demand of the non-aligned states (NAM), negotiations soon encountered what turned out to be insurmountable hurdles. India coupled negotiations of a cut-off with the establishment of an ad hoc committee within the CD on complete nuclear disarmament – a demand that was flatly rejected by the US. As soon as India seemed to show some flexibility after its tests in the spring of 1998, new hurdles emerged in the form of a Chinese demand to establish a committee on the Prevention of Arms Races in Outer Space. Cf. *Müller/Schaper,* US Nuclear Policy after the Cold War, PRIF Reports 69, 2003, p. 30.

inate the fractures within the regime resulting form the existence of undeclared NWS, they could at least be interpreted as first steps towards the much demanded universalization of the treaty. Additionally, an FMCT would contribute to preventing the dissemination of nuclear material to non-state actors. At the same time, these measures would strengthen the legitimacy of the regime and thus prepare the ground for the acceptability of additional safeguard measures as well as restrictions of Article IX pertaining to the withdrawal from the treaty.

Conforming with established patterns at first, the major European states reacted rather reluctantly. The test-moratorium and Clinton's announcement that the US would advance a CTBT took the European nuclear weapon states by surprise. Until the early 1990s, Britain had publicly and repeatedly insisted on the necessity of tests in order to guarantee the safety and reliability of its warheads. After the moratorium had been announced and the American test facilities were no longer available for test explosions, the Thatcher government, being dependent on the Nevada test site, was forced to reverse its policy and declare that Britain's weapons would be safe and reliable without tests. France stubbornly insisted on its right to test and even started new series of underground explosions in the South Pacific right after it had committed itself at the 1995 NPT review and extension conference to the *Principles and Obligations*, including an end to all nuclear tests. Parts of the German government, as well as other non-nuclear Western European states with extensive civilian nuclear industries, expressed reservations concerning the *Additional Safeguards*, complaining that the non-nuclear weapon states had to accept additional burdens while it remained unclear whether and to what extent FMCT would put restrictions on the nuclear industry in NWS.

These attitudes began to change in the second half of the 1990s due to internal adjustments of pivotal European states. By then, Germany had completed its transformation from being the black sheep to playing the role of the white angel of the non-proliferation regime.[10] In Britain, the newly elected Labour-government pushed its ethical foreign policy. Robin Cook, one of the major representatives of this new policy, had roots in the British nuclear disarmament movement. The British Strategic Defense Review, published in 1998, sought to establish a new consensus based on the maintenance of a true minimum deterrence and active promotion of multilateral restraint. At the 2000 NPT review conference, the UK was able to present remarkable progress. Britain had ratified the CTBT in 1998 and had re-

---

10 *Müller/Dembinski/Kelle/Schaper*, From Black Sheep to White Angel? The New German Export Control Policy, PRIF Report 32, 1994.

duced its deterrent to one system (Trident) and a ceiling of 200 operational warheads that had been taken off high alert.[11]

Although France' non-proliferation policy is characterized by continuity, Paris, too, had adjusted its positions in important areas. Having been singled out and heavily criticized for its tests, Paris conducted a U-turn and supported a truly comprehensive CTBT. Like Britain, France had seized the production of fissile material for military purposes and has no intention of reopening the mothballed production facilities at Marcoule and Pierrelatte. Hence, both countries acquired incentives to work for a global cut-off and test-ban treaty. Given these changes in Europe, the second half of the 1990s ushered in a brief period of transatlantic harmony in the area of non-proliferation. Both sides subscribed to the principle of non-proliferation; and both agreed in the desirability and utility of disarmament as a non-proliferation tool. The successful conclusion of the 2000 NPT review conference can be credited to a certain degree to this transatlantic consensus.

Europe's non-proliferation and disarmament diplomacy

European Cooperation in the nuclear field dates back to the early days of the EU. One of the communities established by the Treaty of Rome in 1957 – EURATOM – was tasked with the twofold function of encouraging cooperation in the civilian application of nuclear energy on the one hand and of operating a control and verification system designed to prevent the transfer of fissile material for unauthorized purposes on the other hand.[12] EURATOM and its verification and supply system were basically designed to integrate and, at the same time, control the burgeoning German nuclear industry without jeopardizing the autonomy of the French military nuclear program.

EURATOM regulates both the supply and control of fissile material for the civilian fuel cycles within the EU. Pursuant to Article 86 of the treaty, the EU nominally owns all fissile material that has been produced within its boundaries or has been imported into the European Union. The European Supply Agency (ESA), which is an independent body supervised by the Commission, is tasked with ensuring equal access to nuclear materials for

---

11 *Wisotzki*, Abschreckung ohne Ende? Die ambivalente Nuklearwaffenpolitik Großbritanniens und Frankreichs, HSFK Report 11/2004.
12 The substance of the EURATOM treaty has not been affected by the various treaty revisions. With the fusion of the originally three Commissions, EURATOM has become a department of the Directorate-General of Energy and Transport. Cf. *Schaper*, German Policy Regarding the Possible Elimination of HEU in the Civilian Nuclear Sector, 2006, unpublished manuscript; *Howlett*, EURATOM and Nuclear Safeguards, 1990.

civilian purposes. Chapter VII of the treaty establishes a safeguard system and assigns the responsibility of assuring that nuclear material will not be diverted for undeclared uses to the European Commission. For this purpose, the Commission conducts European-wide material control and accountancy measures.[13]

While EURATOM was designed to prevent proliferation within Western Europe, an EC policy for non-proliferation abroad began to take shape in 1981 with the establishment of a working group on nuclear questions within the framework of the European Political Cooperation (EPC). However, it is revealing that this group was initially set up to deal with the internal repercussions of new external commitments. Member-states had agreed to adhere to the London guidelines (which later became the Nuclear Suppliers Guidelines) and had signed the International Convention for the Physical Protection of Nuclear Materials. The commitments associated with both regimes threatened to create new barriers to the internal market and thus raised complex legal and political issues.

Cooperation in the area of non-proliferation proved difficult due to the above mentioned variety of interests, traditions and viewpoints. Despite its internal differences, the EU was able to score some early successes like a common declaration which linked nuclear supplies to good non-proliferation credentials of the recipient countries.[14] However, politically relevant and visible European actions had to wait until the above mentioned national adjustments were implemented.

New institutions and instruments, too, worked to the advantage of a common approach in the area of non-proliferation. The Maastricht treaty transformed the EC into the EU and created the Common Foreign and Security Policy (CFSP) with new competence and instruments in the form of common positions and joint actions. However, as it turned out in practice, the ambitious goal of a more efficient decision-making system remained elusive. Although the treaty contains provisions for qualified majority voting in the second pillar (Article J.3), member states tacitly agreed to uphold the practice of consensual decisions. Further revisions of the EU treaty in Amsterdam (1997) and Nice (2000) as well as the European Constitution de facto confirm the national veto power in the area of Common Foreign and Security Policy. To the disappointment of supranational actors, the various treaty revisions did not enhance their rather limited role on this policy field. Although competences in the area of non-proliferation cut across pillars,

---

13 European Commission, Directorate-General for Energy and Transport: Europe remains vigilant, Brussels, 2005, available at http://ec.europa.eu/energy/nuclear/safeguards/doc/2006_brochure_nuclear_safeguards_en.pdf.
14 *Müller/van Dassen*, From Cacophony to Joint Action: Successes and Shortcomings of the European Nuclear Non-Proliferation Policy, in: *Holland* (Ed.), Common Foreign and Security Policy. The Record and Reforms, 1997, p. 52-72.

and although the Commission, in addition to its internal non-proliferation competences and competences with regard to export controls, is tasked with the implementation of many of the EU's regional non-proliferation initiatives, its role in preparing policy and in setting the agenda has remained rather limited.[15] The European Parliament is even demoted to an observer, yet a rather articulate one. Non-proliferation is still very much the purview of member states and under the control of the Council. Council working groups sign responsible for the preparation of policy while the Council takes major decisions. The most important institutional innovation occurred when the Amsterdam treaty established the Office of the High Representative. Although the High Representative at the same time serves as Secretary General of the Council Secretariat and is thus directly answerable to the member-states, the holder of the office – Javier Solana – has emerged as the most visible European representative in the area of non-proliferation.

Shortcomings of the institutional reform notwithstanding, nonproliferation became one of the priority areas for CFSP. Prior to the signing of the Maastricht Treaty, the European Council in Rome in 1990 had agreed on a list of possible fields for future common action. This so-called Asolo list mentioned coordination of non-proliferation policy as one of four priorities.[16]

The most important and rather successful initiative during the 1990's was the campaign for the indefinite extension of the NPT at the 1995 Review and Extension conference. At this occasion, the EU not only spoke with one voice but also acted in a coordinated manner. However, in this case success was alleviated by the fact that the US, too, was strongly supportive of an indefinite extension. One year before the start of the conference, the Corfu European Council agreed on a joint action which led to a coordinated series of démarches by the Presidency, the Troika and individual members as well as the formulation of substantial papers for two of the preparatory committees for the extension conference.[17] However, the Joint Action did not cover the review part of the conference and could not prevent EU-member states from breaking ranks and quarrelling publicly over issues like nuclear disarmament and civilian nuclear cooperation.[18]

---

15 *Alvarez-Verdugo*, Mixing Tools Against Prolifertation: The EU's Strategy for Dealing with Weapons of Mass Destruction, in: European Foreign Affairs Review 11, 2006, p. 417-438.
16 European Council, Presidency Conclusion, Rome, 14-15 December 1990.
17 *Müller*, European Nuclear Non-Proliferation after the NPT Extension: Achievements, Shortcomings and Needs, in: *Cornish/van Ham/Krause* (Ed.), Europe and the Challenge of Prolifration (Challiot Papers No. 24), 1996, p. 33-54.
18 Most spectacular, six non-aligned and disarmament-friendly EU-members (Austria, Denmark, Finland, Ireland, the Netherlands and Sweden) followed an established tradition and joint ranks with five non-EU states to form the G-10 (later known as the white angels) to criticize the nuclear weapon states. Cf. *Müller/van Dassen*, p. 66.

After the extension conference, the EU started a couple of diplomatic initiatives in the field of nuclear non-proliferation. Again, its most important undertaking has been the adoption of a common position in the run up to the 2000 NPT Review Conference. The common position envisaged demarches by the EU presidency, the presentation of draft proposals, and statements on behalf of the EU in both the general debate and the three main committees. In this case, the EU tried to avoid the mistakes of the 1995 conference and carefully specified the content of the common position. The position expresses support for the CTBT, an FMCT, further reductions of strategic weapons as well as the continued importance of the ABM treaty.[19]

Other EU initiatives during this period comprise the support of the Korean Peninsula Energy Development Organization (KEDO) with a comparatively small sum of 75 million €, and programs to ensure the safety and security of nuclear materials as well as nuclear know how in the former Soviet Union. Between 1992 and 2001, the Commission and the member states combined spend approximately 550 million € on safety and conversion measures as well as on training programs for scientists formerly employed in the Soviet nuclear weapons complex.

However, other occasions gave testimony to the still limited actorness of the EU in this realm. For example, when India and Pakistan tested nuclear devices in May 1998, the European reaction turned out to be slow and uneven. A Common Position was adopted by the Council only in October. In the meantime, some European countries froze their development aid while others restricted their response to verbal condemnations, arguing that India and Pakistan as non-signatories to the NPT are not legally prevented from acquiring nuclear weapons.[20]

The end of transatlantic cooperation in the area of non-proliferation?

The Bush revolution

As the Bush administration radically altered the United States security policy both as a response to the terrorist attacks and as a consequence of its reservations vis-à-vis international institutions and multilateral arrangements, non-proliferation became a hotly debated and divisive issue within the transatlantic community. Even before September 11, the administration's unilateral inclination and its declared intention to preserve America's military superiority induced it to question negotiated solutions to security

19 *Fisher*, EU Cooperation in Arms Control and Nonproliferation, in: The European Union, Nonproliferation, and Arms Control, Report No. 40, p. 21f.
20 *Portela*, The Role of the EU in the Non-Proliferation of Nuclear Weapons. The Way to Thessaloniki and Beyond, PRIF Report No. 65, 2003, p. 15f.

problems. In simplest terms, some key policymakers doubt that international treaties or institutions like the IAEA will effectively prevent rogue states like North Korea or Iran from acquiring nuclear weapons. According to this view, such institutions constrain »good actors« that are no threats while providing cover to be exploited by »bad actors«.[21] Even if moderate members of the administration continued to value non-proliferation tools like export controls and safeguards, they, too, dismissed the notion of a link between horizontal and vertical proliferation. As a consequence, the administration was heavily inclined to discontinue strategic disarmament negotiations and to withdraw from the ABM-treaty. Likewise, Bush showed no intention whatsoever to spent political capital on the rescue of the stalled negotiations on a CTBT or to compromise with non-aligned states and China in order to disentangle the blockade of the FMCT talks.

After the terrorist attacks, the unilateralist inclinations of the administration interacted with a dramatically reinforced threat perception. Bush's programmatic State of the Union Address set the tone by putting the focus on threats emanating from the combination of 'rogue states', terrorist actors and proliferation of weapons of mass destruction. Following this lead, the National Security Strategy declares that »the overlap between states that sponsor terror and those that pursue WMD compels us to action.« Given this changed threat environment, the administration maintained that the US should no longer solely rely on a reactive posture. »The greater the threat, the greater the risk of inaction – and the more compelling the case for taking anticipatory action to defend ourselves, even if uncertainty remains as to the time and place of the enemy's attack«[22]

The assessment that determined states could evade NPT-safeguards and that WMD in the hand of terrorists pose one of the gravest dangers was neither new nor was it restricted to (neo-) conservative circles in the United States. In fact, a wide chorus of influential voices had been expressing the view that the non-proliferation regime is being challenged by a couple of weaknesses. For example, the Report of the UN High-level Panel on Threats highlighted three scenarios: Firstly, it warned that NNWS parties to the treaty could run clandestine military programs in parallel with their safeguarded programs. Secondly, the panel noted that NNWS parties to the treaty could acquire all the necessary materials and expertise for nuclear weapons within the frame of legitimate civilian use and then withdraw from the treaty at short notice. In this regard, the panel questioned the proliferation resistance of closed fuel cycles and especially of nationally run enrichment and reprocessing programs. Thirdly, the panel warned that private ac-

---

21 *Perkovich*, Transatlantic Cooperation for Nuclear Nonproliferation, in: *Serfaty* (Ed.), Visions of the Atlantic Alliance. The United States, the European Union, and NATO, 2005, p. 193-211 (193).
22 National Security Strategy (see footnote 1), p. 15.

tors could acquire fissile material either with or without the assistance of states or parts of national bureaucracies.[23] The relevance of this scenario was vividly underlined by the revelation that Pakistani scientist, Abdul Qadeer Khan, had set up and administered a clandestine supply network through which enrichment technology had been funneled to Iran, Libya and North Korea.[24]

What distinguished the Bush administration from other governments was its sense of urgency and vulnerability as well as its mistrust of multilateral arrangements and its belief in being able to respond to proliferation challenges alone, if necessary. In fact, American non-proliferation policy has not become less vigorous, but more unilateral and less regime based.[25] Outlines of the new approach became visible with the publication of the Strategy to Combat Weapons of Mass Destruction in December 2002.

This document presented a three-pillared approach to non-proliferation which puts (unilateral) counter-proliferation first, restructured (multilateral) nonproliferation second, and weapons of mass destruction consequence management third.[26] In addition, as the American reaction to India's nuclear program indicates, the administration is renouncing the aspiration to universalize the treaty in favor of a managerial approach to proliferation.

More pronounced than earlier planning papers, the Strategy defines counter-proliferation as a new task for the American military forces. »Counter-proliferation will be fully integrated into the basic doctrine, training and equipment of all forces, in order to ensure that they can sustain operations to decisively defeat WMD-armed adversaries.«[27] In addition to deterrence, the Strategy calls for robust active and passive defenses including the option to preempt the use of weapons of mass destruction.

Concerning non-proliferation diplomacy, the Strategy supports the concept of a FMCT. It announces reinforced efforts to discourage the separation and accumulation of plutonium and the use of highly enriched uranium (HEU) in the civilian industry. Instead, the US will push for more proliferation resistant fuel cycles. Also included under this pillar are denial and disruptive instruments like export controls and sanctions. The Proliferation Security Initiative (PSI), first unveiled by President Bush on 31 May 2003 in Krakow, is one of these disruptive instruments. In essence, the PSI is a

23 See Report of the UN Secretary-General's High-level Panel on Threats, Challenges and Change: A more Secure World. Our Shared Responsibility, New York 2004, para. 108. For a similar assessment see *Perkovich/Mathews/Cirincione/Gottemoeller/Wolfsthal*, Universal Compliance: A Strategy for Nuclear Security, Carnegie Endowment for International Peace 2005, available at www.ProliferationNews.org.
24 *Weiss*, Turning a blind eye again? The Khan Network's History and Lessons for U.S. POlicy, in: Arms Control Today, 35:2, 2005, p. 12-18.
25 *Cirincione*, A New Non-Proliferation Strategy, IAI, 2005, p. 1.
26 National Strategy to Combat Weapons of Mass Destruction, (see footnote 1).
27 ibid, p. 2.

multilateral intelligence-sharing project incorporating coordinated training exercises to improve the chances of interdicting the transfer of weapons of mass destruction to and from states or non-state actors of concern.[28] Originally founded by eleven countries, the legally questionable Initiative has since then been put on a more solid multilateral basis. On April 28th, 2004, the UN Security Council, acting under Chapter VII of the UN Charter, adopted Resolution 1540 which, on the one hand, obliges member states to adopt and enforce effective measures in order to prevent the dissemination of WMD technology and material to non-state actors. On the other hand, the resolution calls upon all states to prevent illicit trafficking in WMD materials.[29]

On 11th February 2004, following up on the proposal to create more proliferation-resistant fuel-cycles, Bush announced that the members of the Nuclear Suppliers Group (NSG) should refuse to transfer reprocessing and enrichment technologies to countries which do not yet possess them. In addition, he proposed that the members of the NSG require the acceptance of the Additional IAEA Verification Protocol by recipient countries as a precondition for the transfer of nuclear material and technology. In return, NSG-members would ensure that states which renounce these sensitive nuclear technologies would have reliable access to fuel and reprocessing services.[30]

These initiatives, however, did not mark a return to multilateral principles. Rather, they are indications of an utilitarian approach to multilateralism. The administration would be willing to work with others on a rule-based approach where such an approach was deemed promising, but would resort to unilateralism whenever necessary. This attitude became apparent in the area of nuclear disarmament. Although the trend of a steady reduction of nuclear weapons continued under the Bush administration, its policy initiatives fell far short if compared with the expectations expressed in the 1995 *Principles and Objectives on Disarmament* and the 2000 *Action Agenda of Thirteen practical steps*.

At the insistence of Russian President Putin and in order to placate Democratic senators, President Bush eventually proposed a semi-formalized nuclear arms reduction mechanism. The Strategic Offensive Reductions Treaty (SORT), signed on 24th May 2002, will bring down deployed strategic weapons to a level of 1.700 – 2.200 warheads within ten years.[31] How-

---

28 *Joseph*, The Proliferation Security Initiative: Can Interdiction Stop Proliferation, in: Arms Control Today, 34:5, 2004, p. 6-13.
29 United Nations, Security Council, Resolution 1540 (2004) adopted by the Security Council at its 4956th meeting, on 28 April 2004.
30 The White House, President Announces New Measures to Counter the Threat of WMD, Washington, February 11, 2004, available at http://www.whitehouse.gov/news/releases/2004/02/print/20040211-4.html.
31 ibid, p. 50f.

ever SORT contains no provisions concerning the access launching vehicles and warheads and no verification measures. It will expire in 2012. The agreement thus allows for maximum freedom of action on both sides.

At the beginning of 2005, the US fielded approximately 5.300 operational nuclear warheads, including 780 non-strategic warheads. Some of these operational warheads were deployed, while others were kept in storage. An additional 5000 warheads have been retained in a 'responsive reserve force' or are in an inactive status, allowing a quick reversal of the disarmament process, if necessary.[32] In June 2004 the Bush administration announced that the nuclear arsenal will be cut in half. At the current termination date of SORT, the number of deployed and deployable American warheads will thus come down to 5000-6000.[33]

Concerning the test-stop, the Bush administration has not made up its mind whether the CTBT would be in America's interest or whether the US would be better off without the treaty and hence should withdraw its signature. The debate within the Administration revolves around three issues: Would the CTBT be verifiable? Will the *Stockpile Stewardship Program* - a compilation of measures to extend the life-span of nuclear weapons - guarantee the safety and reliability of the warheads? Is there or will there be a need for new warheads? And would the development of new warheads require testing? So far, the development of a new generation of low-yield nuclear weapons has not moved beyond the very early stages; and Congress has barred further funds.

Concerning an FMCT, the administration abandoned the notion of verifiability. Following a long internal review, on July 29th, 2004 the US ambassador to the CD, Jackie Sanders, announced that the US continues to support a FMCT, but believes that such a treaty would not be effectively verifiable. An accompanying statement by the Bush administration explained that an effective verification regime would harm national interests of key signatories, citing opposition to provide access to facilities for the production of fuel for naval nuclear reactors.[34] This U-turn is all the more surprising since it contradicts the American standard argument that arms control agreements are desirable only to the extent to which they are verifiable.

Last but not least, the administration has abandoned the goal of achieving universal compliance. As a policy towards India indicates, the Bush administration distinguishes between acceptable and non-acceptable prolifera-

---

32 *Norris/Kristensen*, NRDC Nuclear Notebook, Bulletin of the Atomic Scientists, Jan/Feb. 2005, p. 73-75.
33 *Boese*, Bush Plans to Cut Atomic Arsenal, Arms Control Today, 34:6, July/August 2004, p. 3f.
34 *Boese*, Bush Shifts Fissile Material Ban Policy, Arms Control Today, 34:7, September 2004, p. 20f.

tion. Acceptance of India's nuclear program was at best only partially motivated with a view to bring India in the longer run into the fold of the NPT regime. Instead the guiding aim of this policy is to strengthen India and thus contribute to a balance of power in Asia more to the liking of the United States.

To summarize: American non-proliferation policy under Bush differs in important respects from the policy of his predecessor. Most importantly, American non-proliferation policy has taken a unilateral turn. This turn became most apparent in the rejection of the quid pro quo approach of the late Clinton administration according to which horizontal and vertical non-proliferation would reinforce each other in an auspicious circle.

European responses: The EU as an emerging non-proliferation actor. New initiatives, actors, and procedures.

Although the US policy on Iraq provoked a deep split of Europe, members of the EU were determined to launch a variety of new policies with a view to overcome their internal disagreements and to ensure that such divisions did not happen again. Initiatives in the area of non-proliferation were advantaged by the fact that many European countries, including the UK, followed the American lead not because they shared Bush's unilateral inclinations or his belief in the necessity of a preemptive posture, but because of special relationships or their belief in the indispensability of the American contribution to the European security architecture.

At the informal meeting of EU foreign ministers at Kastellorizo on the island of Rhodes, on 2nd-3rd May 2003, the High Representative Javier Solana was mandated to produce a European strategy concept. On 20th June a first draft was presented to the European Council in Thessaloniki where Solana was commissioned to produce a final version for adoption by the European Council in December of the same year. The paper – »A Secure Europe in a Better World: European Security Strategy« is the first attempt to lay out a European response to global challenges. It identifies threats as well as strategic objectives of the EU and defines policy implications for Europe. Its label as well as its structure identify it as a response to the American National Security Strategy.

Work on the European Security Strategy (ESS) was conducted in parallel with the drafting of the EU Strategy against Proliferation of Weapons of Mass Destruction.[35] Acting on a mandate by the Council, the High Representative, together with the Commission and member states, drew up a set

---

35 The Council of the European Union, EU Strategy against proliferation of weapons of mass destruction (see footnote 2).

of Basic Principles for an EU Strategy against Proliferation of Weapons of Mass Destruction and an accompanying Action Plan.[36] It is reported that Sweden and the UK provided major contributions.[37] On the basis of these documents, the European Council in Brussels (December 2003) adopted the EU Strategy against Proliferation of Weapons of Mass Destruction which integrates both the Basic Principles and the Action Plan. Again, the title and structure of the *European Strategy* indicate that this document has been drafted as a response to the US Strategy.

The ESS and the EU Strategy have been interpreted both as a constructive response and as an alternative to the NSS and the National Strategy.[38] However, given the magnitude of the European disagreements during the Iraq-war, the extent to which both documents differ from their American counterparts is striking. As the Financial Times, noted, this »is the first time the EU has spelt out a systematic alternative to US policy (...)«.[39]

The ESS and the EU Strategy concur with their American counterparts in the definition of threats. The ESS identifies proliferation of weapons of mass destruction as well as the prospect that terrorists will acquire those weapons as »potentially the greatest threat to our security.«[40] However, the European documents present a markedly different approach to non-proliferation. While the ESS recalls in general terms that »the EU is committed to achieving universal adherence to multilateral treaty regimes, as well as to strengthening the treaties«, the EU Strategy is more articulate. Its key statement stresses that »effective multilateralism is the cornerstone of the European strategy for combating proliferation of WMD.« The document expresses member states conviction, »that a multilateralist approach to security, including disarmament and non-proliferation, provides the best way to maintain international order.« To be sure, the strategy mentions coercive measures but stresses the importance of international law and unequivocally determines that »the UN Security Council should play a central role.«

With the adoption of the ESS and the EU Strategy, nonproliferation has been elevated even higher on the priority list of the Common Foreign and Security Policy. The importance attached to this policy field is reflected by the emergence of new actors and institutions. As mentioned above, the High

---

36 Both document are reprinted in: *Missiroli* (Ed.), From Copenhagen to Brussels. European Defence: Core documents, Paris Chaillot Papers No. 67, December 2003, p. 106-118.
37 *Bailes*, The European Security Strategy. An Evolutionary History. SIPRI Policy Paper No. 10, 2005, p. 10.
38 *Müller*, Nukleare Krisen und transatlantischer Dissens. Amerikanische und europäische Antworten auf aktuelle Probleme der Weiterverbreitung von Kernwaffen, HSFK Report 9/2003; *Spear*, The Emergence of a European ‚Strategic Personality', in: Arms Control Today, 33:9, November 2003, p. 13-18.
39 Financial Times, 17. June 2003, p. 3.
40 European Security Strategy (see footnote 2).

Representative and his Policy Unit has shouldered most of the additional workload. In October 2003, Javier Solana appointed Annalisa Giannella his Personal Representative for non-proliferation. Solana and his staff are involved in the preparation of non-proliferation initiatives as well as in the review progress. In addition, Solana and Giannella represent the EU and its non-proliferation policy vis-à-vis third countries. The High Representative, together with the Presidency and the Commission, make up the EU-Troika, where his authority and influence exceeds that of the Commission Representative. Furthermore, Solana became involved in other formats as well, most notably the E3/EU talks with Iran. Most strikingly, the High Representative was mandated by the Council to negotiate as the sole representative of the EU with his Iranian counterpart (see below). Annalisa Giannella, too, is increasingly serving as an interlocutor of the EU. For example, in Spring 2005 Ms. Giannella was sent to Washington to discuss European arms export policy.

Furthermore, the importance attached to Non-Proliferation is reflected by new procedures. The Action Plan which became part of the *EU Strategy* has been designed as a »living« document. It contains a list of rather heterogeneous goals as well as measures to be implemented by member states. At the end of each presidency, the council debates and adopts a progress report. Progress reports are prepared by the Personal Representative for non-proliferation in co-ordination with the Commission services. The Council may, and has actually done so in 2005, task Ms. Giannella with the preparation of a revised list of priorities.[41]

Major European initiatives raised by the Action Plan include the November 2003 decision to mainstream non-proliferation policies into wider relations with other countries. As cooperation agreements are renewed or newly concluded, they will contain a non-proliferation clause, making assistance dependent on the non-proliferation credentials of recipient countries.[42] In addition, the EU has made Non-Proliferation a major issue of its regional dialogues with the United States, India, China, Russia and other countries and organizations.

In addition, the EU is on its way to develop its own threat assessment capabilities. So far, the EU has been dependent on national intelligence or on an exchange of information with the US.[43] The EU Strategy proposes an exchange of information on export controls between the already existing Sit-

---

41 The revised list is added to the December 2005 Progress report. Cf. The Council of the European Union, Progress Report on implementation of the EU Strategy against proliferation of WMD, Brussels, 12 January 2006, Annex to Note 5279/06, available at http://register.consilium.europa.eu/pdf/en/06/st05/st05279.en06.pdf.
42 Council decision 14997/03, Mainstreaming non-proliferation policies into the EU's wider relations with third countries, Brussels, 19 November 2003.
43 *Müller*, Terrorism, Proliferation: A European Threat Assessment, Paris Chaillot Paper No. 58, ISS 2003.

uation Center and like-minded countries. More importantly, it also suggests the setting up of a unit within the Council Secretariat which will function as a monitoring centre, entrusted both with the monitoring of the implementation of the Strategy and with the collection of information and intelligence, in liaison with the Situation Centre. However, limited progress in establishing intelligence capabilities testifies to the uneven implementation of a European non-proliferation infrastructure. While the provision of sensitive information on export controls by member states to the SITCEN is improving, the latest progress report notes little steps forward concerning the creation of a Monitoring Centre. So far, the Personal Representative has prepared and circulated a note on how to implement this part of the mandate to member states.[44]

Other initiatives pertain to efforts to promote the universalisation on the NPT,[45] the ratification of the *Additional Protocol* by third States, a further improvement of the existing export control regimes, the continuation of disarmament assistance in Russia and elsewhere and support for the Comprehensive Nuclear-Test-Ban Treaty Organization.[46]

Assessing the depth of the transatlantic frictions.

At a first glance, the United States and the EU seem to disagree fundamentally on the right strategy how to counter new proliferation challenges. Since the EU has declared non-proliferation a high priority topic and is developing new actors, institutions and procedures to strengthen its own approach, one would expect major conflicts to come. A second glance reveals a different picture. I will show that the scope of commonalities is still wide and increasing. Concerning most issues that are contested like disarmament, the EU itself is internally divided. Despite these still existing commonalities and intra-European frictions, differences between American and

---

44 On the work of the SitCen see: Progress Report, Jan. 2006, p. 11. On the Monitoring Centre see: The Council of the European Union, Implementation of the WMD Strategy - Six monthly Progress Report on the implementation of the EU Strategy against the Proliferation of Weapons of Mass Destruction (2006/1), Brussels, 14 June 2006, Annex to Note 10527/06, available at http://register.consilium.europa.eu/pdf/en/06/st10/st10527.en06.pdf.
45 Council Common Position 2003/805/CFSP of 17 November 2003 on the universalisation and reinforcement of multilateral agreements in the field of non-proliferation of weapons fo mass destruction and means of delivery, Official Jornal of the European Union, L 302/34, 20. November 2003.
46 Council Decision 2003/567/CFSP of 21 July 2003 implementing Common Position 1999/533/CFSP relating to the European Union's contribution to the promotion of the early entry into force of the Comprehensive Nuclear Test-Ban Treaty (CTBT), Official Journal of the European Union, L 192/53, 31. July 2003.

European approaches to non-proliferation will probably persist. These differences are due to internal structures and not to sharply contoured ideological contrasts.

Still working in tandem?

Despite differences expressed in the above mentioned basic documents, the EU and the US still share common ground especially regarding initiatives aimed at strengthening and reinforcing non-proliferation regimes and instruments. A close transatlantic exchange on non-proliferation has been institutionalized in forums such as the EU-US Dialogue, the G-8 and NATO.[47] These regular exchanges bear fruit for example in cooperation on the Proliferation Security Initiative: its eleven founding members comprised eight EU-States including Germany and France.[48] European states and the US cooperate in the G8 global partnership on non-proliferation or in the framework of the EU-US summits to ensure that the *Additional Protocol*, together with the existing Comprehensive Safeguards Agreement, be formally recognized as the new safeguards standard for NNWS parties to the NPT.[49] Likewise, Americans and Europeans share rather similar views on the desireability of more proliferation-resistant fuel cycles. A convergence of views is even observable on formerly rather divisive issues such as Iran.

Performance: Speaking with one voice?

Do these institutional improvements enable the EU to speak with one voice and act together on non-proliferation issues? In order to assess the effectiveness of the European Union in this area, I will briefly discuss three cases relating to the EU's crisis management capacity, its diplomatic capacity and its conference diplomacy.

With the active involvement in the crisis over Iran's nuclear program, the EU for the first time played a leading role in non-proliferation crisis diplo-

---

47 For the EU-U.S. Dialogue see for example the Declaration on the non-proliferation of weapons of mass destruction, Dromoland Castle, 26. Juni 2004. The document is reprinted in:EU security and defence. Core documents 2004, Chaillot Papers No. 75, 2005, pp.157-161.

48 Council of the European Union: Press Office, Non-Proliferation: Support of the Proliferation Security Initiative (PSI), 10052/04 (Presse 189), Brussels, 1 June 2004.

49 See EU-U.S. Declaration on the Non-Proliferation of Weapons of Mass Destruction, (see footnote 47). The document is reprinted in: Institute for Security Studies, EU security and defence. Core documents 2004, Paris Chaillot Papers, No. 75, 2005, p.143-161.

macy. Relations between the EU and Iran date back to December 1992 when the Edinburgh Summit of the European Council decided to commence a critical dialogue with the Islamic Republic. The re-election of President Khatami in 1997 and promising signs of a political thaw in Tehran encouraged the EU to embark on what has then been called the Comprehensive Dialogue. At the Luxembourg Council in 2002, shortly before the eruption of the nuclear crisis, the Commission was even tasked to enter into negotiations with Iran over a Trade and Cooperation Agreement. Negotiations on trade were linked to progress in the political dialogue on human right, proliferation and regional issues, which was conducted by the EU presidency in the usual Troika format. After the IAEA reported on the Iranian infringements of its NPT commitments, negotiations were suspended. Thus, Europe stood to loose significant economic interests and spent political capital.

In October 2003 the Foreign Ministers of the three big EU-states seized the initiative and traveled to Teheran in an attempt to defuse the crisis. It is still unclear whether the three acted spontaneously or on the basis of a mandate.[50] In December 2003, the High Representative was added to the European negotiation team, forming the E3/EU format. Although Solana added a European element to the initiative of the three large EU countries, it took almost two years before the Council on October 2003 confirmed that the E3/EU do indeed represent the European Union.[51] Nevertheless, this format is still causing uneasiness among the other EU-members. On the one hand, the »big three plus Solana« format is seen by many experts as having produced a rare success story for EU non-proliferation policy. On the other hand, it is contested whether this format ensures a sufficient degree of accountability. In September 2006 differences came to the fore when the E3/EU renounced to share a confidential Iranian paper with their colleagues.[52] Despite critical remarks, the Council provided Solana with the mandate to hold face-to-face negotiations with Ali Larijani, Teheran's top nuclear negotiator.

When it became increasingly irrefutable during the Summer of 2006 that diplomacy had failed, the Iran dossier was refered back to the UN Security Council. Although the E3/EU is still involved - Solana actually continued to negotiate not only in the name of EU but also on behalf of the US, China and Russia – it seemed that as sanctions drew closer, the EU was seeking American support, if not American leadership.

One case of nuclear diplomacy occurred when, during his state visit to India in early March 2006, President Bush announced his intention to cut a

---

50 *Posch*, The EU and Iran: a tangled web of negotiations, in: *Posch* (Ed.), Iranian challenges, Paris, Chaillot Paper No. 89, 2006, p. 99-114.
51 ibid, p. 104.
52 EU Members want more openness from Solana on Iran, EUObserver, 02. September 2006.

deal with New Delhi according to which the US would lift its nuclear sanctions in response to India's agreement to divide its nuclear complex into a civilian and a military part and accept international safeguards on the former. Implementation of this promise depends not only on approval by Congress, but also on unanimous support by the 44 member of the NSG to exempt India from the group's rule that a non-nuclear weapon state must allow international verification of its nuclear facilities to be eligible for nuclear imports. Given the European pledges to coordinate policy on export controls, Bush's advance downrightly called for a unified EU response.

Circumstances in this case were actually auspicious for a common approach since this deal had been in the making for over a year. Nevertheless, EU members reacted rather differently to this challenge. The UK and France strongly backed the US proposal on India in the NSG. Jacques Chirac even tried to preempt Bush by paying a flying visit to Dehli on February 19th to conclude a framework agreement for future nuclear technology cooperation.[53] In contrast, NSG members Ireland, Austria, Sweden, Netherlands and Denmark expressed reservations, while Germany was still in the process of making up its mind.[54]

The last test concerns the European position at the 2005 Review conference. During the preparatory work, it had became apparent that issues relating to Article VI would decide on the success of the conference. Many non-aligned countries insisted on the fulfillment of the *Thirteen Steps* as a condition for a further tightening of the safeguards regime and trade system. By then, issues relating to Article VI had also turned into a major intra-European bone of contention. While most European NNWS still perceived a proper combination of horizontal and vertical proliferation as the most promising strategy, the two European nuclear weapon states by then had abandoned this approach.

Changes in the nuclear philosophy had been more distinct in France than in the UK. Of course, 9/11 and the possibility that 'rogue-states' or non-state actors might acquire WMD had affected British nuclear thinking. Indicative of this shift was the FCOs Non-Proliferation Department's change of name to Counter-Proliferation Department. Nevertheless, all in all the British multilateral approach to non-proliferation survived rather unscathed. In France, the 9/11 terrorist attacks had left deeper marks. Ironically, French thinking on WMD threats and nuclear responses increasingly resemble attitudes held in Washington. In fact, most observers ascertain a

---

53 Financial Times, 19. February 2006, p. 6.
54 *Boese,* Congress, NSG Question U.S.-Indian Deal, Arms Control Today, 36:3, April 2006, p. 4. Compare also *Boese,* Nuclear Suppliers still split on U.S.-Indian Deal, Arms Control Today, 36:6, November 2006, p. 44f; *Squassoni,* U.S. Nuclear Cooperation with India: Issues for Congress, Washington, CRS Report to Congress, March 3, 2006, p. 15f.

revolution in French strategic thinking.[55] The trias of regional powers, weapons of mass destruction and terrorism has moved to the center stage of France's threat perception and has influenced nuclear doctrine and strategy. The extent of this revolution became apparent on January 19th, 2006, when President Chirac, during a visit at the Ile Longue headquarters of the Strategic Air and Maritime Forces, revealed a major revision of the nuclear doctrine.[56] In his first major speech on the subject since 2001, he broadened the scope of vital interests to be defended by France's nuclear arsenal beyond the traditional concerns like the protection of national territory to include »strategic supplies and the defense of allied countries«. Instead of the former doctrine of deterrence of the strong by the weak, France's nuclear weapons are directed against regional countries that might acquire weapons of mass destruction and support terrorists. To maximize the deterrent value in such circumstances, the new doctrine stresses gradual responses and limited strikes with weapons of low yield against centers of political control and military power. According to Chirac, even *threats* against France' vital interests could trigger a nuclear response.[57] In accordance with these doctrinal changes, France is pursuing a comprehensive modernization of its nuclear forces.

The repercussion of these doctrinal shifts on the EU's ability to speak with one voice on non-proliferation issues became apparent during the failed 2005 extension conference. Although the EU could make use of standard procedures, agreement on a common position proved to be difficult. During the preparation for the conference, France and, to a lesser extend, the UK tried to move the European position away from the *Thirteen Points* as well as form other positions the EU has held in the past.[58] In spite of these basic disagreements, the EU managed to agree on a Common Position one week before the start of the conference.[59] The Position listed 43 issues which the member-states would pursue in common. However, most of these were repetitions of self-evident and often rehearsed statements. The Position contained a weak hint to the resolutions adopted at the 1995 and 2000 conference. Except from these weak hints controversial issues touching upon the implementation of Article VI were avoided.

55 *Tertrais*, France stands alone, in: Bulletin of the Atomic Scientists, 60:4, 2004, p. 48-55.
56 Frankfurter Allgemeine Zeitung, 20. January 2006, p. 1; FAZ, 21.January 2006, p. 2
57 *Meier*, Chirac Outlines Expanded Nuclear Doctrine, in: Arms Control Today, 36:2, March 2006, p. 43f.
58 *Meier*, The EU at the NPT Review Conference: A Modest Success for the EU's Emerging Policy in Nuclear Nonproliferation, in: Deutsche-Aussenpolitik. Foreign Policy in Dialogue, Newsletter No. 17, 2005, p. 8-14 (19).
59 Council Common Position 2005/329/PESC of 25 April 2005 relating to the 2005 Review Conference of the Parties to the Treaty on the Non-Proliferation of Nuclear Weapons, 2005.

At the conference, France sided with the US on disarmament questions like the bitterly contested issue whether progress since the last review conference should be measured only against the original text of the treaty or also against the *Thirteen Points*. The UK sought to steer a middle course between pursuing its arms control and non-proliferation initiatives and not isolating the US within the Western Group. On the other end of the spectrum, arms control oriented EU members joint disarmament-oriented groupings like the New Agenda Coalition or the G-10.[60] The EU tabled some promising papers like a proposal to clarify the conditions under which states can leave the NPT. In the final analysis, however, the Europeans left a rather divided impression and hence were not able to prevent the failure of the conference. Since then, intra-European divisions have not been bridged. For example, while most European non-nuclear weapon states insist that a cut-off treaty should be verified and cover significant amounts of the existing fissile material, Paris moved closer to the American position. When the US presented a draft for a FMCT in May 2006 which would only cover material produced in the future and which did not contain a verification scheme, Paris agreed.[61]

A distinct non-proliferation policy?

Despite this mixed record, non-proliferation will remain a priority topic on the agenda of the EU's foreign and security policy. By now non-proliferation policy as an issue is well entrenched within the EU political machinery with bureaucratic actors fighting for their competences as well as established procedures. This raises the question what kind of non-proliferation policy the EU will be pursuing and in what way this policy will be distinct and different from policies of nation-states like the US.

The main structural difference pertains to the way policy is generated. In the EU non-proliferation policy, like most other policies directed at the outside world, depends on consensual decisions by 25 member states with different traditions, interests and outlooks which, despite their differences, are increasingly bound to act in common. Furthermore, EU non-proliferation policy is shaped by specific institutions and techniques that have been developed in order to cope with the internal requirement of consensus-building. Two institutions or techniques are worth mentioning: the first concerns the use of past decisions, resolutions, declarations, and other rhetorical devices as guideposts for future policy. It has been mentioned that the CFSP is being stabilized by the framework of this *acquis politique* or that it even

---

60 *Müller*, Vertrag im Zerfall? Die gescheiterte Überprüfungskonferenz des Nichtverbreitungsvertrages und ihre Folgen, HSFK-Report 4, 2005.
61 Frankfurter Allgemeine Zeitung, 20. May 2006, p. 5.

consists of this fund of rhetorical actions.[62] Depending on their theoretical backgrounds, scholars of European foreign policy differ on whether this *acquis* guides behavior because it structures roles actors play or because it works as a rhetorical trap. Important to note here is that states are aware of the binding force of rhetorical acts. In order to cope with uncertainty and to avoid blockages or ineffective lowest common denominator decisions, they even devise declaratory policy in a way as to strengthen its binding effects. For example, member states usually draft declarations with far-reaching ambitions and comprehensive lists of measures. Rather often, they add review mechanisms as well as mechanisms for the dissemination of good practice, peer pressure and beauty contests. The Strategy is a case in point. It describes policy in long time horizons, contains an exhaustive list of goals and measures, arranges for a bi-annual review mechanism and encourages peer review and learning. Concerning the latter aspects, the Strategy requests states to present and compare their export control procedures and to emulate best practice.

However, because states know and fear the binding effect of declarations, their adoption has become a battleground. Rather often common documents represent carefully crafted compromises designed with a view to overcome internal division and not to maximize external effect. As Annalisa Giannella noted: »Achieving unity among 25 member states has become more difficult and sometimes appears to be an end in itself rather than a means to achieve arms control goals«.[63] As a result, many initiatives and declarations lack ambition. Again the Action Program is no exception. Every progress report since the adoption of the National Strategy has been reporting considerable advancements. However, some of the objectives represent aims whose desirability has long been agreed upon and some reflect activity but not necessarily progress in the fight against proliferation. Other have been framed in a way as to cover internal disagreements. For example, the EU Strategy contains a long passage of support for an FMCT but is silent on the most important and contentions issue of its verification.

This internal mechanism of consensus building lends a very distinct feature to the external policies of the EU, providing it with unique strength and weaknesses. On the one hand, this internal mechanism explains the external proclivity for multilateralism. Because the EU needs rules for its internal working, it is inclined to support rule-based approaches in its relations with the external world. Vice versa, externally codified rules to which EU mem-

---

62 *Burghardt/Tebbe*, Die Gemeinsame Außen- und Sicherheitspolitik der Europäischen Union - Rechtliche Strukturen und politischer Prozess, in: Europarecht, 30, 1995, p. 1-20.
63 *Meier*, Between Noble Goals and Sobering Reality: An Interview with EU Nonproliferation Chief Annalisa Giannella, Arms Control Today, 35:7, September 2005, p. 20.

bers have consented are reinforced by the internal mechanisms of the EU. This trait undoubtedly carries advantages. EU non-proliferation policy is predictable and well aligned with the existing multilateral system of regimes.

On the other hand, these internal mechanisms explain the bureaucratic and often ritualistic appearance of its foreign policy, the compromise character of its proposals and the difficulty of the Union to commit its members to policies whenever risks are high and consequences of alternative courses are unclear. They also explain the path dependency of European policy, its limited flexibility, its restricted ability to cope with change and its limited ability to react to new challenges. Given its dependence on precedence and former declarations a guide posts for future action, there is a tendency that the member states of the EU will not be able to find common ground in situations that are new and for which no standard operating procedures are available. This does not imply that the EU will always operate according to the textbook of existing declarations and resolutions. Of course there is room for change as member states, either reacting to changing external circumstances or to internal constellations, try to alter the established *acquis*. However, the European structures are decelerating and delaying change. For example, France and the UK came out in support of accepting the nuclear status of India only after the United States had taken the lead. Moreover, it is rather unconceivable that the EU would take the initiative in this or in a comparable case.

The second mechanism concerns delegation as a response to the challenge of external representation. Speaking not only with one voice but through one voice becomes increasingly necessary as the European nonproliferation policy moves beyond conference diplomacy to include crisis management. However, the delegation authority to negotiate and thus to commit the Union and its member states raises complex issues concerning the proper balance between flexibility and accountability. On the one hand, delegating negotiating-competence to a small group of member states or even to one agent like the High Representative would increase the flexibility and thus the efficiency of negotiations. On the other hand, delegation would raise concerns regarding accountability as well as the agent's power to commit the EU member states. The traditional Troika format is well suited to convey messages on international conferences or at meetings of the various political dialogues. This format is less suited to negotiate and commit the EU on the spot. In these contexts, the Troika format lacks flexibility, continuity and weight, especially if a small state provides the Presidency. The jury is still out on whether the E3/EU format or the 'Solana only' format will provide a better solution for this dilemma. The internal critic at the EU-3 format as well as the Iranian allegation that Solana lacked negotiating flexibility does not augur well. There are probably structural limits to the EU's capacity to negotiate efficiently in crisis situations.

To summarize: the EU will be a force of preservation, rather than of change. It will be a force of upholding and expanding the current multilateral regime, and not of radically reshaping it. The EU will function well on the diplomatic floor of international conferences; it has limits as a leader in crisis management. These limits will be exacerbated as soon as sanctions or even punitive countermeasures are contemplated.

The future of transatlantic cooperation and consequences for the non-proliferation regime

This analysis leads to the conclusion that a stand-off between Europe and the United States in the area of non-proliferation is rather unlikely. The EU will not develop into a countervailing power to America, not even into a competitor of the United States. Even if the US non-proliferation policy were to retain its unilateral trait, a prospect which looks increasingly unlikely, the EU will not contravene American policy.

First, despite differences expressed in basic documents, the EU and the US still share a lot of common ground. Second, the interests and perceptions of EU member states are not as homogeneous and as different from those of the United States as the ESS or the EU Strategy would suggest. Issues relating to Article VI that have formerly divided the transatlantic community are by now complicating the formulation of a common approach within the EU. It is ironic that France, having been one of the most outspoken critic of the Iraq war, by now holds views rather similar to those of the US. Third, with the adoption of the ESS the European Union is moving closer to accepting that in some cases the defense of the non-proliferation regime might require punitive responses. As the internal structures of the EU limit its ability as a crisis manager as well as its ability to commit its members on a confrontational course, it is rather likely that when push comes to shove the Europeans will seek close cooperation with the United States.

What has changed is the configuration of transatlantic cooperation. Whereas in the 1970s and 1980s coordination among Western states occurred bilaterally between the US and individual European States or in forums like the Western Group with America playing a leading role, today coordination is increasingly taking place between the US and the European Union. To be sure, some European States like the UK are still playing the role of a bridge-builder, trying to grind away the sharp edges of a two-pillared relationship. Nevertheless, it is likely that transatlantic coordination on nuclear proliferation issues will increasingly take place between the EU and the US.

Whether this constellation will benefit the non-proliferation regime or whether it will have detrimental effects remains to be seen. However, some speculation might be worthwhile. It has been pointed out that the successful adaptation of the non-proliferation regime in the 1970s and 1980s depended at least to some degree on American leadership. In those days, leadership was reasonably effective because the US could deal with its European partners on a bilateral basis. Europe did not strive for unity in this field and hence did not provide cover for those states which were disinclined to follow the American lead. A counterfactual argument might underline this point. Had the EU already established itself as an actor in the area of non-proliferation during the 1970s, it would have been even more difficult for Washington to induce European cooperation.

It has also been pointed out that the European Union itself will probably not serve as a major force of change. Due to its internal structures, the EU acts as a force of continuity and preservation. It tends to stabilize existing regime structure and will not push for radical change. The EU will rather function as a buffer. It will cushion attempts to radically alter the status quo. Whether this characteristic is regarded as beneficial for the non-proliferation regime or as detrimental depends on how one perceives the state of health of this regime. Those who believe that the multilateral non-proliferation regime is basically on a sound track or at least repairable may welcome the emergence of the EU as an actor on this field. Those who believe that the regime is in a deep crisis and that radically new answers are necessary in order to prevent the spread of nuclear weapons in the future may find the EU less helpful. Unfortunately, after six years of Bush's foreign policy, the non-proliferation regime is in a worse state than before, with the danger of proliferation in 2007 being much higher than it had been in 2000. Whether a return to the quid pro quo achieved at the 2000 extension conference is possible or whether alternative compromises between NWS, NNWS and threshold states can be constructed is at best an open question.

References

Allison, Graham/Carter, Ashton/Miller Steve E./Zelikow, Philip, Cooperative Denuclearization. From Pledges to Deeds, Cambridge, Harvard University 1993.

Alvarez-Verdugo, Milagros, Mixing Tools Against Prolifertation: The EU's Strategy for Dealing with Weapons of Mass Destruction, in: European Foreign Affairs Review, 11, 2006, pp. 417-438.

Bailes, Alyson J.K., The European Security Strategy. An Evolutionary History. Stockholm, SIPRI Policy Paper No. 10, 2005, pp. 10.

Boese, Wade, Bush Plans to Cut Atomic Arsenal, Arms Control Today, 34:6, July/August 2004, p. 33-34.

Boese, Wade, Bush Shifts Fissile Material Ban Policy, Arms Control Today, 34:7, September 2004, p. 20-21.

Boese, Wade, Congress, NSG Question U.S.-Indian Deal, Arms Control Today, 36:3, April 2006, p. 33-34.

Boese, Wade, Nuclear Suppliers still split on U.S.-Indian Deal, Arms Control Today, 36:6, July/August 2006, p.44-46.

Burghardt, Günther/Tebbe, Gert, Die Gemeinsame Außen- und Sicherheitspolitik der Europäischen Union - Rechtliche Strukturen und politischer Prozess, in: Europarecht, 30, 1995, pp. 1-20.

Cirincione, Joseph, A New Non-Proliferation Strategy, IAI, 2005, p. 1.

Council of the European Union, A Secure Europe in a Better World, Euopean Security Strategy, endorsed on 12. December 2003, Annex to Note 78367, available at http://www.consilium.europa.eu/uedocs/cmsUpload/78367.pdf.

Council of the European Union, Common Position 2003/805/CFSP of 17 November 2003 on the universalisation and reinforcement of multilateral agreements in the field of non-proliferation of weapons fo mass destruction and means of delivery, Official Jornal of the European Union, L 302/34, 20.11.2003.

Council of the European Union, Common Position 2005/329/PESC of 25 April 2005 relating to the 2005 Review Conference of the Parties to the Treaty on the Non-Proliferation of Nuclear Weapons, 2005.

Council of the European Union, Decision 14997/03, Mainstreaming non-proliferation policies into the EU's wider relations with third countries, Brussels (19 November 2003).

Council of the European Union, Decision 2003/567/CFSP of 21 July 2003 implementing Common Position 1999/533/CFSP relating to the European Union's contribution to the promotion of the early entry into force of the Comprehensive Nuclear Test-Ban Treaty (CTBT), Official Journal of the European Union, L 192/53, 31. June 2003.

Council of the European Union, EU Strategy against proliferation of weapons of mass destruction, endorsed on 12 December 2003, Annex to Note 15708/03, available at http://consilium.europa.eu/uedocs/cmsUpload/st15708.en03.pdf.

Council of the European Union, Implementation of the EU Strategy against proliferation of WMD, Brussels, 12 January 2006, Annex to Note 5279/06, available at http://register.consilium.europa.eu/pdf/en/06/st05/st05279.en06.pdf

Council of the European Union, Implementation of the WMD Strategy - Six monthly Progress Report on the implementation of the EU Strategy against the Proliferation of Weapons of Mass Destruction (2006/1), Brussels, 14 June 2006.

Council of the European Union, Presidency Conclusion, Rome, 14-15 December 1990.

Council of the European Union: Press Office, Non-Proliferation: Support of the Proliferation Security Initiative (PSI), 10052/04 (Presse 189), Brussels (1 June 2004).

Dembinski, Matthias, Mit START zum Ziel der allgemeinen und vollständigen Abrüstung?, Frankfurt, HSFK-Report 3, 1993.

EU-U.S. Declaration on the non-proliferation of weapons of mass destruction, Dromoland Castle, 26. June 2004, available at http://ec.europa.eu/comm/external_ relations/us/sum06_04/decl_wmd.pdf. EUObserver, 02. September 2006

European Commission, Directorate-General for Energy and Transport: Europe remains vigilant, Brussels, 2005, available at http://ec.europa.eu/energy/nuclear/safeguards/doc/2006_brochure_nuclear_safeguards_en.pdf.

Fisher, Cathleen, EU Cooperation in Arms Control and Nonproliferation, in: The European Union, Nonproliferation, and Arms Control, Washington, The Henry L. Stimson Center, Report No. 40, pp. 21f.

Howlett, Darryl, EURATOM and Nuclear Safeguards, Basingstoke 1990.

Institute for Security Studies, EU security and defence. Core documents 2004, Paris Chaillot Papers, No. 75, 2005, p.143-161

Joseph, Jofi, The Proliferation Security Initiative: Can Interdiction Stop Proliferation, in: Arms Control Today, 34:5, 2004, pp. 6-13.

Kaiser, Karl, The Great Nuclear Debate: American-German Disagreements, in: Foreign Policy, No. 30,1978, pp.83-110.

Kristensen, Hans M. / Handler, Joshua, Changing Targets: Nuclear Doctrine from the Cold War to the Third World, Greenpeace Foundation, 1995.

Lellouche, Pierre, France and the International Nuclear Controversy, in: Orbis, 22:4, 1979, pp. 951-965.

Meier, Oliver, Between Noble Goals and Sobering Reality: An Interview with EU Nonproliferation Chief Annalisa Giannella, Arms Control Today, 35:7, September 2005, p. 20.

Meier, Oliver, Chirac Outlines Expanded Nuclear Doctrine, in: Arms Control Today, 36:2, 2006, pp. 43f.

Meier, Oliver, The EU at the NPT Review Conference: A Modest Success for the EU's Emerging Policy in Nuclear Nonproliferation, in: Deutsche-Aussenpolitik. Foreign Policy in Dialogue, Newsletter No. 17, Trier 2005, pp. 8-19.

Missiroli, Antonio, From Copenhagen to Brussels. European Defence: Core documents, Paris: Chaillot Papers No. 67 (December 2003) pp. 106-118.

Müller, Harald, European Nuclear Non-Proliferation after the NPT Extension: Achievements, Shortcomings and Needs, in: *Cornish, Paul / van Ham, Peter / Krause, Joachim* (Eds.), Europe and the Challenge of Prolifration, Paris, 1996, Challiot Papers No. 24, pp. 33-54.

Müller, Harald, Nukleare Krisen und transatlantischer Dissens. Amerikanische und europäische Antworten auf aktuelle Probleme der Weiterverbreitung von Kernwaffen, Frankfurt. HSFK Report 9/2003.

Müller, Harald, Terrorism, Proliferation: A European Threat Assessment, Chaillot Paper No. 58, Paris, ISS 2003.

Müller, Harald, Vertrag im Zerfall? Die gescheiterte Überprüfungskonferenz des Nichtverbreitungsvertrages und ihre Folgen, Frankfurt, HSFK-Report 4, 2005.

Müller, Harald/Dembinski, Matthias/Kelle, Alexander/Schaper, Annette, From Black Sheep to White Angel? The New German Export Control Policy, Frankfurt, PRIF Report 32, 1994.

Müller, Harald/Schaper, Anette, US Nuclear Policy after the Cold War, Frankfurt, PRIF Reports No. 69, 2003, p.30.

Müller, Harald/van Dassen, Lars, From Cacophony to Joint Action: Successes and Shortcomings of the European Nuclear Non-Proliferation Policy, in: *Holland, Martin* (Ed.), Common Foreign and Security Policy. The Record and Reforms, London: Pinter 1997, pp. 52-72.

National Security Strategy of the United States of America, Washington, September 2002;

National Strategy to Combat Weapons of Mass Destruction, Washiongton, December 2002.

Norris, Robert/Kristensen, Hans, NRDC Nuclear Notebook, Bulletin of the Atomic Scientists, Jan/Feb. 2005.

Nye, Joseph S., Maintaining a Nonproliferation Regime, in: International Organization, 35:1, 1981, pp. 15-38.

Perkovich, George, Transatlantic Cooperation for Nuclear Nonproliferation, in: Serfaty, Simon (Ed.), Visions of the Atlantic Alliance. The United States, the European Union, and NATO, Washington, CSIS Press 2005, p.193-211.

Perkovich, George/Mathews, Jessica/Cirincione, Joseph/Gottemoeller, Rose/Wolfsthal, Jan, Universal Compliance: A Strategy for Nuclear Security, Washington, Carnegie Endowment for International Peace 2005, available at www.ProliferationNews.org..

Portela, Clara, The Role of the EU in the Non-Proliferation of Nuclear Weapons. The Way to Thessaloniki and Beyond, Frankfurt, PRIF Report No. 65, 2003, p. 15f.

Posch, Walter, The EU and Iran: a tangled web of negotiations, in: Posch, Walter (Ed.), Iranian challenges, Paris, Chaillot Paper No. 89, 2006, p. 99-114.

Schaper, Annette, German Policy Regarding the Possible Elimination of HEU in the Civilian Nuclear Sector, Frankfurt 2006, unpublished manuscript.

Spear, Joanna, The Emergence of a European ‚Strategic Personality', in: Arms Control Today, 33:9, November 2003, p. 13-18.

Squassoni, Sharon, U.S. Nuclear Cooperation with India: Issues for Congress, Washington, CRS Report to Congress, March 3, 2006, p. 15f.

Tertrais, Bruno, France stands alone, in: Bulletin of the Atomic Scientists, 60:4, 2004, pp. 48-55.

The White House, Office of the Press Secretary: Statement by the President: Comprehensive Test Ban Treaty, Washington, 11. August 1995.

The White House, President Announces New Measures to Counter the Threat of WMD, Washington, February 11, 2004, available at http://www.whitehouse.gov/news/releases/2004/02/print/20040211-4.html.

United Nations, Report of the Secretary-General's High-level Panel on Threats, Challenges and Change, A more secure World: Our shared responsibility, New York 2004.

United Nations, Security Council, Resolution 1540 (2004) adopted by the Security Council at its 4956th meeting, on 28 April 2004.

Weiss, Leonard, Turning a blind eye again? The Khan Network's History and Lessons for U.S. Policy, in: Arms Control Today, 35:2, 2005, pp. 12-18.

Wisotzki, Simone, Abschreckung ohne Ende? Die ambivalente Nuklearwaffenpolitik Großbritanniens und Frankreichs, Frankfurt, HSFK Report 11/2004.

A Vulnerable Superpower: U.S. Strategy Against Weapons of Mass Destruction in the 21st Century

Derek D. Smith[1]

Introduction

There is widespread agreement that the proliferation of weapons of mass destruction (WMD) represents one of the greatest threats to international security. Less of a consensus exists, however, regarding the appropriate means for responding to this threat. The negotiations over Iran's nuclear program epitomize this diplomatic disunity, as the United States finds itself disagreeing with its European interlocutors and even more at odds with Russia and China.[2] At root, the United States sees itself as a more likely target for terrorism and aggression than its international counterparts, and correspondingly has greater sensitivity to the national security consequences of proliferation. The United States has therefore embarked on a major campaign to prevent, contain, and defend against the spread of WMDs, describing its basic initiatives in a December 2002 document entitled the *National Strategy to Combat Weapons of Mass Destruction*[3] (*National Strategy*). This chapter will analyze the main components of the *National Strategy* and recommend possible avenues for reform.[4]

---

1 Portions of this chapter are adapted from Derek D. Smith, *Deterring America: Rogue States and the Proliferation of Weapons of Mass Destruction* (Cambridge: Cambridge University Press, 2006).
2 See Colum Lynch and Glenn Kessler, »U.S., European Allies ad Odds on Terms of Iran Resolution,« *Washington Post*, October 26, 2006.
3 United States. »National Strategy to Combat Weapons of Mass Destruction.« (December 2002). http://www.whitehouse.gov/news/releases/2002/12/WMDStrategy.pdf (accessed February 16, 2007).
4 The proliferation of WMD is a multi-layered phenomenon, fueled by indigenous research and development, global trade, arms sales, and covert transfers to non-state actors. Defending against such a complex threat, in turns, involves a wide array of legal, institutional, and strategic mechanisms. To clarify and organize these often overlapping subject areas, the *National Strategy* distinguishes nonproliferation (seeking to prevent states from acquiring WMD), counterproliferation (equipping military units to defend against and deter a WMD attack), and consequence management (preparing civilians and military forces to reduce the consequences of a WMD attack). I will use the same general framework in this chapter.

Nonproliferation

Diplomacy

The ideal solution for combating the proliferation of WMD would likely be a series of agreements in which states promised to dismantle existing weapons facilities and abstain from developing any new ones. In December 2003, Libya became a potential role model in this regard by committing to verifiable disarmament.[5] This remarkable turnaround, following a series of secret meetings between Libya, the United States, and the United Kingdom, sparked hopes that a similar outcome was possible with other states such as Iran and North Korea. In particular, some observers searched for a proximate cause of Libya's change of heart and settled on two possibilities: the U.S. invasion of Iraq in March 2003 (Operation Iraqi Freedom) and the September 2003 interception of a freighter bound for Libya with a shipment of parts for centrifuges used in uranium enrichment.[6] Both involved the projection of U.S. military power abroad, leading to the inference that a foreign policy based more on »sticks« than »carrots« might succeed elsewhere.

More likely, Libyan leader Muammar Gaddafi's decision to accept inspections and disarm stemmed from a number of influences.[7] Not only did talks with the United States and the United Kingdom begin well before the September 2003 interdiction mission, but the final agreement included the termination of international sanctions in place since the Lockerbie bombing in December 1988, freeing Libya to open its oil industry to western investment and sales. Behind the scenes, Gaddafi may have feared domestic instability flowing from a faltering Libyan economy more than he feared military intervention from abroad.

Regardless of Libya's true motivations, which only Gaddafi may know, it is unlikely that other states will follow its lead. North Korea, for instance, has withstood decades of isolation and is far more impervious to military threats than Libya given North Korea's countervailing ability to devastate Seoul in response to any attack. The most recent set of multilateral talks with North Korea have foundered with North Korea demanding an end to financial sanctions before it will even consider negotiating ways to carry out the disarmament agreement reached in 2005.[8] Iran, similarly, has never

---

5 See James G. Lakely, »Libya Will Dismantle its Weapons,« *Washington Times*, December 20, 2003.
6 See, e.g., Robin Wright, »Ship Incident May Have Swayed Libya,« *Washington Post*, January 1, 2004.
7 See David Gargill, »The Libya Fallacy: The Iraq War is Not What Disarmed Qadaffi,« *Harper's Magazine*, November, 2004.
8 Edward Cody, »North Korea Nuke Talks End Without Deal,« *Washington Post*, December 22, 2006.

faced the prospect of truly damaging sanctions and appears to view an indigenous nuclear program as an indispensable step toward assuming its rightful place in world affairs. While Iran has expressed willingness to enter into talks regarding inspections of its nuclear program, it has been insistent that any negotiations will not include restraints on uranium enrichment.[9] With these states, although diplomacy should always remain a top priority because local conditions may change over time and lead to greater incentives to compromise, unfortunately the prospects for a comprehensive disarmament deal are dim at present.

Multilateral Regimes

When direct diplomacy is unlikely to bear fruit, the United States historically has turned to multilateral regimes to keep WMD or their precursors away from potential adversaries in the first place. During the Cold War, the United States created the Coordinating Committee for Multilateral Export Controls (CoCom) to deny sophisticated technology to the Soviet Union, and a veritable alphabet soup of arms control agencies and treaties are in place today to limit the spread of WMD, including the Non-Proliferation Treaty (NPT), the Nuclear Suppliers Group (NSG), the Missile Technology Control Regime (MTCR), the Biological Weapons Convention (BWC), and the Chemical Weapons Convention (CWC).

The NPT, entered into force in 1968, was meant to be a grand bargain between those states that acknowledged possessing nuclear weapons – the United States, the Soviet Union (whose obligations Russia has now assumed), the United Kingdom, China and France – and all other non-nuclear-weapon states.[10] To date, only India, Israel and Pakistan have declined to sign the treaty, although North Korea announced its withdrawal in January 2003.[11] Under the NPT, the five nuclear states agreed to not transfer nuclear weapons or development technology to non-nuclear-weapon states, while the non-nuclear states agreed to not acquire or produce nuclear weapons. In return, the nuclear states committed to take steps toward negotiating complete nuclear disarmament. At the same time, non-nuclear-weapon states could develop peaceful civilian nuclear power programs in accord-

---

9 Dafna Linzer, »Iran Pushes for Talks Without Conditions,« *Washington Post*, August 23, 2006.
10 For the text of the Non-Proliferation Treaty, see NPT, »NPT Treaty.« http://www.un.org/events/npt2005/npttreaty.html (accessed February 16, 2007).
11 Joseph Cirincione, Jon B. Wolfsthal, and Miriam Rajkumar, *Deadly Arsenals: Nuclear, Biological, and Chemical Threats*, 2nd ed. (Washington DC: Carnegie Endowment for International Peace, 2005), 28.

ance with safeguard agreements negotiated with the International Atomic Energy Agency (IAEA).[12]

The potential loophole in this system is that states can acquire sophisticated nuclear reactors and technology ostensibly for civilian power production, and then divert the facilities to weapons development either in secret or by violating the IAEA safeguards.[13] This is essentially the model that the United States fears Iran has elected to follow, doubting that such an oil-rich nation truly requires nuclear power to satisfy its energy needs. To close this loophole, there have been an increasing number of proposals to place the supply of fissile material under international control rather than continue to promote complete indigenous development. President George Bush was one of the first world leaders to advocate this approach, calling upon »[t]he world's leading nuclear exporters [to] ensure that states have reliable access at reasonable cost to fuel for civilian reactors, so long as those states renounce enrichment and reprocessing.«[14] A United Nations blue-ribbon commission convened by then Secretary-General Kofi Annan to analyze emerging security concerns and propose reforms came to a similar conclusion.[15] Even Russian President Vladimir Putin has called for a network of uranium enrichment centers that would provide access to nuclear fuel without discrimination.[16]

The primary criticism leveled at the nuclear fuel bank proposal, as recognized by two of its primary proponents, is that it cuts against the original understanding of the NPT, which was premised on unfettered access by non-nuclear states to enrichment and reprocessing facilities.[17] States like Iran claim that their sovereign status entitles them to become self-sufficient in nuclear power generation and not to have to rely on the continued supply

---

12 See »International Atomic Energy Agency.« http://www.iaea.org/ (accessed December 16, 2007).
13 The IAEA lacks physical protection or policing capabilities to prevent states from taking nuclear materials for use in nuclear weapons. Cirincione, Wolfsthal, and Rajkumar, *Deadly Arsenals*, 30.
14 George Bush, »President Announces New Measures to Counter the Threat of WMD: Remarks on Weapons of Mass Destruction Proliferation,« National Defense University Fort Lesley J. McNair, Washington DC, February 11, 2004. http://www.whitehouse.gov/news/releases/2004/02/20040211-4.html (accessed February 16, 2007).
15 See United Nations. »A More Secure World: Our Shared Responsibility.« Report of the Secretary General's High-level Panel on Threats, Challenges and Change. (2004). http://www.un.org/secureworld/ (accessed February 16, 2007), 44.
16 See Fred Weir and Howard LaFranchi, »Russia and the U.S. as Global Nuclear Waste Collectors?,« *Christian Science Monitor*, February 7, 2006.
17 See Richard Lugar and Evan Bayh, »A Nuclear Fuel Bank Advocated,« *Chicago Tribune*, October 22, 2006.

of an international consortium ultimately beyond their control.[18] Unless the international community is willing to back up a new conception of the NPT with the threat of force – an unlikely prospect given the economic benefits that flow to suppliers of nuclear technology[19] – states will continue to exploit this loophole.

Moreover, there is increasing skepticism over the willingness of the existing nuclear states to fulfill their part of the NPT bargain and take steps toward complete nuclear disarmament. If anything, nuclear states are reaffirming the importance of a nuclear arsenal to their national security.[20] In light of this, it is not surprising that non-nuclear states complain of hypocrisy in the NPT system and demand equal treatment. The lingering NPT double standard is also a major reason why the NPT 2005 Review Conference was unable to reach common ground on hardly any of the major nonproliferation issues under consideration.[21]

The NSG, founded in 1975 and now with forty-five member states, seeks to prevent the export of items designed or prepared for nuclear use.[22] The primary means for achieving this objective is via two sets of guidelines: the first covers nuclear material, nuclear reactors, and reprocessing facilities, whereas the second covers civilian items and technologies that could contribute to a covert nuclear program. Operating by consensus, the NSG has no provisions for implementing sanctions against violators of its guidelines. Moreover, as with the NPT, the NSG runs the risk of enshrining a double standard in nuclear possession, a criticism most recently raised in relation to the March 2006 nuclear agreement between the United States and India. That agreement, framed by the parties as a strategic partnership in civilian nuclear cooperation, nonetheless is a major departure from the current arms control regime and will require agreement by the NSG in order to take effect. This is primarily because India is not a member of the NSG and so is prohibited under its terms from receiving nuclear material from member states. If the NSG accedes to this agreement, it may be difficult to explain why a similar exception should not apply to states like Iran. Nota-

---

18 See Nazila Fathi, »Iran Snubs Europe's Nuclear Plan,« *New York times*, May 18, 2006.
19 See Nazila Fathi, »Iran and Russia Sign Accord to Speed Nuclear Power Project,« *New York Times*, December 26, 2002.
20 See, e.g., Walter Pincus, »New Nuclear Weapons Programs to Continue,« *Washington Post*, December 2, 2006; United Kingdom. »The Future of the United Kingdom's Nuclear Deterrent.« (December 2006). http://www.mod.uk/NR/rdonlyres/AC00DD79-76D6-4FE3-91A1-6A56B03C092F/0/DefenceWhitePaper2006_Cm6994.pdf (accessed February 16, 2007).
21 See Rebecca Johnson, »Politics and Protection: Why the 2005 NPT Review Conference Failed,« *Disarmament Diplomacy*, no. 80 (Autumn 2005).
22 See »Nuclear Suppliers Group.« http://www.nuclearsuppliersgroup.org/guide.htm (accessed December 6, 2006).

bly, the NSG itself was founded the year after India's first nuclear test, partly in recognition of the need to limit nuclear cooperation with states that had not signed the Non-Proliferation Treaty.

The MTCR, a multilateral partnership formed in 1987 and now with thirty-four member states, is similar in function to the NSG – operating on the basis of consensus – but it aims to stem the proliferation of unmanned delivery systems for nuclear weapons, developing and implementing a list of controlled items contained in a document known as the MTCR »Annex.«[23] Like the NSG, the MTCR cannot sanction violators of the Annex and also lacks several key missile proliferators in its ranks. China, for instance, has agreed to abide by the original MTCR agreement and Annex, but has rejected full MTCR membership. In November 2002, ninety-three states supplemented the MTCR by subscribing to the International Code of Conduct Against Ballistic Missile Proliferation (ICOC), with a mandate to curb ballistic missile proliferation worldwide.[24] The ICOC is broader in scope than the MTCR because it targets space launch vehicle systems as well as ballistic missiles, recognizing the complementary nature of the two technologies.[25] Like the MTCR, the ICOC has no enforcement mechanism and struggles to avoid the appearance of creating a divide between »have« missile states and »have-nots.«

The BWC and CWC represent international efforts to control the other two parts of the WMD trio: biological and chemical weapons. The BWC, entered into force in March 1975, calls upon its 155 party states to never »develop, produce, stockpile or otherwise acquire or retain« quantities or types of biological agents or toxins (including their means of delivery) »that have no justification for prophylactic, protective, or other peaceful purposes.«[26] The BWC's purpose-based exclusion allows states to retain sufficient stockpiles of prohibited materials in order to develop defensive treatments that can protect against a biological attack. Such a precautionary exception makes sense in light of the inability to reliably verify biological weapon stockpiles (efforts to negotiate a legally binding protocol to the treaty for verification have failed thus far), but it also works against achieving disarmament because states can never be sure that the biological agents another state uses to develop vaccines will not be stored for future offensive

---

23 See »Missile Technology Control Regime.« http://www.mtcr.info/english/ (accessed December 6, 2006).
24 See U.S. Department of State - Bureau of Nonproliferation. »International Code of Conduct Against Ballistic Missile Proliferation.« http://www.state.gov/t/isn/rls/fs/27799.htm (accessed December 3, 2006).
25 See Cirincione, Wolfsthal, and Rajkumar, *Deadly Arsenals*, 95-96.
26 »Convention on the Prohibition of the Development, Production and Stockpiling of Bacteriological (Biological) and Toxin Weapons and on Their Destruction.« http://www.opbw.org/convention/documents/btwctext.pdf (accessed December 22, 2006), art. I.

use, especially when (due to the development of the vaccine) that other state is simultaneously better able to defend itself from retaliation in kind. To reduce this fear of noncompliance, the BWC's review conferences have focused on transparency initiatives and confidence building measures among party states.[27] Despite these reforms, in 2005 the United States still suspected seven states – China, Egypt, Iran, Israel, North Korea, Russia, and Syria – of having some level of offensive biological warfare research programs.[28]

The CWC is a more recent initiative that only entered into force in April 1997. Like the BWC, the CWC aims to strike an appropriate balance between encouraging the use of chemicals for peaceful purposes and preventing the production of chemical weapons. Whereas Article I of the CWC contains a blanket prohibition against the development, production, stockpiling, or use of all chemical weapons, Article VI grants each state party »the right, subject to the provisions of this Convention, to develop, produce, otherwise acquire, retain, transfer and use toxic chemicals and their precursors for purposes not prohibited under this Convention.«[29] To clarify the boundaries between these two endpoints, the CWC includes an Annex that distinguishes between three »Schedules« of chemicals that are either weapons themselves (Schedule 1), can be used to manufacture weapons (Schedule 2), or do have other uses apart from chemical weapons (Schedule 3).[30] Under the CWC Verification Annex, each Schedule has increasingly stringent levels of reporting requirements as well as production and trade restrictions. To date, party states have made disappointingly slow progress in meeting benchmarks for the destruction of prohibited chemical weapons. The Organization for the Prohibition of Chemical Weapons (OPCW), which administers the CWC, recently granted both the United States and Russia a five-year extension beyond their original 2007 deadline to destroy their respective stockpiles.[31] As of June 2006, according to the U.S. ambassador to the OPCW, while the United States had destroyed thirty-seven percent of its chemical weapons, Russia had only destroyed five percent. In-

---

27 See »Biological and Toxin Weapons Convention Website.« http://www.opbw.org/ (accessed December 22, 2006).
28 Cirincione, Wolfsthal, and Rajkumar, *Deadly Arsenals*, 10.
29 See »Convention on the Prohibition of the Development, Production, Stockpiling and Use of Chemical Weapons and on Their Destruction.« http://www.cwc.gov/cwc_treaty_articles.html (accessed December 22, 2006).
30 See »Convention on the Prohibition of the Development, Production, Stockpiling and Use of Chemical Weapons and on their Destruction: Annex on Chemicals.« http://www.opcw.org/html/db/cwc/eng/cwc_annex_on_chemicals.html (accessed February 19, 2007).
31 The Associated Press, »U.S., Russia Granted Five-Year Extensions to Deadline for Destroying Chemical Weapons Arsenal,« *International Herald Tribune*, December 11, 2006.

creased international funding will likely be necessary to meet even the extended deadlines.

Threat Reduction

One of the most likely sources of proliferation is »the large quantities of Soviet-legacy WMD and missile-related expertise and materials.«[32] To control and regulate this area of vulnerability, the United States primarily relies on the Cooperative Threat Reduction Program (CTRP). The CTRP originated in 1991 as legislation sponsored by Senators Sam Nunn and Richard Lugar entitled »The Soviet Nuclear Threat Reduction Act of 1991.«[33] With a budget of approximately $400 million per year, the CTRP seeks to find new employment for former Soviet nuclear scientists and dismantle ageing nuclear forces. As of December 2005, the CTRP had deactivated over 6,000 nuclear warheads, destroyed over 600 intercontinental ballistic missiles, and engaged thousands of former weapons scientists in peaceful work.[34]

Parallel to this effort, in June 2002 the Group of Eight announced the launch of the G-8 Partnership Against the Spread of Weapons of Mass Destruction. According to the summit statement, the priority concerns for the Partnership »are the destruction of chemical weapons, the dismantlement of decommissioned nuclear submarines, the disposition of fissile materials and the employment of former weapons scientists.«[35] To achieve these objectives, the G-8 leaders promised to raise $20 billion by 2012. Unfortunately, four years after the summit, only $3.5 billion had been donated and even less had been appropriated to programs.[36] According to Sam Nunn, one of the original sponsors of the CTRP, »On a scale of one to 10 . . . the G-8 should be given a 10 for rhetoric, seven for pledges, and a two for programs on addressing the most urgent issues.«[37] Among the barriers to further progress are disputes between Russia and donor countries over taxes, legal liability, and access to sensitive national security sites.[38] To break

---

32 »National Strategy to Combat Weapons of Mass Destruction.« 4.
33 See NTI. »The Nunn-Lugar Cooperative Threat Reduction Program.« (2006). http://www.nti.org/db/nisprofs/russia/forasst/nunn_lug/overview.htm (accessed December 22, 2006).
34 »Nunn-Lugar Report.« (August 2005). http://lugar.senate.gov/reports/Nunn-Lugar_Report_2005.pdf (accessed February 16, 2007).
35 »Statement by the Group of Eight Leaders, June 27, 2002.« http://www.fco.gov.uk/Files/kfile/Art%2002%20gp_stat-en.pdf (accessed Feburary 16, 2007).
36 See Bryan Bender, »A Pledge to Track Uranuim Fades,« *Boston Globe*, July 17,, 2006.
37 Bender, »A Pledge to Track Uranuim Fades.«
38 See Sam Nunn and Michele Flournoy, »A Test of Leadership on Sea Island,« *Washington Post*, June 8, 2004.

through this logjam, the Carnegie Endowment recommends establishing a senior coordinator within the White House to give the issue high-level political attention.[39] Without a strategy to gain Russian support on these issues, neither the G-8 Partnership nor the CTRP will make further progress.

Controls on Nuclear Materials

In addition to reducing the amount of fissile material in existence and securing that which remains, the United States seeks »to discourage the worldwide accumulation of separated plutonium and to minimize the use of highly-enriched uranium.«[40] This is because both plutonium and highly-enriched uranium (HEU) are more readily employed in nuclear weapons than low-enriched uranium (LEU), which requires a complex process of enrichment to become fissile material. The only reason HEU came into widespread use was that at the start of President Eisenhower's Atoms for Peace Program, LEU fuel technology was insufficient to provide the desired level of power in foreign research reactors.[41] As a result, the United States and the Soviet Union exported reactors fueled with HEU to approximately forty countries. By the 1970s, LEU technology was adequate and the United States began the process of converting reactors to use LEU instead of HEU. For some time, however, a lack of funding stymied this effort. It was not until 2004 that the U.S. Department of Energy announced the Global Threat Reduction Initiative (GTRI), earmarking $450 million to retrieve any unused uranium fuel and convert any remaining HEU reactors.[42]

The main reason for the resistance to LEU conversion is that HEU reactors produce plutonium which states can reprocess and reuse as new fuel (known as mixed oxide, or MOX).[43] This system is known as a »closed fuel cycle,« as opposed to an »open fuel cycle« that uses an initial batch of uranium and then disposes of the spent fuel.[44] France, Japan, Russia, and India have all made substantial investments in these plutonium-based fuel cy-

---

39 George Perkovich et al., *Universal Compliance: A Strategy for Nuclear Security* (Washington DC: Carnegie Endowment for International Peace, March 2005), 114-115.
40 »National Strategy to Combat Weapons of Mass Destruction.« 4.
41 NTI. »Past and Current Efforts to Reduce Civilian HEU Use.« http://www.nti.org/db/heu/pastpresent.html#gtri (accessed December 22, 2006).
42 See Matthew L. Wald and Judith Miller, »Energy Department Plans A Push to Retrieve Nuclear Materials,« *New York Times*, May 26, 2004.
43 See Charles D. Ferguson, »Risks of Civilian Plutonium Programs,« *Nuclear Threat Initiative Issue Brief*, http://www.nti.org/e_research/e3_52a.html. (accessed February 16, 2007).
44 Ferguson, »Risks of Civilian Plutonium Programs.«

cles.⁴⁵ The problem with this form of »recycling« is that states can separate the resultant excess plutonium and have a ready supply of fissile material for nuclear bombs. This danger led to the proposal of a Fissile Material Cut-off Treaty (FMCT) which would prohibit the production of weapons-grade uranium and plutonium as well as ban enrichment and reprocessing outside international safeguards. Although the United States was initially willing to begin negotiations on the FMCT, it abruptly changed course and declared that the necessary inspections would be too costly and invasive for many states to accept.⁴⁶ Instead, the United States appears to have adopted a »if you can't beat them, join them« strategy of taking spent fuel from foreign countries and reprocessing it into MOX.⁴⁷ Unlike separated plutonium, this mixed form of fuel is too radioactive for terrorists to handle and so is more proliferation-resistant. The United States is also advocating the development of new types of reactors – known as »pebble-bed reactors« – that would not produce spent fuel accessible to the recipient country.⁴⁸ Given the difficulty with turning back the clock on current users of a closed fuel cycle, this may be the most realistic way forward.

Export Controls

In April 2004, the Security Council unanimously passed Resolution 1540, requiring all states to »adopt and enforce appropriate effective laws« to preclude providing assistance to nonstate actors and to »establish domestic controls to prevent the proliferation of [WMD].«⁴⁹ A special committee of the Security Council is responsible for monitoring the resolution's implementation based on reports from member states, the first of which were due in October 2004.⁵⁰ Unfortunately, by the October deadline, only fifty-four countries had submitted their reports, a response rate of less than one-third.⁵¹ As of February 2006, that number had risen to 124 countries, but

---

45 Perkovich et al., *Universal Compliance*, 101-102.
46 Dafna Linzer, »U.S. Shifts Stance on Nuclear Treaty,« *Washington Post*, July 31, 2004; John Zarocostas, »U.S. Seeks Treaty to Ban Fissile Material,« *Washington Times*, July 30, 2004.
47 Peter Baker and Dafna Linzer, »Nuclear Energy Plan Would Use Spent Fuel,« *Washington Post*, January 26, 2006.
48 Baker and Linzer, »Nuclear Energy Plan Would Use Spent Fuel.«
49 United Nations. »Security Council Resolution 1540.« Un Doc. S/RES/1540. (2004).
50 »Security Council Resolution 1540.« para. 1.
51 See Andrew K. Semmel, »The U.S. Perspective on UN Security Council Resolution 1540: Remarks to the Asia-Pacific Nuclear Safeguards and Security Conference,« Sydney, Australia, November 8, 2004. http://www.state.gov/t/isn/rls/rm/38256.htm (accessed February 15, 2007).

seventy still had not reported.⁵² The Security Council extended the committee's mandate until April 2008 and intends to increase compliance through outreach and greater technical assistance.⁵³

It remains to be seen how the international community will interpret Resolution 1540. The Carnegie Endowment has called for the development of a model law on export controls to guide states in meeting Security Council requirements.⁵⁴ Even if all states adopted such a model, however, export controls are only as effective as those who enforce them. The United States, for instance, allowed its major export control legislation to lapse in 1989 and has only periodically reauthorized it for short periods of time.⁵⁵ The challenge is that increasingly proliferation is fueled by »dual-use« items – goods with civilian purposes that also have military applications.⁵⁶ For example, in 2000 Japan imposed export controls on its PlayStation2 video game system because it could process high quality images quickly, a feature much in demand for advanced missile guidance systems.⁵⁷ While restricting video games may not create an international incident, blocking equipment such as centrifuges or x-ray machines can be extraordinarily politically sensitive given the humanitarian benefits of their legitimate medical use. Also, companies and governments, often more attuned to the immediate prospect of financial gain than the long-term security risks of questionable sales, do not always ensure that buyers are using exported products for their intended purpose.⁵⁸ Despite these significant hurdles, the success of the international arms bazaar led by Pakistani nuclear mastermind Dr. A. Q. Khan demonstrates how crucial it is to prevent a future repetition of such proliferation.⁵⁹

---

52 NTI. »WMD 411: Provisions of Resolution 1540.« http://www.nti.org/f_wmd411/f2n1.html (accessed December 23, 2006).
53 »WMD 411: Provisions of Resolution 1540.«
54 Perkovich et al., *Universal Compliance*, 117-118.
55 Ian F. Fergusson, »The Export Administration Act: Evolution, Provisions, and Debate,« *CRS Report for Congress*, May 5, 2005, http://www.fas.org/sgp/crs/secrecy/RL31832.pdf. (accessed February 16, 2007).
56 David Albright, »A Proliferation Primer,« *The Bulletin of Atomic Scientists* 49, no. 5 (June 1993): 14.
57 See Patrick M. Morgan, *Deterrence Now* (Cambridge: Cambridge University Press, 2003), 234.
58 U.S: General Accounting Office. »Post-Shipment verification Provides Limited Assurance That Dual-Use Items Being Properly Used, GAO-04-357.« (January 2004).
59 See William J. Broad and David E. Sanger, »Pakistani's Black Market May Sell Nuclear Secrets,« *New York Times*, March 21, 2005; David E. Sanger and William J. Broad, »From Rogue Nuclear Programs, Web of trails Leads to Pakistan,« *New York Times*, January 3, 2004.

Sanctions

Sanctions have always been a controversial component of the U.S. nonproliferation repertoire. Critics charge that the penalties rarely have any impact on the leaders of targeted countries, with innocent civilians bearing the brunt of the burden. Even the *National Strategy* acknowledged that at times »sanctions have proven inflexible and ineffective.«[60] These challenges, however, have not stopped attempts to tailor sanctions to minimize their collateral impact. In the wake of the North Korean nuclear test in October 2006, the United Nations Security Council unanimously adopted Resolution 1718, directing all member states to »prevent the direct or indirect supply, sale or transfer« to North Korea of certain military hardware and luxury goods.[61] The latter prohibition was meant to target North Korean leader Kim Jong Il and his reported penchant for fine cognac and expensive automobiles. These sanctions were in addition to the financial restrictions the United States had already imposed on Banco Delta Asia, the Macao bank believed to be the hub of North Korea's money laundering and counterfeiting activities.[62]

The hope was that these »sticks« could become »carrots« by serving as bargaining chips that the North Koreans would grant concessions to remove. Unfortunately, as mentioned above, North Korea has made lifting the financial sanctions a virtual pre-requisite for further talks on its nuclear program. Moreover, South Korea has been especially reluctant to impose the U.N. sanctions given its attempts to create cross-border business projects with North Korea and thereby reduce tensions from the Cold War.[63] The true linchpin to imposing meaningful sanctions on North Korea has always been China, which provides an estimated 80-90 percent of North Korea's oil imports at a reportedly steep discount from world market prices.[64] China, though, is reluctant to push North Korea too far toward the brink as the effects of any economic or political collapse would inevitably spill over and affect China as well. Sanctions will thus likely remain a largely symbolic tool of nonproliferation enforcement.

---

60 »National Strategy to Combat Weapons of Mass Destruction.« 5.
61 United Nations. »Security Council Resolution 1718.« UN Doc. S/RES/1718. (2006), para. 8.
62 See Helene Cooper and David E. Sanger, »U.S. Signals New Incentives for North Korea,« *New York Times*, November 19, 2006.
63 See Glenn Kessler, »Rice Presses S. Korea to Pursue Full Sanctions,« *Washington Post*, October 20, 2006.
64 Joseph Kahn, »China May Press North Koreans,« *New York Times*, October 20, 2006.

Counterproliferation

Interdiction

Interdiction, according to the *National Strategy,* »is a critical part of the U.S. strategy to combat WMD and their delivery means. We must enhance the capabilities of our military, intelligence, technical, and law enforcement communities to prevent the movement of WMD materials, technology, and expertise to hostile states and terrorist organizations«[65] Recognizing this need, President Bush announced in May 2003 the Proliferation Security Initiative (PSI), a multinational effort to equip states to prevent WMD proliferation.[66] The founding participants of the PSI issued a »Statement of Interdiction Principles,« identifying specific areas for cooperation, particularly in sharing intelligence information and providing mutual consent in interdiction missions.[67] Already the PSI has had some notable successes, including the aforementioned September 2003 interception of a freighter bound for Libya with a shipment of centrifuge parts.[68]

The PSI is meant to »be consistent with existing national legal authorities and international law and frameworks.«[69] Generally, while a state has complete jurisdiction over its airspace, territory, and internal waters, its authority diminishes in relation to the distance from its coastline.[70] Except under very limited circumstances, the UN Convention on the Law of the Sea (UNCLOS) bars any state from intercepting another state's vessel on the high seas without the consent of the ship's flag state. The potential consequences of this restriction were brought into sharp relief in December 2002, when U.S. intelligence services identified an unflagged North Korean freighter (the *So San*) crossing the Arabian Sea and contacted the Spanish govern-

---

65 »National Strategy to Combat Weapons of Mass Destruction.« 2.
66 See U.S. Department of State – Bureau of Nonproliferation. »The Proliferation Security Initiative.« (July 28, 2004). http://www.state.gov/t/isn/rls/other/34726.htm (accessed February 19, 2007).
67 See The White House – Office of the Press Secretary. »Proliferation Security Initiative: Statement of Interdiction Principles.« (September 4, 2003). http://www.state.gov/t/isn/rls/fs/23764.htm (accessed February 19, 2007).
68 See also Nicholas Kralev, »Rice Says Initiative Bolsters Security,« *Washington Times*, June 1, 2005.
69 U.S. Department of State – Bureau of Nonproliferation. »Proliferation Security Initiative Frequently Asked Questions (FAQ).« (January 11, 2005). http://www.state.gov/t/isn/rls/fs/32725.htm (accessed February 19, 2007).
70 See Daniel H. Joyner, »The Proliferation Security Initiative: Nonproliferation, Counterproliferation and International Law,« *Yale Journal of International Law* 30, no. 2 (Summer 2005): 525-526.

ment to request that its navy stop the vessel and inspect it for illicit cargo.[71] Spanish special forces boarded the ship, uncovering a cache of Scud missiles hidden beneath sacks of cement. Shortly thereafter, Yemeni government officials came forward and claimed ownership, declaring that they had purchased the missiles from North Korea for defensive purposes. Since international law does not bar such a sale, the United States and Spain allowed the *So San* to proceed, accepting an agreement from the Yemeni president not to make further purchases. This incident was disturbing not for its specific facts – the boarding itself was legal because the ship was flagless – but rather because it highlighted the limited legal authority that would exist for similar operations in the future. If the *So San* had been flying a North Korean flag, and refused to consent to boarding, UNCLOS would prohibit interdiction, even if there was a strong certainty that it carried WMD.

Making the best of its limited legal authority, the PSI is focusing on streamlining the process for acquiring the consent of flag states to board their vessels, thereby bypassing UNCLOS altogether. Besides the provisions addressing mutual consent in the PSI's »Statement of Interdiction Principles,«[72] the United States has signed six ship-boarding agreements including some of the world's major shipping registry states, establishing bilateral procedures for boarding vessels suspected of carrying WMD or related materials.[73] Modeled after counter-narcotics arrangements, these agreements have the effect of limiting the number of flag states a proliferating state can rely upon in transporting illicit materials under the protection of UNCLOS. Indeed, by August 2005 the PSI had ship boarding agreements with states representing more than sixty percent of the global commercial shipping fleet.[74] Despite this initial progress, securing the assent of the remaining key shipping registry states could be difficult given that many states that offer »flags of convenience« (allowing registration with little regulation or oversight) are highly dependent on the earnings from such

---

71 See Jofi Joseph, »The Proliferation Security Initiative: Can Interdiction Stop Proliferation?,« *Arms Control Today* 34, no. 5 (June 2004): 7; Thom Shanker, »Threats and Responses: Arms Smuggling; Scud Missiles Found on Ship of North Korea,« *New York Times*, December 11, 2002.
72 »Proliferation Security Initiative: Statement of Interdiction Principles.«
73 The United States has signed agreements with Liberia (February 11, 2004), Panama (May 12, 2004), the Marshall Islands (August 13, 2004), Croatia (June 1, 2005), Cyprus (July 25, 2005), and Belize (August 4, 2005). Each of these agreements enables a party to request that the other confirm the nationality of the ship in question and, if needed, authorize interdiction. For the text of the agreements, see the U.S. Department of State. »Ship Boarding Agreements.« http://www.state.gov/t/np/c12386.htm (accessed December 23, 2006).
74 See U.S. Department of State - Office of the Spokesman. »The United States and Belize Proliferation Security Initiative Ship Boarding Agreement.« (August 4, 2005). www.state.gov/r/pa/prs/ps/2005/50787.htm (accessed February 19, 2007).

transactions and may be reluctant to grant consent.[75] Unless the United States can reach ship-boarding agreements with virtually all flag states, traffickers will retain options for shipping WMD effectively immune from interdiction authority.[76] Moreover, even if universal participation were possible, the most likely proliferators, such as Pakistan, Iran and North Korea, could always elect to transport WMD shipments under their own flag, thereby guaranteeing that consent would not be forthcoming.

The limitations of the PSI are apparent in the efforts to enforce the sanctions against North Korea in U.N. Security Council Resolution 1718 (mentioned above). In order to ensure compliance with the Resolution's trade restrictions, »all Member States are called upon to take, in accordance with their national authorities and legislation, and consistent with international law, cooperative action including through inspection of cargo to and from [North Korea], as necessary.«[77] These terms provide plenty of wiggle room, and China has already indicated that although it may participate in certain inspections, it does not view interceptions as consistent with the principle of freedom of the high seas.[78] South Korea has likewise ruled out joining any PSI interdictions.[79] Without a resolution mandating universal participation, it will be up to the PSI member states alone to enforce Resolution 1718, a daunting task given the extraordinary intelligence, timing, and coordination required for such missions.

Deterrence

It does not necessarily follow that if some states acquire WMD, they will elect to use them. One might expect that the fear of devastating retaliation from a military superpower like the United States would dampen any aggressive impulses on the part of a regional power with WMD. In fact, it is very plausible that states like Iran and North Korea desire nuclear capabilities solely to deter the United States from intervening in their affairs or initiating an invasion similar to that carried out against Iraq. The trouble with this perspective is that it risks neglecting the role of third-party actors; a re-

75 See Andreas Persbo and Ian Davis, *Sailing Into Uncharted Waters? The Proliferation Security Initiative and the Law of the Sea* (British American Security Information Council Research Report: June 2004), 8-9.
76 See Joel A. Doolin, »Operational Art for the Proliferation Security Initiative,« *unfinished final paper at the Naval War College*, http://www.fas.org/man/eprint/doolin.pdf. (accessed February 19, 2007).
77 »Security Council Resolution 1718.« para. 8 (f).
78 See Maggie Farley, »China Reverses its Refusal to Seach N. Korean Cargo,« *Los Angeles Times*, Ocotber 17, 2006.
79 Norimitsu Onishi, »South Korea Won't Intercept Cargo Ships From the North,« *New York Times*, November 14, 2006.

gime like the Taliban in Afghanistan may have been effectively deterred from attacking the United States, but it did not feel compelled to move against Al Qaeda, enjoying sanctuary within its borders at the time.

Other states unwilling to face the virtually certain retaliation that a direct strike would invite may be willing to run the risk that an indirect attack might be difficult to trace to its origin. Even if a proxy attack is not a state's intention, there may be financial incentives for states to attempt to sell nuclear materials on the black market. This would be a remarkably dangerous game to play, but a state like North Korea may feel that it has no other choice given its dire economic situation.[80] That is why commentators like Graham Allison at Harvard University place such great emphasis on achieving »nuclear accountability;« the ability to trace down the source of a weapon is the best bet to deter the supplier from transferring it in the first place.[81] The United States certainly has the capability to communicate a credible deterrent threat, so the real danger is it not knowing who to retaliate against.

Missile Defenses

Given the enormous challenges inherent in interdiction and the reluctance to wholly rely on deterrence, U.S. government officials are giving much more attention and funding to national missile defense (NMD) programs.[82] Often maligned as a pipe dream that seeks to »hit a bullet with a bullet,« skeptics claim that the low reliability of such a system,[83] combined with its susceptibility to countermeasures,[84] mean that it is unlikely to provide many

---

80 North Korean WMD sales are not merely a pessimistic hypothetical. In negotiations with the United States, a North Korean official threatened that its willingness to sell nuclear materials would depend on U.S. actions. Donald Kirk, »N. Korea Flirts With ›Red Line‹,« *Christian Science Monitor*, May 28, 2004.
81 See Bill Powell, »What to Do When Outlaws Get the Bomb,« *Time*, October 23, 2006.
82 See Bill Gertz, »U.S. Test Missile Hits a Korean Bulls-Eye,« *Washington Times*, September 2, 2006; James Glanz, »This Time It's Real: An Antimissile System Takes Shape,« *New York Times*, May 4, 2004; Bradley Graham, »General Says Missile Defense Could Be Ready Soon,« *Washington Post*, April 28, 2004.
83 Thus far, test results of the fledgling missile defense system have not been promising. See John Mintz and Joby Warrick, »U.S. Unprepared Despite Progress, Experts Say,« *Washington Post*, November 8, 2004; Peter Spiegel, »For N. Korean Missile, U.S. Defense is Hit or Miss,« *Los Angeles Times*, June 22, 2006; David Stout and John H. Cushman, »Defense Missile for U.S. System Fails to Launch,« *New York Times*, December 6, 2004.
84 See, e.g., William J. Broad, »Achilles' Heel in Missile Plan: Crude Weapons,« *New York Times*, August 27, 2001.

strategic benefits.⁸⁵ One group of analysts asserts, »Confidence in the effectiveness of the planned NMD system would not be high enough to increase U.S. freedom of action beyond the level already achieved through deterrence.«⁸⁶ Other skeptics of NMD, including nuclear deterrence theorist Robert Powell, believe that a moderately effective NMD will decrease American security by making the United States bolder in its interactions with other states, thereby increasing the risk of a nuclear attack in response.⁸⁷ Still other critics point out that if American NMD ambitions are too extensive or seen as too effective, Russia and China may compensate by building up their missile arsenals, possibly producing an overall net loss in security.⁸⁸

On the opposing side of this debate are those who feel that any uncertainty over accuracy will affect the enemy as well, and it is worth »raising the admission price« of potential WMD attacks as high as possible.⁸⁹ According to this position, U.S. missile defenses could act as a »psychological deterrent,« providing important insurance against attack by raising the prospect in an adversary's mind that using its WMD-missile force could bring about all of the costs inherent in U.S. retaliation without any of the »benefit« of causing damage to American interests.⁹⁰ As James Lindsay and Michael O'Hanlon put it, »even a porous missile defense could enhance deterrence by forcing an attacker with limited capability to contemplate the possibility that any attack would be futile and fatal.«⁹¹ With such a system in place, states would be less inclined to engage in blackmail or extreme coercive measures under the cover of deterrence, realizing that the United States might feel secure enough to respond with military force regardless of whether the threat was a bluff or not. This viewpoint meshes with Robert

---

85 Richard L. Garwin, »A Defense That Will not Defend,« *The Washington Quarterly* 23, no. 2 (Summer 2000): 110; Gordon R. Mitchell, *Strategic Deception: Rhetoric, Science, and Politics in Missile Defense Advocacy* (East Lansing, MI: Michigan State University Press, 2000).
86 George Lewis, Lisbeth Gronlund, and David Wright, »National Missile Defense: An Indefensible System,« *Foreign Policy*, no. 117 (Winter 1999-2000): 128.
87 Robert Powell, »Nuclear Deterrence theory, Nuclear Proliferation, and National Missile Defense,« *International Security* 27, no. 4 (Spring 2003): 88.
88 Dean Wilkening, *Ballistic-Missile Defence and Strategic Stability*, ed. International Institute for Strategic Studies, *Adelphi Paper 334* (Oxford: Oxford University Press, 2000), 8.
89 Henry Kissinger, *Does America Need a Foreign Policy?* (New York: Simon & Schuster, 2001), 69.
90 Jerome H. Kahan, »Deterrence and Warfighting in an NBC Environment,« in *The Niche Threat: Deterring the Use of Chemical and Biological Weapons*, ed. Stuart E. Johnson (Washington DC: National Defense University Press, 1997), 100.
91 James M. Lindsay and Michael E. O'Hanlon, *Defending America: The Case for Limited National Missile Defense* (Washington DC: Brookings Institution Press, 2001), 20.

Powell's central premise – that robust defense capabilities would make the U.S. willingness to use force offensively more credible – but reaches the opposite conclusion that greater freedom of action is advantageous to American foreign policy. The prospect of such an outcome has resulted in much of the international opposition to NMD by those interested in keeping American military might as constrained as possible.

Both sides of the argument have merit, and ultimately the decision will come down to technical feasibility, and what level of insurance against missile attack is worth the expense involved. In brinksmanship decisions, if an adversary is hoping to deter the United States, will it likely rely heavily on a long-range missile threat? Given the wide range of alternative means for harming the United States, as demonstrated by the September 11th attacks, there is an understandable concern that missile defenses might embody a »Maginot Line« mentality that aggressive states could easily bypass altogether. Moreover, as an alternative to long-range missiles, rogue states may develop cruise missiles that are far more difficult to defend against and perfectly suited for carrying biological weapons.[92] Nevertheless, the unique coercive power of missiles justifies further testing of new defensive technologies, especially with the greater success of boost-phase and air-borne laser defense systems.[93] Stripping states of a secure belief in their ability to deliver WMD by missile will undoubtedly reduce the force of their deterrent threats. The crucial issue will be how NMD technologies develop and whether they are cost-effective compared to the other threats faced by the United States.

Passive Defenses

Considering the fallibility of missile defenses, should a WMD attack ever occur it is imperative to try and limit its destructiveness through the use of passive defenses. On the battlefield, the ability of U.S. military forces to survive a WMD attack and continue with the mission (which would then likely include regime change) will make other leaders more reluctant to put deterrence to the test. Military gaming exercises show that chemical and bi-

---

92 Kathleen C. Bailey, *Doomsday Weapons in the Hands of Many: The Arms Control Challenge of the 90s* (Chicago: University of Illinois Press, 1991), 103; Rex R. Kiziah, *Assessment of the Emerging Biocruise Threat, Future Warfare Series No. 6* (Maxwell Air Force Base, AL: Air War College, August 2000); Barry R. Schneider, *Future War and Counterproliferation: U.S. Military Responses to NBC Proliferation Threats* (Westport, CT: Praeger, 1999), 126.
93 See Frank J. Gaffney, »Go Navy Missile Defense,« *Washington Times*, March 1, 2005; James T. Hackett, »Needed: Lasers in the Sky,« *Washington Times*, April 6, 2006.

ological weapon (CB) detection and defense capabilities can significantly boost U.S. resolve, giving soldiers confidence that they can fight and win in a contaminated environment.[94] Reversing perspectives, war games in which teams were assigned to play the role of a regional adversary revealed that the U.S. ability to operate in a WMD environment had a major impact on the adversary's decision over whether to resort to unconventional weapons.[95] Similar to the psychological deterrence power of missile defenses, effective passive defense measures are likely to create uncertainty in the mind of an adversary that their WMD use would succeed, causing them to fear inviting repercussions without any military gain.

To reinforce this perception, the U.S. Department of Defense is developing and fielding a range of sensors, masks, decontamination systems, and medical kits for soldiers in combat.[96] New protective suits are standard issue for American infantry, and many soldiers receive vaccinations against smallpox.[97] The U.S. military is also gradually expanding its training for operations involving WMD, including the use of simulations, the construction of Humvees that protect against and detect CB, the creation of special response teams and medical units, and the exploration of new operational tactics to limit vulnerability.[98] One project involved a competition sponsored by the Defense Advanced Research Projects Agency that set a $1 million reward for a team that could construct an unmanned land vehicle capable of navigating across 200 miles of open desert without any human assistance.[99] While there are certainly shortcomings in certain areas and significant room for improvement, assessments that coalition soldiers in Operation Iraqi Freedom were reasonably well prepared to withstand a chemical

---

94 Robert G. Joseph, »The Role of Nuclear Weapons in U.S. Deterrence Strategy,« in *Deterrence in the 21st Century*, ed. Max G. Manwaring (London: Frank Cass, 2001), 58.
95 Robert G. Joseph and John F. Reichart, »NBC Military Planning: Lessons Learned from Analysis and Wargaming,« in *Countering the Proliferation and Use of Weapons of Mass Destruction*, ed. Vincent J. Jodoin and Alan R. Van Tassel (New York: McGraw-Hill, 1988), 185.
96 See U.S. Department of Defense. »Chemical and Biological Defense Program.« Annual Report to Congress. (March 2006). http://www.fas.org/irp/threat/cbdp2006.pdf (accessed February 19, 2007).
97 Matthew Cox and William Matthews, »The Best Protective Gear in the World?,« *Air Force Times*, February 24, 2003; Vicki Kemper, »Vaccine Program Going Well, Military Reports,« *Los Angeles Times*, February 14, 2003.
98 »Chemical and Biological Defense Program.«
99 See Rene Sanchez, »Robot Race is Giant Step for Unmanned Kind,« *Washington Post*, March 10, 2004.

weapons attack reflected well on America's progress in CB defense capabilities.[100]

Preemption

Fearing that none of these largely defensive measures will be adequate, some commentators maintain that the risk of certain states using WMD or supplying them to terrorists may be substantial enough to justify disarmament by air strikes or outright invasion.[101] The *National Strategy* noted that the U.S. capability to defend against WMD-armed adversaries includes »in appropriate cases through preemptive measures.«[102] Generally speaking, this option is not new to U.S. military planners, who seriously contemplated contingency plans to destroy the nuclear facilities of the Soviet Union at the start of the Cold War[103] and China in the early 1960s.[104] After a period of limited interest over the subsequent few decades, the build-up to Operation Iraqi Freedom brought renewed attention to the strategic and legal aspects of forcible disarmament. Then Secretary of Defense Donald Rumsfeld articulated a modern version of the classic preemption doctrine, claiming »[i]t is not possible to defend against every threat, in every place, at every conceivable time. Defending against terrorism and other emerging threats requires that we take the war to the enemy.«[105]

The challenge will be how to make this offensive outlook militarily successful and politically viable, given that »we can expect future WMD target sets to be large, extremely difficult to find, hardened, well-protected, and

---

100 Peter Baker, »But What if the Iraqis Strike First?,« *Washington Post*, January 23, 2003; Tony Capaccio, »Iraq Probably Can't Mount Major Chemical Attack, General Says,« *Bloomberg.com*, March 4, 2003; Romesh Ratnesar, »Can They Strike Back?,« *Time*, February 3, 2003.
101 See, e.g., Michael J. Glennon, »Preempting Terrorism: The Case for Anticipatory Self-Defense,« *The Weekly Standard*, January 28, 2002.
102 »National Strategy to Combat Weapons of Mass Destruction.« 3.
103 See Russell D. Buhite and William Christopher Hamel, »War for Peace: The Question of an American Preventive War Against the Soviet Union, 1945-1955,« *Diplomatic History* 14, no. 3 (Summer 1990).
104 See William Burr and Jeffrey T. Richelson, »Whether to 'Strangle the Baby in the Craddle': the United States and the Chinese Nuclear Program, 1960-1964,« *International Security* 25, no. 3 (Winter 2000-2001): 54-55, 68.
105 Donald H. Rumsfeld, »Transforming the Military,« *Foreign Affairs* 81, no. 3 (May/June 2002).

located next to things or people we do not want to damage or injure.«[106] Iran's suspected enrichment facilities, for instance, are effectively immune from air strikes, hidden in large government complexes and other secret locations.[107] Novel tunneling techniques have given states the ability to bury bunkers and compartments, reinforced to withstand intensive bombing, far beneath the Earth's surface; indeed, there are now more than 1,100 such facilities known be in existence.[108] To be fair, advances have taken place on the detection side as well – including sophisticated techniques such as hyperspectral imaging, seismic sensing, and gravimetry – that may help uncover even well-hidden underground construction efforts.

Confronted with the prospect of deeply buried targets, the U.S. Department of Defense is reconsidering the employment of tactical nuclear weapons, leading to fierce debate in Congress over whether to fund further research, development, and possible testing of such an option.[109] Some analysts argue that only nuclear weapons are powerful enough to penetrate shielded and hardened facilities, and could have the added advantage of creating temperatures likely to incinerate any chemical or biological weapons contained therein.[110] Furthermore, advocates of tactical nuclear weapons believe that by being »usable« and thereby more credibly threatened, they will contribute to deterrence more than thermonuclear devices that would create unacceptable levels of damage.[111] However, there is a growing con-

---

106 Robert W. Chandler and Robert Jl. Trees, *Tomorrow's War, Today's Decision: Iraqi Weapons of Mass Destruction and the Implications of WMD-Armed Adversaries for Future U.S. Military Strategy* (McLean, VA: AMCODA Press, 1996), 156.; see also Marc Dean Millot, »Facing the Emerging Reality of Regional Nuclear Adversaries,« *The Washington Quarterly* 17, no. 3 (Summer 1994): 48.
107 See Sharon Squassoni. »Iran's Nuclear Program: Recent Developments.« Congressional Research Service. (March 2004) http://www.fas.org/sgp/crs/nuke/RS21592.pdf (accessed February 19, 2007).
108 Michael A. Levi, *Fire in the Hole: Nuclear and Non-Nuclear Options for Counterproliferation*, Working Paper No.31 (Washington DC: Carnegie Endowment, November 2002), 8; Eric M. Sepp, *Deeply Buried Facilities: Implications for Military Operations*, Occasional Paper No. 14 (Maxwell Air Base, AL: Air War College, May 2000), 5.
109 See Helen Dewar, »Senate Passes $447 Billion Defense Bill,« *Washington Post*, June 24, 2004; Bill Gertz, »Defense Seeks Raise, Rock-Penetrating Nuke,« *Washington Times*, February 8, 2005; Associated Press, »Senate Approves Money for New Nuclear Weapon,« *Los Angeles Times*, July 2, 2005.
110 Thomas Dowler and Joseph S. Howard II, »Stability in a Proliferated World,« *Strategic Review* 23, no. 2 (Spring 1995): 28. Conventional weapons, by contrast, may simply only succeed in dispersing the CB materials, causing widespread collateral damage.
111 Richard T. Cooper, »Making Nuclear Bombs,« *Los Angeles Times*, February 3, 2003; David. G. Savage, »Nuclear Pant Meant to Deter,« *Los Angeles Times*, March 11, 2002; Amy Scott Tyson, »Nuclear Plan Changes Calculus of Deterrence,« *The Christian Science Monitor*, March 14, 2002.

sensus that such a strategy will fall prey to the same flaws that have foiled plans for tactical nuclear weapons before, from nuclear artillery to neutron bombs: no matter how tiny, they simply cannot be used without causing intolerable radioactive fallout.[112] As an alternative, military research labs are developing new conventional options such as penetrating »thermobaric« bombs (called BLU-118Bs), advanced munitions that can repeatedly strike the same precise location to reach far beneath the surface, and bombs that employ a »hard target smart fuze« to delay detonation until deep underground.[113]

Even if the United States could contain the fallout from a nuclear strike, there is still the serious danger of releasing WMD from the attack and causing collateral damage. During Operation Desert Fox in 1998, then Secretary of Defense William Cohen left many Iraqi CB facilities off the target list, remarking, »We're not going to take a chance and try to target any facility that would release any kind of horrific damage to innocent people.«[114] This is a significant lesson for any state hoping to secure sanctuary for its WMD. As a result, extensive research is underway on technologies like high-power microwave weapons (that would disable the electricity and communications of a facility), high-temperature incendiaries (that would burn up any released material) and special foam (that would seal off a site and render it unusable without releasing its contents) to disable a target without emitting WMD.[115] Given that even the most protected underground sites require contact with the surface, the prospects for »functional defeat,« or isolating a facility by destroying its electronics or support systems, are rather promising.[116]

In the end, if there are too many targets to be able to place confidence in even the most thorough of air campaigns to destroy them all, then a preemptive attack runs the risk of provoking the very attack it intended to foreclose. The reliability of target identification ought to be tempered by the experience of the 1990-1991 Gulf War, after which target planners were shocked

---

112 See Michael M. May and Zachary Haldeman, *Effectiveness of Nuclear Weapons Against Buried Biological Agents* (Stanford, CA: Center for International Security and Cooperation, June 2003).

113 John F. Burns and Eric Schmitt, »U.S. Forces Join Big Assault on Afghan Stronghold,« *New York Times*, March 3, 2002; Andrew Koch, »Dual Delivery is Key to Buried Targets,« *Jane's Defence Weekly*, March 8, 2000; Levi, *Fire in the Hole*, 17-20; Andre C. Revkin, »Advanced Armaments,« *New York Times*, December 3, 2001.

114 Steven Lee Myers, »The Targets: Jets Said to Avoid Poison Gas Sites,« *New York Times*, December 18, 1998.

115 David A. Fulghum, »Microwave Weapons May Be Ready for Iraq,« *Aviation Week & Space Technology*, August 5, 2002; John Hendren, »U.S. Studies Foam Bombs Among Options to Isolate Chemicals,« *Los Angeles Times*, July 18, 2002; Michael Smith, »Saddam to be Target of Britain's 'E-Bomb',« *London Daily Telegraph*, August 26, 2002.

116 See Levi, *Fire in the Hole*, 21.

at how badly they underestimated the number of Iraqi WMD facilities.[117] Conversely, the apparent overestimation of Iraqi WMD stockpiles during Iraqi Freedom also does little to instill faith in the ability of the intelligence community to develop an accurate target set.[118] Granted an outright invasion would probably bypass the uncertainties of intelligence and collateral damage problems, uprooting a state's WMD development in its entirety, but it would also likely increase the risk of devastating reprisals and last resort attacks. The heavy burdens of occupation, as demonstrated by the aftermath of Iraqi Freedom, would also serve as a severe limiting factor on carrying out missions of regime change and disarmament.

Consequence Management

According to the *National Strategy*, »[d]efending the American homeland is the most basic responsibility of our government.«[119] This responsibility is incredibly difficult to carry out, given that the United States is a soft target with numerous points of vulnerability. America's agriculture is vulnerable to bioterrorism, its public events are vulnerable to chemical attacks, and the specter of a suitcase nuclear bomb makes even entire cities vulnerable. Particularly after the anthrax attacks in the autumn of 2001 and subsequent reports of a plot to detonate a »dirty bomb« in a U.S. city, the threat of WMD has without question become a U.S. domestic concern. In response, the United States is beginning to mirror the kind of training, investment, and innovation directed toward its military forces in homeland security efforts to improve the skills and equipment of first-responders and civil support teams in major cities.[120] When compared to the billions of dollars spent on national missile defense, these efforts can justifiably be described as offering »more 'anti-bang' for the buck.«[121] Unfortunately, despite significant progress in some areas, many experts believe that the United States

---

117 See Andrew Cockburn and Patrick Cockburn, *Out of the Ashes: The Resurrection of Saddam Hussein* (London: Verso, 2000), 96.
118 Walter Pincus, »U.S. Has Still Not Found Iraqi Arms,« *Washington Post*, April 26, 2003.
119 »National Strategy to Combat Weapons of Mass Destruction.« 5.
120 See Richard A. Falkenrath, Robert D. Newman, and Bradley A. Thayer, *America's Achilles' Heel: Nuclear Biological, and Chemical Terrorism and Covert Attack* (Cambridge, MA: MIT Press, 1998).
121 Richard Betts, »Universal Deterrence or Conceptual Collapse? Liberal Pessimism and Utopian Realism,« in *The Coming Crisis: Nuclear Proliferation, U.S. Interests, and World Order*, ed. Victor A. Utgoff (Cambridge, MA: MIT Press, 2000), 79.

has a long way to go in providing an adequate homeland security framework.[122]

This is not to say that the United States has failed to take steps to protect itself; at least on the surface the Bush Administration appears to understand the need for developing defensive technologies, having requested billions of dollars to protect the nation against bioterrorism and other threats. Project Bioshield, for example, is meant to encourage private firms to conduct research into new vaccines against threats such as anthrax, and to experiment with novel techniques like artificial antibodies to potentially treat smallpox after infection.[123] Likewise, the Department of Homeland Security has implemented many important reforms, particularly in the area of border control.[124] Through the Container Security Initiative, the United States has revised its customs rules to require every shipping company importing cargo to provide U.S. officials with advance information on each container on their ships, along with other security measures.[125] Under the Secure Freight Initiative, the U.S. Departments of Energy and Homeland Security announced that six foreign seaports will install radiation-detection equipment and x-ray machines to scan U.S.-bound containers for WMD.[126] Portable pager-sized nuclear detection devices that can sense minute amounts of radioactive material are also substantially aiding border control at land crossings.[127] Unfortunately, producing comparable biological weapon detectors is proving much more of a challenge, prompting research into advanced technologies such as tissue-based biosensors as well as specialized environmental and public health monitoring systems to improve

---

122 Ceci Connolly, »Readiness for Chemical Attack Criticized,« *Washington Post*, June 4, 2003; Spencer S. Hsu, »Anthrax Alarm Uncovers Response Flaws,« *Washington Post*, March 17, 2005; Shaun Waterman, »Test Reveals Wide Failures in Terror Response Abilities,« *Washington Times*, December 21, 2003.

123 Will Dunham, »U.S. Congress Approves Bioterrorism Preparedness Bill,« *Reuters*, December 9, 2006; Vicki Kemper, »Senate Approves $5.6 Billion for 10-Year 'Bioshield' Project,« *Los Angeles Times*, May 20, 2004.

124 See U.S. Department of Homeland Security. »National Response Plan.« (December 2004). http://www.dhs.gov/xlibrary/assets/NRP_FullText.pdf (accessed February 19, 2007); U.S. Department of Homeland Security. »Securing Our Homeland: U.S. Department of Homeland Security Strategic Plan.« (2004). https://www.dhs.gov/xlibrary/assets/DHS_StratPlan_FINAL_spread.pdf (accessed February 19, 2007).

125 Mark Hosenball and Evan Thomas, »High-Seas Hunting,« *Newsweek*, December 23, 2003.

126 Chris Strohm, »Six Foreign Ports to Scan Cargo For Nuclear Devices,« *Govexec.com*, December 7, 2006. http://www.govexec.com/dailyfed/1206/120706tdpm1.htm (accessed February 19, 2007).

127 Philip Shenon, »Border Inspectors to Look for Radioactive Material,« *New York Times*, March 1, 2003.

detection speed and sensitivity.[128] These homeland security measures are far from a failsafe, but they are a prudent and often cost-effective way to save American lives if the unthinkable does occur.

Conclusion

Returning to the opening theme of this chapter, one of the major challenges to U.S. counterproliferation efforts is that other states do not feel the same sense of urgency to stop and perhaps roll back the spread of WMD. The dilemma is that any traditional methods of counterproliferation – diplomacy, export controls, sanctions, interdiction, etc – need multilateral participation to be effective. The *National Strategy* has a section that addresses international cooperation, but it is only two sentences long: »WMD represent a threat not just to the United States, but also to our friends and allies and the broader international community. For this reason, it is vital that we work closely with like-minded countries on all elements of our comprehensive proliferation strategy.«[129] This passage's assumption of a common perception of threat and a common sense of purpose is simply not borne out in reality. Admittedly, it is not an easy task to craft a unified counterproliferation strategy, as the difference in threat perception is there for a reason: the United States is a far more visible and controversial actor in world affairs than most states. To the extent that the United States can moderate this image, it may be able to lessen the threats arrayed against it and have an easier time gaining adherents to its policies. But retreating from the world stage is not an option, and the United States must persuade its allies that they share a vital interest in avoiding a future of nuclear anarchy. Otherwise, the United States will find itself inescapably drawn to the areas of counterproliferation it can most control on its own: defense and preemption. This would be an unfortunate outcome as the two strategies may form a vicious cycle, requiring greater and greater defensive measures as preemption sparks further proliferation.

---

128 Spencer S. Hsu, »Sensors May Track Terror's Fallout,« *Washington Post*, June 2, 2003; Judith Miller, »U.S. is Deploying a Monitor System for Germ Attacks,« *New York Times*, January 22, 2003.
129 »National Strategy to Combat Weapons of Mass Destruction.« 6.

References

Albright, David. »A Proliferation Primer.« *The Bulletin of Atomic Scientists* 49, no. 5 (June 1993): 14-23.

Bailey, Kathleen C. *Doomsday Weapons in the Hands of Many: The Arms Control Challenge of the 90s*. Chicago: University of Illinois Press, 1991.

Baker, Peter. »But What if the Iraqis Strike First?« *Washington Post*, January 23, 2003.

Baker, Peter, and Dafna Linzer. »Nuclear Energy Plan Would Use Spent Fuel.« *Washington Post*, January 26, 2006.

Bender, Bryan. »A Pledge to Track Uranuim Fades.« *Boston Globe*, July 17, 2006.

Betts, Richard. »Universal Deterrence or Conceptual Collapse? Liberal Pessimism and Utopian Realism.« In *The Coming Crisis: Nuclear Proliferation, U.S. Interests, and World Order*, edited by Victor A. Utgoff. Cambridge, MA: MIT Press, 2000

»Biological and Toxin Weapons Convention Website.« http://www.opbw.org/ (accessed December 22, 2006).

Broad, William J. »Achilles' Heel in Missile Plan: Crude Weapons.« *New York Times*, August 27, 2001.

Broad, William J., and David E. Sanger. »Pakistani's Black Market May Sell Nuclear Secrets.« *New York Times*, March 21, 2005.

Buhite, Russell D., and William Christopher Hamel. »War for Peace: The Question of an American Preventive War Against the Soviet Union, 1945-1955.« *Diplomatic History* 14, no. 3 (Summer 1990): 367-384.

Burns, John F., and Eric Schmitt. »U.S. Forces Join Big Assault on Afghan Stronghold.« *New York Times*, March 3, 2002.

Burr, William, and Jeffrey T. Richelson. »Whether to 'Strangle the Baby in the Craddle': the United States and the Chinese Nuclear Program, 1960-1964.« *International Security* 25, no. 3 (Winter 2000-2001): 54-99.

Bush, George. »President Announces New Measures to Counter the Threat of WMD: Remarks on Weapons of Mass Destruction Proliferation.« National Defense University Fort Lesley J. McNair. Washington DC, February 11, 2004. http://www.whitehouse.gov/news/releases/2004/02/20040211-4.html (accessed February 16, 2007).

Capaccio, Tony. »Iraq Probably Can't Mount Major Chemical Attack, General Says.« *Bloomberg.com*, March 4, 2003.

Chandler, Robert W., and Robert Jl. Trees. *Tomorrow's War, Today's Decision: Iraqi Weapons of Mass Destruction and the Implications of WMD-Armed Adversaries for Future U.S. Military Strategy*. McLean, VA: AMCODA Press, 1996.

»Convention on the Prohibition of the Development, Production, Stockpiling and Use of Chemical Weapons and on their Destruction: Annex on Chemicals.« http://www.opcw.org/html/db/cwc/eng/cwc_annex_on_chemicals.html (accessed February 19, 2007).

Cirincione, Joseph, Jon B. Wolfsthal, and Miriam Rajkumar. *Deadly Arsenals: Nuclear, Biological, and Chemical Threats*. 2nd ed. Washington DC: Carnegie Endowment for International Peace, 2005.

Cockburn, Andrew, and Patrick Cockburn. *Out of the Ashes: The Resurrection of Saddam Hussein*. London: Verso, 2000.

Cody, Edward. »North Korea Nuke Talks End Without Deal.« *Washington Post*, December 22, 2006.

Connolly, Ceci. »Readiness for Chemical Attack Criticized.« *Washington Post*, June 4, 2003.

»Convention on the Prohibition of the Development, Production and Stockpiling of Bacteriological (Biological) and Toxin Weapons and on Their Destruction.« http://www.opbw.org/convention/documents/btwctext.pdf (accessed December 22, 2006).

»Convention on the Prohibition of the Development, Production, Stockpiling and Use of Chemical Weapons and on Their Destruction.« http://www.cwc.gov/cwc_treaty_articles.html (accessed December 22, 2006).

Cooper, Helene, and David E. Sanger. »U.S. Signals New Incentives for North Korea.« *New York Times*, November 19, 2006.

Cooper, Richard T. »Making Nuclear Bombs.« *Los Angeles Times*, February 3, 2003.

Cox, Matthew, and William Matthews. »The Best Protective Gear in the World?« *Air Force Times*, February 24, 2003.

Dewar, Helen. »Senate Passes $447 Billion Defense Bill.« *Washington Post*, June 24, 2004.

Doolin, Joel A. »Operational Art for the Proliferation Security Initiative.« *unfinished final paper at the Naval War College*, http://www.fas.org/man/eprint/doolin.pdf. (accessed February 19, 2007).

Dowler, Thomas, and Joseph S. Howard II. »Stability in a Proliferated World.« *Strategic Review* 23, no. 2 (Spring 1995): 26-37.

Dunham, Will. »U.S. Congress Approves Bioterrorism Preparedness Bill.« *Reuters*, December 9, 2006.

Falkenrath, Richard A., Robert D. Newman, and Bradley A. Thayer. *America's Achilles' Heel: Nuclear Biological, and Chemical Terrorism and Covert Attack*. Cambridge, MA: MIT Press, 1998.

Farley, Maggie. »China Reverses its Refusal to Seach N. Korean Cargo.« *Los Angeles Times*, Ocotber 17, 2006.

Fathi, Nazila. »Iran and Russia Sign Accord to Speed Nuclear Power Project.« *New York Times*, December 26, 2002.

–. »Iran Snubs Europe's Nuclear Plan.« *New York times*, May 18, 2006.

Ferguson, Charles D. »Risks of Civilian Plutonium Programs.« *Nuclear Threat Initiative Issue Brief*, http://www.nti.org/e_research/e3_52a.html. (accessed February 16, 2007).

Fergusson, Ian F. »The Export Administration Act: Evolution, Provisions, and Debate.« *CRS Report for Congress*, May 5, 2005, http://www.fas.org/sgp/crs/secrecy/RL31832.pdf. (accessed February 16, 2007).

Fulghum, David A. »Microwave Weapons May Be Ready for Iraq.« *Aviation Week & Space Technology*, August 5, 2002.

Gaffney, Frank J. »Go Navy Missile Defense.« *Washington Times*, March 1, 2005.

Gargill, David. »The Libya Fallacy: The Iraq War is Not What Disarmed Qadaffi.« *Harper's Magazine*, November, 2004.

Garwin, Richard L. »A Defense That Will not Defend.« *The Washington Quarterly* 23, no. 2 (Summer 2000): 109-123.

Gertz, Bill. »Defense Seeks Raise, Rock-Penetrating Nuke.« *Washington Times*, February 8, 2005.

–. »U.S. Test Missile Hits a Korean Bulls-Eye.« *Washington Times*, September 2, 2006.

Glanz, James. »This Time It's Real: An Antimissile System Takes Shape.« *New York Times*, May 4, 2004.

Glennon, Michael J. »Preempting Terrorism: The Case for Anticipatory Self-Defense.« *The Weekly Standard*, January 28, 2002.

Graham, Bradley. »General Says Missile Defense Could Be Ready Soon.« *Washington Post*, April 28, 2004.

Hackett, James T. »Needed: Lasers in the Sky.« *Washington Times*, April 6, 2006.

Hendren, John. »U.S. Studies Foam Bombs Among Options to Isolate Chemicals.« *Los Angeles Times*, July 18, 2002.

Hosenball, Mark, and Evan Thomas. »High-Seas Hunting.« *Newsweek*, December 23, 2003.

Hsu, Spencer S. »Anthrax Alarm Uncovers Response Flaws.« *Washington Post*, March 17, 2005.

–. »Sensors May Track Terror's Fallout.« *Washington Post*, June 2, 2003.

»International Atomic Energy Agency.« http://www.iaea.org/ (accessed December 16, 2007).

Johnson, Rebecca. »Politics and Protection: Why the 2005 NPT Review Conference Failed.« *Disarmament Diplomacy*, no. 80 (Autumn 2005).

Joseph, Jofi. »The Proliferation Security Initiative: Can Interdiction Stop Proliferation?« *Arms Control Today* 34, no. 5 (June 2004): 6-13.

Joseph, Robert G. »The Role of Nuclear Weapons in U.S. Deterrence Strategy.« In *Deterrence in the 21st Century*, edited by Max G. Manwaring. London: Frank Cass, 2001.

Joseph, Robert G., and John F. Reichart. »NBC Military Planning: Lessons Learned from Analysis and Wargaming.« In *Countering the Proliferation and Use of Weapons of Mass Destruction*, edited by Vincent J. Jodoin and Alan R. Van Tassel. New York: McGraw-Hill, 1988.

Joyner, Daniel H. »The Proliferation Security Initiative: Nonproliferation, Counterproliferation and International Law.« *Yale Journal of International Law* 30, no. 2 (Summer 2005): 507-548.

Kahan, Jerome H. »Deterrence and Warfighting in an NBC Environment.« In *The Niche Threat: Deterring the Use of Chemical and Biological Weapons*, edited by Stuart E. Johnson. Washington DC: National Defense University Press, 1997.

Kahn, Joseph. »China May Press North Koreans.« *New York Times*, October 20, 2006.

Kemper, Vicki. »Senate Approves $5.6 Billion for 10-Year 'Bioshield' Project.« *Los Angeles Times*, May 20, 2004.

–. »Vaccine Program Going Well, Military Reports.« *Los Angeles Times*, February 14, 2003.

Kessler, Glenn. »Rice Presses S. Korea to Pursue Full Sanctions.« *Washington Post*, October 20, 2006.

Kirk, Donald. »N. Korea Flirts With 'Red Line'.« *Christian Science Monitor*, May 28, 2004.

Kissinger, Henry. *Does America Need a Foreign Policy?* New York: Simon & Schuster, 2001.

Kiziah, Rex R. *Assessment of the Emerging Biocruise Threat, Future Warfare Series No. 6*. Maxwell Air Force Base, AL: Air War College, August 2000.

Koch, Andrew. »Dual Delivery is Key to Buried Targets.« *Jane's Defence Weekly*, March 8, 2000.

Kralev, Nicholas. »Rice Says Initiative Bolsters Security.« *Washington Times*, June 1, 2005.

Lakely, James G. »Libya Will Dismantle its Weapons.« *Washington Times*, December 20, 2003.

Levi, Michael A. *Fire in the Hole: Nuclear and Non-Nuclear Options for Counterproliferation*, Working Paper No.31. Washington DC: Carnegie Endowment, November 2002.

Lewis, George, Lisbeth Gronlund, and David Wright. »National Missile Defense: An Indefensible System.« *Foreign Policy*, no. 117 (Winter 1999-2000): 120-137.

Lindsay, James M., and Michael E. O'Hanlon. *Defending America: The Case for Limited National Missile Defense.* Washington DC: Brookings Institution Press, 2001.

Linzer, Dafna. »Iran Pushes for Talks Without Conditions.« *Washington Post*, August 23, 2006.

–. »U.S. Shifts Stance on Nuclear Treaty.« *Washington Post*, July 31, 2004.

Lugar, Richard, and Evan Bayh. »A Nuclear Fuel Bank Advocated.« *Chicago Tribune*, October 22, 2006.

Lynch, Colum, and Glenn Kessler. »U.S., European Allies ad Odds on Terms of Iran Resolution.« *Washington Post*, October 26, 2006.

May, Michael M., and Zachary Haldeman. *Effectiveness of Nuclear Weapons Against Buried Biological Agents.* Stanford, CA: Center for International Security and Cooperation, June 2003.

Miller, Judith. »U.S. is Deploying a Monitor System for Germ Attacks.« *New York Times*, January 22, 2003.

Millot, Marc Dean. »Facing the Emerging Reality of Regional Nuclear Adversaries.« *The Washington Quarterly* 17, no. 3 (Summer 1994): 41-71.

Mintz, John, and Joby Warrick. »U.S. Unprepared Despite Progress, Experts Say.« *Washington Post*, November 8, 2004.

«Missile Technology Control Regime.« http://www.mtcr.info/english/ (accessed December 6, 2006).

Mitchell, Gordon R. *Strategic Deception: Rhetoric, Science, and Politics in Missile Defense Advocacy.* East Lansing, MI: Michigan State University Press, 2000.

Morgan, Patrick M. *Deterrence Now.* Cambridge: Cambridge University Press, 2003.

Myers, Steven Lee. »The Targets: Jets Said to Avoid Poison Gas Sites.« *New York Times*, December 18, 1998.

NPT. »NPT Treaty.« http://www.un.org/events/npt2005/npttreaty.html (accessed February 16, 2007).

NTI. »The Nunn-Lugar Cooperative Threat Reduction Program.« (2006). http://www.nti.org/db/nisprofs/russia/forasst/nunn_lug/overview.htm (accessed December 22, 2006).

NTI. »Past and Current Efforts to Reduce Civilian HEU Use.« http://www.nti.org/db/heu/pastpresent.html#gtri (accessed December 22, 2006).

NTI. »WMD 411: Provisions of Resolution 1540.« http://www.nti.org/f_wmd411/f2n1.html (accessed December 23, 2006).

»Nuclear Suppliers Group.« http://www.nuclearsuppliersgroup.org/guide.htm (accessed December 6, 2006).

»Nunn-Lugar Report.« (August 2005). http://lugar.senate.gov/reports/Nunn-Lugar_Report_2005.pdf (accessed February 16, 2007).

Nunn, Sam, and Michele Flournoy. »A Test of Leadership on Sea Island.« *Washington Post*, June 8, 2004.

Onishi, Norimitsu. »South Korea Won't Intercept Cargo Ships From the North.« *New York Times*, November 14, 2006.

Perkovich, George, et al. *Universal Compliance: A Strategy for Nuclear Security.* Washington DC: Carnegie Endowment for International Peace, March 2005.

Persbo, Andreas, and Ian Davis. *Sailing Into Uncharted Waters? The Proliferation Security Initiative and the Law of the Sea*. British American Security Information Council Research Report, June 2004.

Pincus, Walter. »New Nuclear Weapons Programs to Continue.« *Washington Post*, December 2, 2006.

–. »U.S. Has Still Not Found Iraqi Arms.« *Washington Post*, April 26, 2003.

Powell, Bill. »What to Do When Outlaws Get the Bomb.« *Time*, October 23, 2006.

Powell, Robert. »Nuclear Deterrence theory, Nuclear Proliferation, and National Missile Defense.« *International Security* 27, no. 4 (Spring 2003): 86-118.

Press, Associated. »Senate Approves Money for New Nuclear Weapon.« *Los Angeles Times*, July 2, 2005.

Press, The Associated. »U.S., Russia Granted Five-Year Extensions to Deadline for Destroying Chemical Weapons Arsenal.« *International Herald Tribune*, December 11, 2006.

Ratnesar, Romesh. »Can They Strike Back?« *Time*, February 3, 2003.

Revkin, Andre C. »Advanced Armaments.« *New York Times*, December 3, 2001.

Rumsfeld, Donald H. »Transforming the Military.« *Foreign Affairs* 81, no. 3 (May/June 2002): 20-32.

Sanchez, Rene. »Robot Race is Giant Step for Unmanned Kind.« *Washington Post*, March 10, 2004.

Sanger, David E., and William J. Broad. »From Rogue Nuclear Programs, Web of trails Leads to Pakistan.« *New York Times*, January 3, 2004.

Savage, David. G. »Nuclear Pant Meant to Deter.« *Los Angeles Times*, March 11, 2002.

Schneider, Barry R. *Future War and Counterproliferation: U.S. Military Responses to NBC Proliferation Threats*. Westport, CT: Praeger, 1999.

Scott Tyson, Amy. »Nuclear Plan Changes Calculus of Deterrence.« *The Christian Science Monitor*, March 14, 2002.

Semmel, Andrew K. »The U.S. Perspective on UN Security Council Resolution 1540: Remarks to the Asia-Pacific Nuclear Safeguards and Security Conference.« Sydney, Australia, November 8, 2004. http://www.state.gov/t/isn/rls/rm/38256.htm (accessed February 15, 2007).

Sepp, Eric M. *Deeply Buried Facilities: Implications for Military Operations*, Occasional Paper No. 14. Maxwell Air Base, AL: Air War College, May 2000.

Shanker, Thom. »Threats and Responses: Arms Smuggling; Scud Missiles Found on Ship of North Korea.« *New York Times*, December 11, 2002.

Shenon, Philip. »Border Inspectors to Look for Radioactive Material.« *New York Times*, March 1, 2003.

Smith, Derek D. *Deterring America: Rogue States and the Proliferation of Weapons of Mass Destruction*. Cambridge: Cambridge University Press, 2006.

Smith, Michael. »Saddam to be Target of Britain's 'E-Bomb'.« *London Daily Telegraph*, August 26, 2002.

Spiegel, Peter. »For N. Korean Missile, U.S. Defense is Hit or Miss.« *Los Angeles Times*, June 22, 2006.

Squassoni, Sharon. »Iran's Nuclear Program: Recent Developments.« Congressional Research Service. (March 2004). http://www.fas.org/sgp/crs/nuke/RS21592.pdf (accessed February 19, 2007).

»Statement by the Group of Eight Leaders, June 27, 2002.« http://www.fco.gov.uk/Files/kfile/Art%2002%20gp_stat-en.pdf (accessed Feburary 16, 2007).

Stout, David, and John H. Cushman. »Defense Missile for U.S. System Fails to Launch.« *New York Times*, December 6, 2004.

Strohm, Chris. »Six Foreign Ports to Scan Cargo For Nuclear Devices.« *Govexec.com*, December 7, 2006. http://www.govexec.com/dailyfed/1206/120706tdpm1.htm (accessed February 19, 2007).

The White House - Office of the Press Secretary. »Proliferation Security Initiative: Statement of Interdiction Principles.« (September 4, 2003). http://www.state.gov/t/isn/rls/fs/23764.htm (accessed February 19, 2007).

U.S: General Accounting Office. »Post-Shipment verification Provides Limited Assurance That Dual-Use Items Being Properly Used, GAO-04-357.« (January 2004).

U.S. Department of Defense. »Chemical and Biological Defense Program.« Annual Report to Congress. (March 2006). http://www.fas.org/irp/threat/cbdp2006.pdf (accessed February 19, 2007).

U.S. Department of Homeland Security. »National Response Plan.« (December 2004). http://www.dhs.gov/xlibrary/assets/NRP_FullText.pdf (accessed February 19, 2007).

U.S. Department of Homeland Security. »Securing Our Homeland: U.S. Department of Homeland Security Strategic Plan.« (2004). https://www.dhs.gov/xlibrary/assets/DHS_StratPlan_FINAL_spread.pdf (accessed February 19, 2007).

U.S. Department of State. »Ship Boarding Agreements.« http://www.state.gov/t/np/c12386.htm (accessed December 23, 2006).

U.S. Department of State - Office of the Spokesman. »The United States and Belize Proliferation Security Initiative Ship Boarding Agreement.« (August 4, 2005). www.state.gov/r/pa/prs/ps/2005/50787.htm (accessed February 19, 2007).

U.S. Department of State - Bureau of Nonproliferation. »International Code of Conduct Against Ballistic Missile Proliferation.« http://www.state.gov/t/isn/rls/fs/27799.htm (accessed December 3, 2006).

U.S. Department of State - Bureau of Nonproliferation. »The Proliferation Security Initiative.« (July 28, 2004). http://www.state.gov/t/isn/rls/other/34726.htm (accessed February 19, 2007).

U.S. Department of State - Bureau of Nonproliferation. »Proliferation Security Initiative Frequently Asked Questions (FAQ).« (January 11, 2005). http://www.state.gov/t/isn/rls/fs/32725.htm (accessed February 19, 2007).

United Kingdom. »The Future of the United Kingdom's Nuclear Deterrent.« (December 2006). http://www.mod.uk/NR/rdonlyres/AC00DD79-76D6-4FE3-91A1-6A56B03C092F/0/DefenceWhitePaper2006_Cm6994.pdf (accessed February 16, 2007).

United Nations. »A More Secure World: Our Shared Responsibility.« Report of the Secretary General's High-level Panel on Threats, Challenges and Change. (2004). http://www.un.org/secureworld/ (accessed February 16, 2007).

United Nations. »Security Council Resolution 1540.« Un Doc. S/RES/1540. (2004).

United Nations. »Security Council Resolution 1718.« UN Doc. S/RES/1718. (2006).

United States. »National Strategy to Combat Weapons of Mass Destruction.« (December 2002). http://www.whitehouse.gov/news/releases/2002/12/WMDStrategy.pdf (accessed February 16, 2007).

Wald, Matthew L., and Judith Miller. »Energy Department Plans A Push to Retrieve Nuclear Materials.« *New York Times*, May 26, 2004.

Waterman, Shaun. »Test Reveals Wide Failures in Terror Response Abilities.« *Washington Times*, December 21, 2003.

Weir, Fred, and Howard LaFranchi. »Russia and the U.S. as Global Nuclear Waste Collectors?« *Christian Science Monitor*, February 7, 2006.

Wilkening, Dean. *Ballistic-Missile Defence and Strategic Stability.* Edited by International Institute for Strategic Studies, *Adelphi Paper 334*. Oxford: Oxford University Press, 2000.

Wright, Robin. »Ship Incident May Have Swayed Libya.« *Washington Post*, January 1, 2004.

Zarocostas, John. »U.S. Seeks Treaty to Ban Fissile Material.« *Washington Times*, July 30, 2004.

The EU-3 and the Iranian Nuclear Program

Anthony Seaboyer and Oliver Thränert

Introduction

The proliferation of nuclear weapons is not a new issue to rank high on the international agenda. Since the 1960ties there is concern, that evermore nuclear weapon states would destabilize international relations and finally nuclear war might occur. Although the international community was able to create the Nuclear Nonproliferation Treaty (NPT) of 1970, banning nuclear arms for all its states parties, except the United States, Russia, China, France and the United Kingdom, this multilateral arms control agreement faces a severe crisis for several reasons. One is that the nuclear have-nots are disappointed because the nuclear powers did not meet their nuclear disarmament pledges under the NPT. Another reason is the fact that two NPT signatories conduct nuclear programs, that either already led to the development of nuclear weapons – such was the case with North Korea – or are suspected of following the aim to establish such weapons in the future, as is the case with Iran.

The issue of how to respond to nuclear proliferation and prevent it more effectively has caused intense debate not only within the international community in general, but also – and particularly – between the transatlantic partners. On the European side, many governments disagree with the Bush Administration's nonproliferation approach, often characterized as being »neo-conservative«. In 2003 the European Union on its part agreed to its own nonproliferation strategy based on »effective multilateralism«. At the same time, after the detection of two clandestine nuclear facilities in Iran in August 2002, the Europeans became aware that the Iranian nuclear program poses a significant threat to the NPT and might cause a nuclear arms race in the European neighborhood region of the Middle East. Therefore, France, Germany, and the UK decided to put effective multilateralism to a test. In October 2003 the foreign ministers of these three countries traveled to Tehran and signed a document with representatives of the Iranian government that paved the way for further negotiations on the Iranian nuclear issue.

What later was labeled the EU-3 evolved spontaneously without any conceptual model. In any case, this new approach was very innovative in character. However, as it turned out in the course of the negotiations with Iran, the three countries were solely unable to solve a problem of the dimension of the conflict over the Iranian nuclear program. A common strategy together with the US and other partners was necessary.

In this article, we ask how the United States and the European governments cooperated in their approach to curb Iran's nuclear ambitions. Thereby we concentrate on the European part of the picture. How did the EU-3 evolve and what did they achieve?

Prior to the analysis of these main questions we ask if Iran really aims at nuclear weapons and discuss possible Iranian motives for its nuclear program. We also analyze why it is of major importance to prevent Iran from developing nuclear weapons.

Subsequently, we look into the European approach towards the issue by reviewing the EU-3 platform, from its inception as an initiative, up to December 2006 when the UN Security Council imposed sanctions for the first time,, because Tehran did not meet its safeguards requirements with the International Atomic Agency (IAEA). We furthermore discuss what led to the creation of the EU-3, its strategy, and analyze its results.

Finally we specifically focus on transatlantic cooperation as part of the EU-3 initiative starting with determinants of US-Iran relations and their effect on US cooperation with the EU-3, before we ask what else influenced transatlantic cooperation in dealing with the Iranian nuclear program. Against this background we ask how the EU-3 and the US actually cooperated on the issue. Because the books are not yet closed on this issue, our findings can only be seen as preliminary in character.

The Iranian Nuclear Program

Does Iran really aim at nuclear weapons?

To estimate the urgency of the issue, it is necessary to know, if Iran really aims to achieve nuclear weapons, and if so, how close the regime actually is to reaching this goal.

The brief answer is that the IAEA so far is still not in the position to prove weather Iran has reported all elements of its nuclear program that are declarable. Instead, serious doubts remain. The Agency, therefore, has no complete picture, particularly concerning Iranian centrifuge activity as part of its uranium enrichment program. Most importantly, the Agency is still seeking additional assurance that, as stated by Iran, no P-2 centrifuge program which would allow for faster uranium enrichment was conducted between 1995 and 2002 (Perkovich 2006a).

Undoubtedly, some circumstantial evidence suggests that Iran is indeed aiming at nuclear weapons. Iran did not comply with its safeguard agreement with the IAEA for 18 years. Tehran did not declare the import of uranium and centrifuges or the conduct of enrichment experiments, not to mention the facilities where this research took place. Moreover, the regime received most of its centrifuges and blue prints through the Khan-network, which is not particularly known for doing business in the field of purely civilian nuclear programs. Apparently, Iran received documents including partial instructions for the casting and machining of uranium metal which could be used to design critical parts of a nuclear weapon. Tehran argues that it had not asked for such information and only recently became aware that these documents were in its files. These explanations hardly sound convincing.

Furthermore, Iran is building an uranium enrichment facility at Natanz, officially for the production of fuel rods, to be utilized in Iranian light-water reactors. So far there is only one light-water reactor near Busher, that is about to be completed (Barnaby 2006). The fuel rods for this reactor will be delivered by Russia under a bilateral Iranian-Russian contract. Although Iran has further plans to develop more nuclear reactors, the country in any case does not possess enough natural uranium to support such a civilian nuclear program. However, its natural uranium resources are sufficient to run a significant military nuclear program.

Uranium enrichment technology itself is of dual-use nature. Such facilities can be used for either producing low enriched uranium for civilian purposes or highly enriched uranium for military applications. Most countries possessing enrichment facilities today are also nuclear weapon states.[1]

In addition, Iran plans the construction of a heavy-water research reactor. Such reactors are ideally applicable for the production of weapon plutonium. At the same time, Iran is not known to have a reprocessing program which would make the use of such reactors coherent (Amineh 2004).

Furthermore, Iran has been running an intense ballistic as well as a cruise missile program since the 1980s. Its newest version of the Shahab-3 is described as having a range of up to 1.500 km. It is hard to believe that Iran would invest so many efforts in a missile program, over such a long period of time, without having in mind to be able to later equip them with the most effective mounting: nuclear warheads (Thränert 2005a).

Moreover, Mark Fitzpatrick identifies ten indicators for military participation in what is described as a purely civilian nuclear program by Iranian officials. These include military involvement in an uranium mine and mill, experiments with Polonium 210, applicable in weapons, and military controlled centrifuge workshops (Fitzpatrick 2006a: 8). Another interesting

---

1 At this point, the only two non-nuclear weapon countries running enrichment facilities under national control are Japan and Brazil. Germany and the Netherlands participate in a trilateral consortium together with the UK, named URENCO, that also produces low-enriched uranium for civilian purposes.

fact is that, according to UN Security Council resolution 1736, there is apparently one military individual that is involved in the nuclear program and in Iran's ballistic missile program. This strongly supports suspicions that there are military connections to Iran's nuclear program.

However, at this point it is impossible to correctly estimate when Iran might have reached this point. Again, it is Mark Fitzpatrick (Fitzpatrick 2006a) who lists the following areas of uncertainty:

- It is not exactly known how long it will take Iran to produce enough centrifuges and to operate those efficiently over a long enough period of time, for producing enough weapons grade uranium for at least one weapon.
- It is unknown what warhead design would be preferred by Iran so that we do not know, how much highly-enriched uranium would be needed.
- Another unknown is whether and in what time Iran is capable of producing uranium hexafluoride in large amounts that is not contaminated and therefore can be used in large centrifuge cascades.

However, the latest estimates of the IISS says that: »If and when Iran does have 3,000 centrifuges operating smoothly, the IISS estimates it would take an additional 9–11 months to produce 25 kg of highly enriched uranium, enough for one implosion-type weapon. That day is still 2–3 years away at the earliest« (Langton 2007).

In any event, European capitals agree with the view held in Washington, that Iran indeed does aim at approaching the nuclear weapons option. Other than for instance in the case of Saddam Hussein, there is no fundamental transatlantic difference about how the Iranian nuclear program is to be estimated (Shaw/Albright 2006: 1).

What are motives for a possible Iranian nuclear weapon program?

While the exact status of Iran's nuclear activities is difficult to determine (Allison 2006) and remains to be unclear, Iranian motivations are more accessible. Various motives referring to different policy fields – from security-related concerns to economic and status-related issues – could motivate Tehran to further implement its civilian nuclear program or, as assumed by many, even seek the military option.

Both the former Iranian President Chatami and the current Iranian President Ahmadinejad argue that access to modern technologies, such as nuclear power plants, is essential for the overall development of Iran's economy. Moreover, Iran argues that it needs access to nuclear technology for civilian purposes to compensate its ever increasing domestic energy consumption, enabling the country to continue exporting most of its oil reserves to international markets in exchange for hard currency. This argument is strongly disputed, as nuclear power can only allow Iran to replace electricity-producing fuels. About 18% of Iran's electricity is currently produced by petroleum. Freeing this small percentage for export does not amount to as much, as that the referring costs would be economically justifiable (Bradford 2007).

Regarding a possible military use, first steps were already taken in the Shah era, when as much as today, many people perceived nuclear weapons as a very valuable status symbol capable of supporting Iran's rise to a leading regional power (Thränert 2003: 16). As the nuclear question in general is strongly related to the Iranian self-image, many believe that Iran could only significantly enhance its status if it also becomes a nuclear weapon country (Bahgat 2006: 323). In particular, the fact that Pakistan already has a nuclear arsenal is viewed as not acceptable by many Iranians as long as Iran does not possess nuclear arms. Furthermore, most international experts agree, that nuclear weapons would provide Iran with an opportunity to dominate the region (Cordesman 2006).

Most importantly, nuclear weapons are seen by many Iranians as the ultimate instrument of deterrence. Proponents cite North Korea, arguing that Pyongyang has managed not to be attacked by the US due to its nuclear status. There is no doubt that Iran is currently already pursuing a policy of deterrence, by arguing that any military strike against Iran would be far more costly, than that it would be effective (Devine/Schofield 2006: 142).

However, according to public sources, it is not clear, whether the Iranian political and religious elite has already made a decision to build nuclear weapons. Most experts believe, however, that Iran wants to come as close as possible to a nuclear weapons option (Fitzpatrick 2006a: 5).

Why is it so important to prevent an Iranian nuclear weapon?

Many analysts estimate, that Iran will sooner or later procure nuclear weapons. Most strikingly, an Iranian nuclear weapons program could cause a nuclear arms race in the Middle East, with Saudi-Arabia and Egypt as the first candidates that could also go nuclear (Rosen 2006). Consequently, the NPT, already in an intense crisis, could be severely damaged or even entirely corroded so that – without the nuclear nonproliferation norm – we might, in a very short period of time, live in a world of 15 or more nuclear weapon countries (Cirincione 2006).

In any event, without the NPT, Europe would loose its core instrument to prevent nuclear proliferation by diplomatic means. Although the Bush Administration does not have a strong multilateral arms control record, the

US has an interest in maintaining the nuclear nonproliferation norm, in part to keep nuclear weapons out of the hands of terrorists. Even if the plausibility of such an incident has to be estimated very carefully (Daase 2005), we know that Iran actively supports terrorists even with Katyusha rockets (Hughes 2007). Although this does not imply that Tehran would also sell nuclear weapons, the international community cannot afford to take the chance. Furthermore, a nuclear Iran could try to dominate the region and put pressure on Israel which would not remain unanswered (Thränert 2003: 28). If, in addition to nuclear weapons, Iran also developed missiles capable of reaching central Europe, the security situation of the continent would dramatically change. Most importantly, in case of Iranian aggression, Europe would likely lose its ability of military intervention in the region when trying to reestablish international order (Seaboyer/Thränert 2006). Such an incident may not necessarily take place, but it cannot be ruled out entirely. Likewise, the US needs to keep the option for military intervention open in order to protect its allies in the region. Opinions in Washington and European capitals may differ, but against the above mentioned background, neither the US nor Europe – or any other Western country – seem ready to accept an Iranian nuclear weapons option, let alone a nuclear weapon.

The EU-3 initiative

A brief history of the EU-3 initiative

The founding of the EU-3 in October 2003 happened spontaneously. After two secret Iranian nuclear complexes were detected by an Iranian opposition group, Tehran for the first time had to admit that it had been carrying out a covert uranium enrichment and heavy water program. Even though the two constructions in Natanz and Arak were, at the admitted status of completion, not declarable under the NPT-safeguards, the international community had strong doubts about a peaceful Iranian intention behind these endeavors.

At that time, great concern about the Iranian nuclear program – but also about further conflict escalation with Iran – motivated the foreign ministers of France, Britain and Germany to engage diplomatically (Denza 2005: 304). Although details about how exactly the three foreign ministers came together remain unclear, the initiative was from the beginning supported by the High Representative for European Common Foreign and Securtiy Policy (CFSP), Javier Solana. The High Representative coordinated the initiative with the other EU member states. However, it took nearly two years before the EU-Council in October 2005 officially confirmed that the EU was behind the EU-3 approach. This was also when the initiative was finally officially defined as the 'E3/EU' initiative (Posch 2006: 103).

Already in autumn 2003, there was a strong tendency on the US side to report the Iranian case to the UN Security Council. But the governments of France, Germany and the UK felt that after the dispute over Iraq in 2002/03 they could not afford another fierce confrontation on how to respond to the Iranian nuclear challenge. Therefore, the Europeans hesitated to follow the US approach. In their view, confrontations about the Iran dossier in the Council would have had the potential to drastically further weaken the UN. Hence, in summer 2003, the EU initially sought to keep the issue away from the Security Council at least for the time being.

Therefore, the three European foreign ministers followed an Iranian invitation to Tehran (Samore 2004). The foreign ministers of Britain Jack Straw, of France Dominique de Villepin, and of Germany Joschka Fischer thereby October 21st reached an »Agreed Statement« with Iran in which Tehran ensured »to engage in full cooperation with the IAEA to address and resolve through full transparency all requirements and outstanding issues to the Agency« (IAEA 2003). Most importantly, Iran agreed to suspend all uranium enrichment and reprocessing activities as defined by the IAEA. This was a first important EU-3 success. The subsequent Iranian cooperation with the IAEA enabled the international community to gain significant insight into Tehran's program, which had lacked almost completely so far.

In the course of the negotiations that followed the EU-3 aimed at agreeing with Iran on a long-term co-operation providing all parties with satisfactory assurances relating to Iran's nuclear power program. Initial signs for a further success were promising. However, doubts emerged in February 2004. A report by the IAEA Director General revealed that Iran had not declared designs for P-2 centrifuges and had also experimented with polonium-210 (IAEA 2004c). An IAEA resolution of March 2004 announced that Iranian declarations furthermore contained omissions and lacked a complete picture of the program. In the resolution, Tehran was accused of having left various questions unresolved (IAEA 2004a). Three months later, the IAEA found that »Iran's cooperation had not been as full, timely and proactive as it should have been« (IAEA 2004b). Iran reacted vigorously to this IAEA resolution by accusing the EU-3 of not keeping their promise to seriously try finding a solution that did not lead to a transfer to New York (Borda 2005: 4). When Tehran informed the IAEA that it would break its »voluntary suspension« as a response, the negotiations reached a low. The EU-3 reacted by tabling a resolution adopted by the IAEA Board of Governors that not only stated serious concerns about Iran's uranium enrichment activities, but also included an implicit threat of referring Iran to the UN Security Council (IAEA 2004d).

Despite these unpromising developments, a few months later the EU-3 did manage to achieve yet another significant agreement with Iran, even far more specific than the one of October 2003. With the Paris Agreement of November 15th, 2004, the Europeans finally convinced Iran both to sign the additional protocol to its safeguards agreement and to abstain from further uranium enrichment and other activities, that would lead to a full nuclear fuel cycle. Both sides reaffirmed their commitment to the NPT in this document. Working groups were set up to prepare a final long-term agreement. The signing of the additional protocol and the voluntary enrichment suspension were widely perceived as serious Iranian concessions. Accordingly, the Paris Agreement was a very significant success (Posch 2006: 105).

At the same time, irritating developments could not be overlooked. Soon after the IAEA officially declared that Iran had verifiably suspended enrichment activities, Tehran expressed that it wanted to continue enrichment activities in a much smaller dimension for research purposes. For the first time, it became clearly apparent, that Iran followed a strategy that can be described best as a »salami slicing«. Iran also began to gradually turn the nuclear issue into a matter of national pride and status. The Iranians argued that it was a sign of disrespect, that the West denied Iran's right to the peaceful use of nuclear technology, it earned according to article IV of the NPT. The EU-3 on their part thought they were offering extensive cooperation, especially regarding technology and trade.

On the 5th August 2005, the EU-3 submitted an extensive proposal for a long term settlement of relations to Tehran (Thränert 2006c). Therein all signing parties were obligated to abstain from the threat or the use of violence, not consistent with United Nations principles. France and Britain also offered to reaffirm there negative and positive security guarantees to all non-nuclear states parties to the NPT, including Iran. The EU-3 even announced to directly support the civilian use of nuclear technology in Iran as long as it would act according to its IAEA safeguards. In return, Iran was asked to restrict its nuclear program to light water reactors, not to withdraw from the NPT and to provide access for IAEA inspectors to facilities and allow interviews with staff members, as considered necessary to clarify all outstanding issues concerning the Iranian nuclear program. Concluding, the EU-3 proposed a review process to take place within ten years. The parties then would value whether confidence had been built. If so, parts of the agreement could be altered. With this review process the EU-3 meant to keep the door open for Iran to return to its uranium enrichment program, once confidence was built, that it would not be used for military purposes.

But Tehran rejected this extensive offer harshly, without really verifying it or considering it as a starting point for further negotiations (Perthes/Wagner 2006: 3). Instead the offer was described as an insult to the Iranian nation, for which the Europeans should excuse themselves – a diplomatic move, nearly unprecedented. Even more, in a letter to the foreign ministers of France, Britain and Germany, Iran declared that it would resume the production of uranium hexafluoride. This, as the European foreign ministers consequently wrote in a letter to the Iranian regime, clearly violated the Paris Agreement. After two years of tough negotiations, in which the Iranian side indicated that it was prepared to compromise, in order to solve the issue, this development not only surprised but also seriously disappointed the Europeans. While Tehran argued that it was still acting according to the Paris Agreement, the EU-3 perception was fundamentally different. »This episode marked a turning point in the E3/EU negotiations since now the Iranians had crossed a 'red line'«(Posch 2006: 106).

Already prior to these developments, the situation had been further complicated by the election of the new Iranian president Mahmoud Ahmadinejad in June 2005. EU-3 relations to Tehran were not only complicated by the fact that the new president was perceived as a radical by the West, but also because the new president himself rapidly navigated towards drastic changes in the negotiations (Huntley 2006: 731). He replaced all diplomats in the delegation dealing with the EU-3 and even went as far as to exchange the whole Iranian diplomatic corps in capitals important for the negotiations. Instead, he posted diplomats in Vienna, London, Paris and Berlin, who, at least partially, were known as revolutionary extremists (Randow/Ladurner 2006: 153). He managed to add to this confrontation and seriously worsen Western relations by repeatedly denying the Holocaust and the right of the close Western ally Israel to exist. His additional disrespect for the UN Security Council did not improve the situation either (Overhaus 2006: 7).

These drastic changes coincided with a shift of Tehran's perception of the EU-3. Impressions in Tehran, in terms of Europe not delivering what Iran really needed, were gaining popularity. From the Iranian perspective, »Europe's ambiguous stance towards the issue of regime change, Europe's inability to help heal the Iranian-American rift and the EU's lack of timely and sufficiently strong support for the reform movement – all these factors lead to the Iranians wondering what the EU-3 were exactly good for (Reissner 2006: 121).«

Indeed, statements of senior US officials, such as Vice President Dick Cheney, referring to regime change as the only sustainable solution added to these concerns. But their policy orientations where never supported by the Europeans. Simultaneously, European and – more importantly – US patience was slowly running out. A severe and now openly visible lack of confidence between the negotiating parties emerged. »Neither the Iranians trusted the Europeans nor the Europeans the Iranians« (Posch 2006: 106).

Moreover, Tehran altered its negotiation strategy. From the very beginning of the EU-3 – Iran negotiation process, Tehran had sought to separate the Europeans from the US. Now it even aimed at dividing the EU-3 from other EU members. Knowing that Italy and Spain were increasingly unsatisfied that they were not directly involved in the negotiations with Iran, Iranian officials began criticizing, the non-integration of EU members such as Spain and Italy were in the negotiation process. Iran's new policy soon included seeking to significantly increase the number of countries with which it wanted to negotiate. Now Russia, China and members of the Non-Aligned Movement (NAM) were also proposed. Iran thus put considerable pressure on the EU-3 by claiming that they alone were not sufficient.

In September 2005, the IAEA Board of Governors adopted an even harder position on Iran. Vienna clearly stated that Iran was not complying with its Safeguards Agreement and also expressed the »absence of confidence that Iran's nuclear program is exclusively for peaceful purposes« (IAEA 2005a). This shift is widely seen as the final turning point. Nevertheless, the IAEA again did not refer Iran to the UN Security Council. Again, it was the EU-3 that – acting against US pressure – prevented the reference to New York in order to keep the door open for further consultation. But as Iran defied the resolution by announcing it would break IAEA seals on facilities for enriching uranium and end its moratorium on enrichment, the EU-3 negotiating efforts finally failed (Rogers/Holt 2006: 7). As Tehran removed the seals from its facilities and restarted enrichment on January 9th, 2006, all that was left for the EU-3 was to inform the IAEA that »discussions with Iran have reached an impasse« and to call for an extraordinary IAEA Board meeting (IAEA 2006a). On February 4th, 2006, the IAEA reported Iran to the UN Security Council (IAEA 2006b).

The first activity of the Council was a presidential statement of March 29th. It »notes with serious concern Iran's decision to resume enrichment-related activities, including research and development, and to suspend cooperation with the IAEA under the additional Protocol« (UN 2006c).

In the meantime, the three European countries where able to achieve what can be described as their most significant success. At a meeting of the foreign ministers of Germany, the UK, France, the US, Russia and China in Vienna on the first of June 2006, these governments agreed to confront Iran with a clear choice: either open negotiations that could lead to an improvement of relations, including political and economic cooperation and suspending all activities that would lead to full nuclear fuel cycle; or pursue with such projects, but then face severe sanctions, as a result of respective UN Security Council resolutions.

Javier Solana thereafter delivered the so far most extensive offer to Iran, now in the name not only of the EU-3 but also of the US, Russia and China. This by far most extensive offer ever submitted to Tehran, for the first time included a possible direct participation of the United States in negotiations. Moreover Washington even announced its willingness to support Iran with nuclear technology if it would suspend uranium enrichment. Finally, the offer made it much clearer, than in the European proposal of August 2005, that Iran in the future could run an uranium enrichment program if the international community could be sure that it would not be misused for military purposes. Despite the offer, Iran continued uranium enrichment and the construction of new centrifuges (IAEA 2006c).

Due to intense EU-3 negotiations with Russia, China and the US in the following months, the UN Security Council, on 31st July 2006, was able to agree on resolution 1696 (UN 2006a) in which Iran was demanded to suspend uranium enrichment by 31st August 2006. As the Director General of the IAEA on 31st August had to report, that Iran had not suspended uranium enrichment, the EU-3 started another negotiating initiative trying to reach consensus for the implementation of UN Security Council sanctions against Iran. During various talks in the following, the High Representative for the CFSP Javier Solana tried to convince Iran to return to the negotiation table and thereby avoid sanctions imposed by the Security Council, but in the end he was not successful. Not alone, but also as a result of intense EU-3 negotiating engagement, the UN Security Council agreed on Sanctions against Iran in its resolution 1737 (UN 2006b) on December 23, 2006.

What led to the EU-3?

Factors that contributed to the emergence of the EU-3 can be divided into external and EU-internal. As far as external factors are concerned, the Europeans saw a strong necessity to support rule-based multilateral arms control regimes in general and the NPT in particular (Harnisch 2006: 1). It was also especially important for them to send out a signal to the region, as the very fragile balance of power in the Middle East would be severely damaged by Iranian nuclear weapons. Already the prospect of Iranian nuclear weapons has the potential to not only cause an arms race, but serious tensions that in the long term could lead to war in the already seriously troubled region. The future of this European neighborhood therefore was a strong motivator for engaging into the conflict over Iran's nuclear program.

From a more global perspective, the UN's authority was also seriously at stake. One more dispute in the UN Security Council, emerging over the next issue of high relevance after the Iraq disaster of 2002/03 and demonstrating again the Security Council's inability to act, would have had the potential to significantly further weaken the UN's credibility. Such a development would have clearly run contrary to European interests. Not only because France and Britain, which enjoy to have a permanent seat at the UN Security Council, would have had their international role damaged, but also because there is a basic understanding among Europeans that the UN system should be strengthened, not weakened, in order to deal effectively with international crises and conflicts. Not only because of their honorable ethical position, but also for the very pragmatic reason that they themselves as middle powers have no other way to influence international politics, the EU member states are true multilaterals.

At the very least, Europeans wanted to make sure that international coalition building could take place before the Iranian dossier would be transferred to New York, avoiding another struggle at the highest international authority (Thränert 2006a: 2).

EU internal factors also led to the EU-3 initiative. Most importantly, the Iranian crisis appeared exactly at a time, when the EU was in the process of discussing the future of the European Common Foreign and Security Policy (CFSP). Since its beginning with the Maastricht Treaty in 1992, the CFSP has always been subject of intense debate. Its effectiveness, among other issues, is most prominently criticized as decisions must be unanimous. This procedure has often proved to be a barrier difficult to overcome. Additionally, the Kosovo experience of the 1990ies was widely interpreted as showing, in particular, a significant need for a more autonomous European foreign policy less dependent on the US. More recently, during the debate over European support for US-engagement in Iraq, deep trenches appeared within the EU. The member states not being able to agree on which measures to apply, or if a military engagement at all was the appropriate answer, demonstrated a significant lack of EU operability. Adding to this crisis, some EU member states began publicly criticizing others for their position in dealing with the US request for support in Iraq. In sum, the EU's common foreign and security policy had just experienced one of its most serious crises. In this setting, the EU-3 recognized an opportunity not only to develop and demonstrate a common European answer to the next urgent issue, but also to prove that their own crisis was overcome. Discord on the next major issue would have been a further disaster for the EU. Above all, an incapability of action in two consecutive major international crises would have had unpredictable consequences for the further existence of CFSP. In order to no less then retain the credibility of the CFSP, if not the EU itself, it was absolutely necessary to prevent such a development.

Last but not least, some intentions were directly related to the three participating governments themselves. As Germany for example played a very fruitful role within the EU-3 initiative, its engagement is widely seen as very successful. It was the first time ever, that Germany engaged in a non-European crisis of high relevance on such a prominent political level. In doing so, Germany improved its reputation and regarding the Iran issue almost received the reputation of a permanent member to the UN Security Council. In France, the government was very eager to take a leading role in strengthening the EU as a global security actor (Rieker 2006: 524). The UK wanted to bridge the transatlantic gap that appeared after the Iraq crisis 2002/03 and at the same time regain influence in European affairs.

Last but not least, the Europeans wanted to avoid another transatlantic division. A further conflict would have not only posed a severe challenge to EU unity, it would have severely damaged transatlantic relations as well – an option unacceptable for most EU-member states. In order to also prevent also any further conflict with the most important European ally the aim was to find a way around confrontation with the US on the Iranian issue.

How did the structure evolve?

As much as the EU-3 initiative was not planned, but rather emerged spontaneously, its structure evolved similarly. No design existed giving ideas for how the initiative should be executed or which procedures should be implemented. In fact, the lack of institutionalization is symptomatic for the initiative. Diplomats involved in the EU-3 initiative agree that this main difference from often overregulated other European foreign policy procedures, was a significant factor for its relative successes. It occurred, because from the beginning on, the initiative was not designed to exist permanently but only to solve the conflict over Iran's nuclear program (Posch 2006: 111). Although it was foreseeable that a longer process would be necessary, it was never intended to create a self-supporting structure, deployable in other cases. Whenever thoughts were raised about such a possibility, EU member states not directly involved in the EU-3 initiative expressed strong rejection.

Throughout its process, the initiative benefited significantly from existing structures. On the working level, members of the French, British and German foreign ministries cooperated closely, within well established working relations. Initially, from a pragmatic perspective, there was also no need for any formal structure.

As success was achieved relatively early in the negotiation process, officials did not want to change a winning horse. Later during the negotiations, as the EU-3 experienced problems in reaching an adequate agreement with the Iranian delegation, causes therefore were referred rather to other factors such as a lack of adequate US support or the Iranian attitude towards the issue instead of to the EU-3's structure.

Only when some EU member states complained about their marginal role in the process, their limited influence and the little information that was provided to them, ideas about changes on a structural level were discussed. However, the solution provided was to more prominently integrate the High Representative for the CFSP Javier Solana. This enabled him to coordinate the negotiation process more closely with the other EU member states.

Involved diplomats see the EU-3's informal organization as a clear advantage because its structure could evolve freely, just as needed, without having to fulfill the demands of any theoretical blueprint dictating what an EU initiative should ideally look like in order to please everybody. However, this »organically« grown structure remained to be problematic as it by far did not please all EU member states. Nevertheless, in the end, the achievements of the process, combined with the assurance that this format would not be institutionalized, poured oil on troubled waters.

How did Europe attempt to solve the conflict?

From the very beginning in October 2003, when the Foreign Ministers of France, Germany and the UK went to Tehran, their aim was to convince Iran to regain international trust and confidence through a voluntary suspension of its uranium enrichment and heavy-water projects. In other words: the nuclear issue was never dealt with as a purely legal, but as a political matter. According to the NPT, it is the legal right of Iran as a non-nuclear state to use nuclear technology peacefully as long as it meets its IAEA safeguards obligations. At the same time, following a prudent legal approach, the IAEA Board of Governors would have brought the Iranian file to the attention of the UN Security Council very early after the detection of Iranian violations of its safeguards agreement. The EU-3 aimed at a double suspension: Iran would suspend its nuclear fuel cycle activities, and the EU-3 would suspend Iran's referral to the UN Security Council.

The EU-3's diplomatic strategy heavily relied on »carrots« in the form of economic offers. Intense efforts and even more intense patience were characteristic for the European approach. The EU-3 thereby negotiated with Tehran as much as with Washington, trying to bring the crucial US support in to an offer the Iranians would agree on. In practice, this turned out to be very difficult. On the one hand, the US did not have a consistent strategy and instead allowed their course to change from time to time. On the other hand, the Iranian »salami slicing« tactic, combined with more than unhelpful rhetoric towards the US and Israel, did its share to complicate the negotiations. Nevertheless, the EU-3, time and again, ran an extra mile to give Tehran further chances to find a solution. This very patient approach not only came from European good will, but was also largely due to the fact that there were no alternatives to a diplomatic approach according to the European perception. Military options never played a role in the European debate. The downside of this approach was that Iran as well gained more time to pursue its endeavors.

Some critics contend, that initial EU-3 incentives offered to Iran were far too little compared to what Tehran was asked to abandon. Despite there being some truth to this position, the question remains if the EU-3 themselves could have ever offered what Tehran was really interested in. Particularly, when it comes to security concerns and Iran's claim for security guarantees, Europe – without a common transatlantic strategy backed by the US – has little to offer.

What did the EU-3 achieve?

While the main aim of the EU-3 initiative was to prevent Iran from acquiring a nuclear weapons option, there were a number of other Europeans intentions folded within its efforts. These can be differentiated into goals referring to the Iranian nuclear program, the UN and multilateral crises management, the EU and its foreign and security policy, and to the reputation of the three participating governments themselves.

After Iran admitted that it had a secret enrichment program in late 2003, the main long-term goal of the three European foreign ministers undoubtedly was to convince Tehran diplomatically to stop developing a nuclear weapons option. The short-term goal was thus to stop Iran, at least temporarily, from establishing a complete nuclear fuel cycle (Thränert 2004: 2). A mid-term goal was to persuade Tehran to start repairing damage stemming from the breach of IAEA regulations and enable the international community to regain confidence in Iranian declarations by providing transparency. The latter was a very important goal as the EU-3 aimed at further understanding the intentions behind the Iranian nuclear program (Delpech 2006: 68).

The Paris Agreement of 2004, in which Tehran reaffirmed its commitment to the NPT, was definitely the most impressive achievement. Therein Iran agreed on much further reaching concessions then it did in 2003. The agreement was more detailed and explicitly mentioned all steps of uranium enrichment (Randow/Ladurner 2006: 151). Over long periods of time, the EU-3 were also able to convince Iran of the necessity to cooperate with the IAEA (Posch 2006: 104). Iran's approval of implementing the additional IAEA protocol was crucial. Although Tehran did not ratify the additional protocol, it did implement it for quite a while, enabling the international community to gain valuable information on Tehran's activities (Thränert 2005b). That said, the EU-3 managed to persuade Iran to agree on concessions, that not only bought time, but also helped the international community to learn a lot more about Iran's nuclear program.

The EU-3 were successful in keeping the IAEA Board of Governors from referring the conflict to the UN Security Council. This gained considerable time, enabling the international community to prepare negotiations in the Security Council. This extra time could be used for discussions with the

Bush Administration and also for intense bargaining with Russia and China. As a result, a common strategy evolved. The EU-3 were very successful in this regard. They significantly contributed to enabling consensus on the Security Council resolutions of July and December 2006 directed against Iran (Dupré 2007). The creation of such an international coalition was definitely not expected by the Iranians. Therefore, for the time being, the European strategy of international coalition building proved to be successful, as opposed to the Iranian strategy of dividing the EU from the US, Russia and China through its salami slicing tactics. That said, the EU-3 initiative was very successful.

The EU-3 also was successful in reaching their aims concerning the EU. While these objectives might not be of such urgent international importance, to the EU they are very relevant. With the initiative, the EU-3 and therewith also indirectly the EU established itself as a valuable negotiating partner in one of the most urgent international crisis of the time. None of the three EU-3 countries alone would have gained this opportunity. This example shows the success EU member states can achieve when acting together. In turn, the messages sent to EU citizens on an almost daily basis through media reporting served to portray a capable and cooperative European Union. With the EU's crises over the CFSP and more generally over its constitutional process, such a prominent and positive picture of its influence was more than welcome. Critics could also be confronted with a clear example of European capability to act, in stark contrast to the »trauma of total inability to act« (Mauer 2006: 16) during the crisis over Iraq. With their performance Europeans not only impressed critics on the continent but also in Britain, the United States and even in Iran (Posch 2006: 113). The governments of the EU-3 for themselves were also successful. Germany clearly improved its standing as an internationally well respected actor. France contributed to improve the international reputation of the EU with a view to its CFSP. Finally London regained influence on the continent. The UK was also especially influential in transferring European ideas to Washington.

In general, it appears that aims achievable within the sole competence of the EU-3 were reached. Those that lay beyond the EU's competence, for instance because the EU-3 alone could not provide what the Iranians basically wanted, were not obtained. Nevertheless, given that the list of the EU-3's achievements is much longer than that of its failures, the picture of the EU-3's success can be painted in bright colors. What was not reached was mainly beyond the EU-3's own abilities.

The United States and the EU-3

From the beginning of the EU-3 initiative, Iran sought to divide the transatlantic partners. Negotiating with the three most important European nations as representatives of the entire EU, Iran tried to counterbalance US international importance and at the same time widen the by that time existing gap in transatlantic relations. Given the fall out over the Iraq invasion, prospects for this strategy initially were very promising. Although the transatlantic partners had announced the end of their dispute at the G-8 meeting of June 2003 in Evian, transatlantic relations were still going through one of their most serious crises ever as the EU-3 initiative began (Sauer 2004: 129). Given that Iran's intent to divide the transatlantic partners appeared so promising, did Tehran succeed in widening the already exceptionally large transatlantic gap?

After 9/11, the aim to prevent the spread of nuclear weapons ranked even higher on the US foreign policy agenda then before (Sagan 2006). In the 2002 State of the Union Address, President George W. Bush referred to an »axis of evil«. Besides Iraq and North Korea, Iran was labeled as a member. According to President Bush, these countries had in common not only that they ran illegal WMD programs, but also that they supported international terror organizations.

Besides Iraq, Iran certainly causes the Bush Administration the most headaches (Fitzpatrick 2006b). US relations with Iran are strongly dominated by the fact that no diplomatic relations between the US and the Islamic Republic of Iran exist since 1979, when Iranian students occupied the US Embassy in Tehran. Iran is also not willing to accept the existence of the closest ally of the US in the region, Israel, and insists on calling for an end to the Israeli state. Furthermore, Iran also supports terror organizations financially as well as with weapon systems that fight against Israel. Finally, Tehran is not playing a constructive role in Iraq. Instead of supporting the US goal of rebuilding the neighboring country, Iran supports organizations fighting against US troops (Ganji 2006).

Finally, Iran has a long record of human rights abuses. Its political system can be described as a theocratie rather than a democracy, a fact, which makes the country a target to US democratization strategies. With the democratization of the Middle East a foremost aim of the Bush Administration, prospects for Washington and Tehran moving towards each other are very limited. The Iranian Presidential elections of June 2005 only worsened the situation. The new President Mahmoud Ahmadinejad repeatedly mentioned that Israel should be wiped off the map. With his radical aims he clearly moved Iran into the direction of an Islamist country.

For the Bush Administration it appeared to be very difficult to agree on a consistent Iran strategy. Throughout the entire conflict about the Iranian nuclear program, there were at least two different camps within the Bush Administration (Chubin 2006: 90). The first consisted of neo-conservatives such as Vice President Dick Cheney who did not at all want to deal with the Iranian government but instead preferred regime change strategies. The second school of thought, which can be described as realist, tended to support the European negotiation process. Would this concept fail, the Iran dossier would be transferred to the UN-Security Council to adopt sanctions directed against Tehran. Over time, the latter camp gained the upper hand.

At the beginning of the debate about the Iranian nuclear program, a common transatlantic negotiating strategy was not foreseeable (Müller 2003). US policy was diffuse and partially simply passive (Perkovich 2006b). Therefore, it was left to the Europeans, to find a sustainable strategy more or less on their own. Given Iran's request for direct US participation and most importantly Iran's claim for security guarantees only the US could provide, the lack of a common transatlantic approach severely hindered the European initiative (Perthes/Wagner 2006). In fact, even though the US later in the negotiation process provided more support to the EU-3, the absence of a real common action had a very decisive – and negative – effect on the success of the EU-3 initiative.

US – EU-3 cooperation in dealing with the Iranian nuclear program can best be distinguished in a first phase from the beginning of the EU-3 until the end of President Bush's first term and a second, from Bush's re-election until today.

Given the history of US-Iranian relations the prospects for a direct dialogue or even a serious support of a diplomatic approach were of the EU-3 negotiations very limited from the beginning (Bayat-Philipp 2004; Thränert 2006b). The common goal of preventing Iran from achieving nuclear weapons was always clear. The Bush Administration was dominated by reservation towards extensive political offers to Tehran, because of the nuclear program itself, Iranian support of terror organizations, the regime's attitude towards Israel, and because of its general human rights policy. Individuals such as John Bolton, who as Undersecretary of State was an influential figure concerning the Iran dossier, were simply not interested in creating a diplomatic approach towards Tehran. For instance, when representatives of the EU-3 met him in Washington, prior to their planned meeting with the Iranians in Paris in November 2004, Bolton was almost completely ignoring European arguments in favor of signing yet another document with the Iranians that could pave the way for further negotiations. Bolton only wanted to discuss sanctions to be adopted by the UN Security Council, nothing else.

But Bush's re-election marked a turning point (Wolfsthal/Hamilton 2006). One of the Administration's foremost aims now was to achieve better relations with the European allies. In his first State of the Union Address after re-election in 2004, the President announced that he wanted to convince Iran to suspend uranium enrichment. In order to reach that aim, Bush showed to be prepared to more closely cooperate with its European partners. In the same speech, however, he also made reference to the superior goal of his second term in office, of supporting the spread of democracy worldwide. He directly addressed the Iranian people and promised support for their struggle for freedom. The Administration thereby more strongly emphasized the aim of regime change and the promotion of democracy in Iran, a policy clearly not in line with the European strategy of negotiating with the regime. Seeking a cooperative solution together with the Europeans on the one hand and regime change on the other, hardly makes for compatible policies. Therefore, room for cooperation with the EU-3 was clearly limited.

The Europeans, for their part, tried to benefit from Bush's announcement of closer cooperation with Europe, by even more trying to bring the US directly into the negotiation process. Bush, though, rejected the strategy of direct negotiations with Iran, mainly due to concerns about such a policy being interpreted as an acceptance of the regime in Tehran. Nevertheless, a new policy of the second Bush Administration emerged, indicating that Bush would, if not directly participate in, at least more actively support European efforts. Most notably, a new mindset towards European endeavors appeared as Bush during his visit to Europe after re-election thanked former German Chancellor Gerhard Schröder for taking a lead role, together with France and Britain, in trying to solve the conflict over Iran's nuclear program. Moreover, the President announced that the US, together with its European partners, would work towards convincing Tehran to stop its nuclear ambitions.

Although a common transatlantic strategy was still elusive, members of the US administration convinced that economic incentives could be part of the solution did gain influence. British Prime Minister Tony Blair in particular managed to convince Bush of the advantages of a common transatlantic approach (Wright 2005). While the US and the EU-3 had initially been far apart in their ideas on how to deal with the conflict over Iran' nuclear program, they now began to move much closer together. This shift was largely due to the new Secretary of State Condoleezza Rice, who Bush appointed in his second term. The new Secretary of State believed in advantages of – at least initially – giving diplomacy a real chance. The fact that she was very close to the President allowed for a reconsideration of the Administration's approach. National Security Advisor Stephen Hadley also strongly believed that the EU-3's economic carrots could convince Iran to suspend its nuclear program if the US backed the Europeans. However, the most influential opponents to the policy shift were Vice President Dick Cheney and then Secretary of Defense Donald Rumsfeld. Both held the view that, in the end, neither the Iranians nor the Europeans could really be trusted. As such, the

Vice President and the Secretary of Defense formed a very strong front both against the negotiation process itself, as just as much as against any serious cooperation with the EU-3. In fact, the majority of the Administration at that time supported economic incentives for the Iranians but did not really believe in the ability of the strategy to succeed. Instead, they counted on the fact that once such a policy failed, the Europeans would then have no choice but to support a transfer of the issue to New York (Kaplan 2005).

Yet it soon became apparent, how small political room for maneuver really was. Neither were the Administration's offers – negotiations over an Iranian WTO membership and a loosening of sanctions on spare parts for civil aircrafts – especially interesting to Tehran. Nor was Washington really willing to conclude an agreement before the upcoming Iranian presidential elections in June 2005. After the elections, however, such approval became a lot less likely. The West had hoped for the election of the well-known former President Akbar Hashemi Rafsanjani, who had announced his desire to improve relations with the West and particularly with the US. Instead, the new President Mahmoud Ahmadinejad lobbied for the nuclear program, rejected a suspension of uranium enrichment projects (Reissner 2005), and showed no interest in improving relations with Washington. Furthermore, the perception that he was elected in a fraudulent process became widespread within the Bush Administration. As a result, Washington again began to reconsider its policy of supporting negotiations with Iran.

The Iranians did their share to bring Washington's reconsideration process to an abrupt end as they started the production of uranium hexafluoride in August 2005 (Adam/Dinmore/Bozorgmehr 2005). At this point, the US and the EU-3 again pulled at the same strings. Bush accepted the European resolution at the special meeting of the IAEA Board of Governors of September 24th, which once again requested Iran to suspend the production of uranium hexafluoride (IAEA 2005b).

What followed was the transfer of the Iranian dossier to the UN Security Council. This body unanimously approved two resolutions directed against Iran. But despite this unity, Tehran did not meet the Council's request to suspend its fuel cycle activities.

When dividing transatlantic cooperation on the Iran issue into two phases, intermitted by President Bush's re-election, we find a first phase, in which US support existed, but was hesitant. In Bush's second term he clearly moved much closer to the EU-3 position. At the same time the EU-3 increasingly moved towards the stricter US position. Undoubtedly the Iranians failed in reaching their goal to further separate the transatlantic partners. Quite to the opposite, the transatlantic partners managed to overcome their crisis over Iraq and to move increasingly closer towards a common position in dealing with Iran.

Conclusion

The Iranian nuclear program is one of the greatest challenges to the international community. In dealing therewith, the EU-3, the governments of France, Germany and the UK, played a significant role in establishing an international coalition directed against the Iranian nuclear threat. This includes close cooperation between the Europeans and the US. But also Russia and China, the two other permanent members of the UN Security Council, are part of the effort. Enabling this broad coalition building to become possible can be described as the most significant success of the EU-3 initiative, which was created spontaneously in October 2003.

Although the EU, that closely cooperated with the EU-3 governments, could show a high political profile in dealing with one of the most urgent current international crises it remains questionable whether such an approach will also be applicable in future crises. This is because EU members outside of the EU-3 are suspicious that they would be ousted from the future development of the CFSP as a result of yet another EU-3 case.

Clearly transatlantic discord existed at the beginning of the EU-3 negotiating initiative in October 2003 as the US strongly pushed for a direct transfer of the Iranian dossier to the UN Security Council while the Europeans tried to avoid such a referral. Tehran on its part sought to widen the gap between the transatlantic partners coming from the dispute over Iraq. Yet Iran failed to drive the allies further apart. Quite the opposite: Europe and the US did come a long way in moving their policies very close together during and after the EU-3 negotiations. As such, the EU-3 initiative had very positive effects on the development of transatlantic relations.

Despite the positive performance of the EU/EU-3, the Iranian nuclear issue could not be settled. On the contrary - Tehran continues to follow its nuclear path, thereby coming ever closer to a weapons option. How long it would take Iran to reach the point of no return is an open question that includes a couple of unknowns. In the meantime, the UN Security Council, the highest international authority, should try to put more pressure on Iran, as appropriate, to stress that the international community is not willing to accept Iranian nuclear weapons. At the same time, the door for cooperative diplomatic efforts needs to be kept open. Whether the international coalition, including strong transatlantic cooperation, will keep its act together is a question that can hardly be answered at this juncture. In any event, the contribution of the EU/EU-3 remains to be important.

References

This article is based on interviews with experts involved in the EU-3 initiative within the IAEA and foreign ministries as well as on the following:

Adam, Christopher/ Dinmore, Guy/Bozorgmehr, Najmeh (2005): Iran defies warning on uranium activity. In: The Financial Times. 09.08.2005.

Allison, Graham (2006): How good is American Intelligence on Iran's Bomb? In: Yale Global. 2006:13. P. 1-4.

Amineh, Mehdi Parvizi (2004): Demokratisierung und ihre Feinde im Iran. In: Aus Politik und Zeitgeschichte. 2004:9. P. 25-28.

Bahgat, Gawdat (2006): Nuclear Proliferation: The Islamic Republic of Iran. In: Iranian Studies. 39:3. P. 308-327.

Barnaby, Frank (2006): Iran's Nuclear Activities. In: Oxford Research Group. 2006: February. P. 1-6.

Bayat-Philipp, Mangol (2004): Die Beziehungen zwischen den USA und Iran seit 1953. In: Aus Politik und Zeitgeschichte. 2004:9. P. 29-38.

Borda, Aldo Zammit (2005): The Iranian nuclear issue and EU3 negotiations. In: Fornet Working Paper. 2005:8. P. 1-24.

Bradford, Peter (2007): Assessing Iran's Nuclear Power Claim. Carnegie Endowment Proliferation Analysis. Available at: www.carnegieendowment.org/publications/index.cfm?fa=view&id=18951&prog=zgp&proj=znpp. 09.07.06.

Chubin, Shahram (2006): Iran's Nuclear Ambitions. Washington.

Cirincione, Joseph (2006): No Military Options. In: Carnegie Issue Brief. 2006: February. P. 1-2.

Cordesman, Anthony H. (2006): Iran's Nuclear and Missile Programs: A Strategic Assessment. In: CSIS Report. P. 1-68.

Daase, Christopher (2005): Terrorgruppen und Massenvernichtungswaffen. In: Aus Politik und Zeitgeschichte. 48: 2005. P. 31-38.

Delpech, Thérèse (2006): Iran Case Study: Time is Running Out. In: Triangle Papers. 2006: 60. P. 59-84.

Denza, Eileen (2005): Non-proliferation of Nuclear Weapons: The European Union and Iran. In: European Foreign Affairs Review. 2005:10. P. 289-311.

Devine, James/Schofield, Julian (2006): Coercive Counter-Proliferation and Escalation: Assessing the Iran Military Option. In: Defense & Security Analysis. 22:2. P. 141-157.

Dupré, Bruno (2007): Iran Nuclear Crisis: The Right Approach. Carnegie Endowment Proliferation Analysis. Available at: http://www.carnegieendowment.org/publications/index.cfm?fa=view&id=19002&prog=zgp&proj=znpp. 02.02.07.

Fitzpatrick, Mark (2006a): Assessing Iran's Nuclear Program. In: Survival. 48:3. P. 5-26.

Fitzpatrick, Mark (2006b): Iran and North Korea: The Proliferation Nexus. In: Survival. 48:1. P. 61-80.

Ganji, Babak (2006): A Shi'i Enclave? Iranian Policy towards Iraq. In: Conflict Studies Research Center Middle East Series. 06:09. P. 1-27.

Harnisch, Sebastian (2006): Safeguarding the Non-Proliferation Regime: An Action Plan for the E3/EU and the Security Council on Iran. Available at: www.deutsche-aussenpolitik.de/digest/op-ed_inhalt_27.php. 15.10.2006.

Hughes, Robin (2007): Iran replenishes Hizbullah's arms inventory. In: Janes Defence Weekly. 44:1. P. 17.
Huntley, Wade L. (2006): Rebels without a cause: North Korea, Iran and the NPT. In: International Affairs. 82:4. P. 723-742.
IAEA (2003): IAEA and Iran, Statement by the Iranian Government and visiting EU Foreign Ministers, 21 October 2003. Available at: www.iaea.org/NewsCenter/Focus/IaeaIran/statement_iran21102003.shtml. 10.06.2006.
IAEA (2004a): Board of Governors Resolution GOV/2004/21. Implementation of the NPT Safeguards Agreement in the Islamic Republic of Iran. Available at: www.iaea.org/Publications/Documents/Board/2004/gov2004-21.pdf. 22.03.2006.
IAEA (2004b): IAEA Board of Governors Resolution GOV/2004/49. Implementation of the NPT Safeguards Agreement in the Islamic Republic of Iran. Available at: www.iaea.org/Publications/Documents/Board/2004/gov2004-49.pdf. 22.03.2006.
IAEA (2004c): Board of Governors Resolution GOV/2004/11. Implementation of the NPT Safeguards Agreement in the Islamic Republic of Iran. Available at: www.iaea.org/Publications/Documents/Board/2004/gov2004-11.pdf. 22.06.06.
IAEA (2004d): IAEA Board of Governors Resolution GOV/2004/79. Implementation of the NPT Safeguards Agreement in the Islamic Republic of Iran. Available at: www.iaea.org/Publications/Documents/Board/2004/gov2004-79.pdf. 22.03.06.
IAEA (2005a): IAEA Board of Governors Resolution GOV/2005/77. Implementation of the NPT Safeguard Agreement in the Islamic Republic of Iran. Available at: www.iaea.org/Publications/Documents/Board/2005/gov2005-77.pdf. 01.10.06.
IAEA (2005b): Implementation of the NPT Safeguards Agreement in the Islamic Republic of Iran and related Board resolutions GOV/2005/77. Available at: www.iaeo.org/Publications/Documents/Board/2005/gov2005-77.pdf. 12.10.2006.
IAEA (2006a): IAEA Information Circular INFCIRC/662. Communication dated 13 January 2006 received from the Permanent Missions of France, Germany and the United Kingdom to the Agency. Available at: www.iaea.org/Publications/Documents/INfcircs/2006/infcirc662.pdf. 14.09.2006.
IAEA (2006b): IAEA Board of Governors Resolution GOV/2006/14. Implementation of the NPT Safeguards Agreement in the Islamic Republic of Iran. Available at: www.iaea.org/Publications/Documents/Board/2006/gov2006-14.pdf. 23.09.06.
IAEA (2006c): IAEA Board Report by the Director General GOV/2006/38. Implementation of the NPT Safeguards Agreement in the Islamic Republic of Iran. Available at: www.iaea.org/Publications/Documents/Board/2006/gov2006-38.pdf. 15.06.06.
Kaplan, Lawrence F. (2005): Teheran Twist. Bush's new Iran Policy. In: The New Republic. 28.03.2005.
Langton, Christopher (2007): The Military Balance 2007. The International Institute for Strategic Studies. London.
Mauer, Victor (2006): Die Sicherheitspolitik der Europäischen Union. In: Aus Politik und Zeitgeschichte. 43: 2006. P. 10-16.
Müller, Harald (2003): Nukleare Krisen und transatlantischer Dissens. In: HSFK Report. 2003:9. P. 1-33.
Overhaus, Marco (2006): Analytical Introduction to the Dossier »European Diplomacy and the Conflict over Iran's Nuclear Program.« Available at: www.deutsche-aussenpolitik.de/resources/dossiers/iran06/Introduction.php. 13.06.2006.
Perkovich, George (2006a): Five Scenarios for the Iranian Crisis. In: Proliferation Papers. IFRI Security Studies Department. Winter: 2006. P. 1-29.
Perkovich, Goerge (2006b): »Democratic Bomb«: Failed Strategy. In: Carnegie Endowment Policy Brief. 2006: 49. P. 1-7.

Perthes, Volker/Wagner, Eva (2006): Enriching the Options: Europe, the United States, and Iran. In: SWP Discussion Paper. 2006: May. P. 1-13.

Posch, Walter (2006): The EU and Iran: a tangled web of negotiations. In: Chaillot Paper. 2005: 89. P. 99-114.

Randow, Gero von/Ladurner, Ulrich (2006): Die iranische Bombe. Hamburg.

Reissner, Johannes (2005): Irans neue Distance zum Westen. SWP Comments. 2005:A 32. P. 1-8.

Reissner, Johannes (2006): EU-Iran relations: options for future dialogue. In: Chaillot Paper. 89: 2006. P. 115-126.

Rieker, Pernille (2006): From Common Defence to Comprehensive Security: Towards the Europeanization of French Foreign and Security Policy? In: Security Dialogue. 37:4. P. 509-528.

Rogers, Mike/Holt, Rush (2006): Recognizing Iran as a Strategic Threat: An Intelligence Challenge for the United States. Staff Report of the House of Permanent Select Committee on Intelligence, Subcommittee on Intelligence Policy. August 23, 2006. Available at: http://intelligence.house.gov/Media/PDFS/Release082306.pdf. 23.08.06.

Rosen, Peter (2006): After Proliferation: What to Do If more States Go Nuclear. In: Foreign Affairs. September/October: 2006. P. 1-4.

Sagan, Scott D. (2006): How to Keep the Bomb From Iran. In: Foreign Affairs. 2006: September/October. P. 1-8.

Samore, Gary (2004): Meeting Iran's Nuclear Challenge. In: The Weapons of Mass Destruction Commission Paper. 2004: 21. P. 1-18.

Sauer, Tom (2004): The »Americanization« of EU Nuclear Non-proliferation Policy. In: Defense and Security Analysis. 2004:20. P. 113-131.

Seaboyer, Anthony/Thränert, Oliver (2006): What Missile Proliferation means for Europe. In: Survival. 48:2. P. 85-96.

Shaw, Jacqueline/Albright, David (2006): Iran's Nuclear Program: Flawed House Intelligence Committee Report Should be Amended or Withdrawn. In: ISIS Report. 2006: November . P. 1-4.

Thränert, Oliver (2003): Der Iran und die Verbreitung von ABC-Waffen. SWP Research Paper. 2003:S 30. P. 1-36.

Thränert, Oliver (2004): Ending Suspicious Nuclear Activities in Iran. In: SWP Working Paper. 2004:3. P. 1-6.

Thränert, Oliver (2005a): Die Verbreitung von Raketen und Marschflugkörpern. SWP Research Paper. 2005:S 15. 1-32

Thränert, Oliver (2005b): Die Iranische Bombe verhindern. Der europäische Weg. In: Die Neue Gesellschaft / Frankfurter Hefte. 2005:1 + 2. P. 1-4.

Thränert, Oliver (2006a): Iran before the Security Council. In: SWP Comments 2006:C 02. P. 1-4.

Thränert, Oliver (2006b): A Simmering Crusade. Die Bush-Administration und das iranische Atomprogram. In: Hils, Jochen/Wilzewski, Jürgen (Hrsg.): Defekte Demokratie - Crusader State? Die Weltpolitik der USA in der Ära Bush. Trier. P. 461-482.

Thränert, Oliver (2006c): Das große internationale Iran-Puzzle. In: Internationale Politik. August: 2006. P. 28-35.

UN (2006a): United Nations Security Council Resolution S/RES/1696. Available at: www.un.org/News/Press/docs/2006/sc8792.doc.htm. 01.08.2006.

UN (2006b): United Nations Security Council Resolution S/RES/1737. Available at: http://daccessdds.un.org/doc/UNDOC/GEN/N06/681/42/PDF/ N0668142.pdf?OpenElement. 30.01.2006.

UN (2006c): Security Council Presidential Statement SC/8679. Available at: www.un.org/News/Press/docs/2006/sc8679.doc.htm. 06.04.2006.

Wolfsthal, Jon B./Hamilton, Jennifer (2006): The EU-US Summit and the Challenge of Iran's Nuclear Program. In: CSIS Commentary. 2006: June. P. 1-2.

Wright, Robin (2005): U.S. Allies May Have to Wait Out Iran Elections. In: Washington Post. 12.03.2005.

The EU and Counter-Terrorism: A Reliable Ally in the 'War on Terror'?

David Brown[1]

Introduction

Tony Blair, in outlining a twenty-first century orientation for UK foreign policy, envisaged it as some form of 'bridge', holding together the US and the EU. While the UK's self-appointed role has not been accepted by either 'side' of the bridge[2] – and has been criticised even from within his own Cabinet[3] - the image has its uses. For the transatlantic counter-terrorist relationship to be successful in tackling the developing and mutating Islamist threat, with its perceived global scope and increased lethality, both sides of the 'bridge' have to be stable and secure. A significant amount of research has been carried out on the Bush administration's self-declared 'war on terror', particularly in relation to the controversial decision to invade Iraq.[4] Yet, it is equally important to consider how the EU's counter-terrorist framework has developed, identifying the progress made and highlighting the problems that still remain to be tackled. In order to fully comprehend how the EU has countered the terrorist threat, the key trends that coloured the Third Pillar's first decade will briefly be sketched out, before moving on to the post September 11 phase. Having identified three key trends – the issue of relative prioritisation, the perceived 'implementation gap' between declared intentions and actual reality on the ground and the problematic labelling of such co-operation as a 'matter of common concern', both in terms of the perceived threat and the likely responses – the second half of the chapter will explore how these have developed in the post September 11 era.

---

1 The views expressed here are personal and do not represent the opinions or views of the British Government, Ministry of Defence or the Royal Military Academy Sandhurst.
2 See Dr Kendall Myers comments in Tom Baldwin, »Blair's bridge between Europe and the US? It's falling down and he is left with nothing,« *The Times*, 30 November, 2006.
3 See Robin Cook, *The Point of Departure* (London: Simon and Schuster, 2003), 133.
4 See, for example, Ron Suskind, *The One Percent Doctrine: Deep inside America's pursuit of its enemies since 9.11* (London: Simon and Schuster, 2006); Bob Woodward, *State of Denial: Bush at War Part III* (London: Simon and Schuster, 2006).

The Pre-September 11 era: A shaky foundation?

Counter-terrorism was not at the top of the Third Pillar agenda when the new institutional structures were created. In fact, it was not listed as one of nine separate 'common concerns', relegated instead to an overarching category of 'police co-operation', centred on the European Police Office (Europol).[5] This was a somewhat ironic development, given that counter-terrorism was then initially excluded from Europol's remit. Such decisions highlight the lack of prioritisation of counter-terrorism. A more detailed study of the Third Pillar's legislative instruments reinforces this point. Between 1992 and 2000, of 509 registered legislative instruments – both binding and non-binding – only fourteen were dedicated primarily to counter-terrorism.[6] In fact, in 1997, there were no registered counter-terrorism instruments at all, which is ironic, given that the Treaty of Amsterdam made counter-terrorism a separate and distinct competency in the same year. Not only that, but, had events elsewhere not intervened, there were few plans to change this situation, as the Scoreboard indicates. The Scoreboard, an initiative intended to prioritise the implementation phase of the decision-making process, gives a clear indication of the EU's longer-term counter-terrorist priorities. There was only one direct reference to counter-terrorism in any of the pre-September 11 iterations, namely a commitment to prepare 'common definitions and penalties' by the third quarter of 2001.[7]

In terms of implementing legislation, the pre-September 11 record is unimpressive, with Bures noting that 'practical implementation was often painfully slow'.[8] It is necessary to take a wider view, not only because the problem is endemic across the Third Pillar, but also because, in its initial years, the limited counter-terrorist measures tended to be non-binding in nature. Across the internal security spectrum, only one convention out of twenty-five had actually been fully ratified, let alone implemented in full.[9] While the Europol Convention has significant relevance for counter-terrorism, at least post 1999, when terrorism became a specific part of its remit, it remains the exception to the general rule. In fact, partly as a result of such

---

5 See Article K: 1 (9) TEU.
6 For details, see the »Justice and Home Affairs Acquis 1993-2000 «. (2001). http://www.statewatch.org/semdoc/acquis.htm (accessed 1 December 2006).
7 See, for example, European Commission. »Biannual update of the Scoreboard to review progress on the creation of an area of freedom, security and justice in the European Union (First Half of 2001).« Brussels. (2001).
8 Oldrich Bures, »EU counter-terrorism policy: A paper tiger?,« *Terrorism and Political Violence* 18, no. 1 (2006): 59.
9 Joanna Apap and Sergio Carrera, »Progress and obstacles in the area of freedom, security and justice in an enlarging Europe: An overview,« in *Justice and Home Affairs in the European Union*, ed. Joanna Apap (Northhampton: Edward Elgar, 2004), 10.

a poor ratification record, the EU has moved away from utilising Conventions, in favour of Framework Decisions, which are binding in terms of the agreed objectives, but leave up to the member states how they achieve said objectives. In fact, one suggestion for developing Europol involves changing the decision-making base from a Convention to a Council Decision by the end of 2007.[10] Such a poor historical legacy undermines the EU's credibility, as it attempts to demonstrate that it 'adds value' to the efforts of its individual member states.

A possible explanation for this poor record lies with the third noted trend of the initial period, namely the questionable labelling of counter-terrorism as a 'matter of common concern' for the EU as a whole. While the Treaty on European Union (TEU) used such labels, there was little to denote exactly what made an issue one of 'common concern'.[11] While such phrases offer the comforting veneer of togetherness, the reality for counter-terrorism may be less straight-forward. In the pre-September 11 era, eight of the then fifteen member states registered a terrorist incident, with the remaining seven, thankfully, free of terrorist activity. In fact, when a qualitative element is added, the situation becomes even more complex. For example, both France and Italy, during that period, had effectively tackled their predominant left wing threat, either through effective policing or the fragmentation of the terrorist group from within. Also, Denmark, included within the eight, registered only one incident in the total reporting period.[12] As such, the actual level of commonality may be even lower, perhaps closer to Verbruggen's assessment, that Spain was 'the only EU member state with deeply entrenched domestic terrorist activity still as the prime concern of both politics and law enforcement'.[13] It should also be remembered that the nature of the threat is likely to differ slightly from state to state, depending on the terrorists' ideological motivation. Overall, when taken in conjunction with the poor implementation record and the relative lack of priority accorded to counter-terrorism matters within the Third Pillar, it does not form a particularly stable foundation for the EU to build upon.

---

10 Council of the European Union. »Draft Justice and Home Affairs Council Conclusions on the future of Europol on 25 October 2006.« Brussels. (October 2006).
11 Having conducted an extensive search of JHA documentation, and consulted with senior figures within the European institutions, I have been unable to ascertain a formal, agreed definition of 'common concern'.
12 For full figures, see US Department of State. »Patterns of Global Terrorism 1994-2001.« (1995-2002).
13 F. Verbruggen, »Bull's Eye? Two remarkable EU Framework Decisions in the fight against terrorism,« in *Legal instruments in the fight against international terrorism: A transatlantic dialogue*, ed. C. et al Fininaut (Leiden: Martinus Nijhoff, 2004), 300.

New Priorities – The impact of September 11

In the wake of September 11, the international community, both institutionally and as individual member states, began an almost frenetic (in most cases) legislative and operational response. This was most starkly (and understandably) seen in the US, where the Bush administration reacted in a more aggressive way than its predecessors[14], both in terms of the greater use of military force and in shifting the balance between security concerns and civil liberties, as seen, for example, in the rapid adoption of the Patriot Act. Equally, a number of key EU member states also overhauled their own national security arrangements, with the UK, for example, even going as far as to declare a 'state of emergency', in order to reintroduce indefinite detention without trial.[15] The EU also responded swiftly across an array of issue areas, ranging from tackling radicalisation to civil protection. The 2005 EU Counter-Terrorist Strategy alone contains 90 separate measures, subdivided into four areas of activity – to prevent against, protect from, respond to and pursue terrorists, primarily, although not exclusively, Al Qaeda and affiliate networks.[16] Unsurprisingly, therefore, given the changed international environment, the EU has significantly increased the level of attention given to terrorism related matters, substantively improving on its relatively limited performance in the Third Pillar's opening years.

This has led some to make even more optimistic predictions about the future development of the European level of decision-making in Justice and Home Affairs (JHA). It is necessary to address these concerns, to place the post September 11 era into context. Monar, for example, has highlighted significant growth in the wider JHA area, citing not only its expanding remit – helped along by the EU's widened membership – but also the greater number of meetings undertaken specifically to address JHA matters. The Council Secretariat, for example, estimates that 40% of its meetings are either directly or indirectly associated with JHA matters.[17] While such activity is indeed symbolic of greater attention being paid to JHA related matters, there is a danger in reading too much into such procedural aspects. Given the increased complexity of EU decision-making in this area, with its

---

14 It is worth recalling that members of the Clinton administration believed that they were also at 'war with terrorism'. See Thomas J. Badey, »US Anti-terrorism Policy: The Clinton Administration,« *Contemporary Security Policy* 19, no. 2 (1998).

15 For further details on both the UK and a number of other key member states' responses at the national level, see Kirstin Archick, *European approaches to Homeland Security and Counter-terrorism* (Washington DC: Congressional Research Service, July 2006).

16 For details, see the public version of »The European Union Counter-Terrorist Strategy.« Brussels. (November 2005).

17 See Jorg Monar, »An emerging regime of European Governance for Freedom, Security and Justice,« *ESRC One Europe or Several? Programme briefing note 2/99*.

array of agencies, committees and institutional arrangements, an increase in the volume of JHA related activity is to be expected.

Some, such as Kaunert, have taken a step further and concluded, in effect, that a norm has been established accepting the efficacy of the European decision-making level. He bases this assessment, not on the establishment of a separate internal security pillar as part of the TEU, nor on the entrenching of the longer term vision of an 'Area of Freedom, Security and Justice' (AFSJ) (established as an EU objective as part of the Treaty of Amsterdam), but on the rather more shaky foundations of the proposed European Constitution. It is true that, if fully implemented, the Constitution would bring about significant changes to the way JHA matters were handled within the EU, not least in relation to the abolition of the Third Pillar. This would lead to increased roles for the Community institutions, changes to the right of initiative (whereby the default position would be with the Commission, with an individual member state requiring the support of a quarter of the total membership to introduce new legislation) and alterations to existing European police and judicial agencies, such as permitting Europol access to intelligence material and the possible creation of a European Public Prosecutor.[18] Coupled with the September 2005 European Court of Justice (ECJ) decision regarding the legality of the Commission outlining the need for criminal penalties, at least in the specific area of environmental protection, such proposals have led one commentator to forecast that 'the EU becomes the primary holder of competence in the area of judicial and police co-operation'.[19] This coincides with Kaunert's suggestion that, after the events of July 7th 2005, 'decision-makers do not regard the national sovereignty concerns to be of any use in the fight against terrorism'.[20]

There are a number of concerns with this model for progression, not least of which is the current status of the European Constitution, following its double rejection at the hands of the French and Dutch voters. While it remains to be seen what will eventually emerge to take its place, it is notable that, given the chance to rescue elements of the internal security package at Tampere in 2006, the EU member states were unable to reach a consensus on the matter. As The Economist noted, 'in 1999, ministers decided in principle to put parts of Europe's national criminal justice and policing systems under the control of common institutions in Brussels...last weekend, they

---

18 For details of the »Treaty establishing a Constitution for Europe.« http://europa.eu/constitution/en/lstoc1_en.htm (accessed 1 December 2006).
19 M. Kaiafa-Gbandi, »The Treaty Establishing a Constitution for Europe and challenges for Criminal Law at the commencement of the 21st Century,« *European Journal of Crime, Criminal Law and Criminal Justice* 13, no. 4 (2005): 491.
20 Christian Kaunert, »The Area of Freedom, Security and Justice: The construction of a 'European Public Order',« *European Security* 14, no. 4 (2005): 481.

decided in practice not to'.[21] There has been a similarly fierce response to the ECJ decision, with a number of member states determined to limit the potential scope of the ruling.[22]

Equally, there are countervailing trends within JHA matters that need to be considered. As Monar has correctly noted, the historical development of JHA co-operation has been based, at least in part, on the development of 'laboratories', such as TREVI, Interpol and the Schengen system.[23] In the latter case, its development came about because the opportunities for ensuring the removal of internal border controls within the then EC were obstructed, notably by the UK. As such, committed member states established less formal bodies outside the EC/EU structures, to advance proposals and make progress (with the Schengen acquis eventually adopted by the EU at Amsterdam). Arguably, similar processes are at work once again, inspired to some extent by the widening of the EU to embrace 12 new member states. The development of the G5 (now G6, with the inclusion of Poland) and the signing of the Treaty of Prum in May 2005 can be seen, not as indicators of the successful functioning of the European level, but of the desire to seek new solutions and locate new 'laboratories' at a less formal, multinational level. In the latter case, the Prum states have begun to establish new policing arrangements, forming new rules for DNA sharing, fingerprint data and airline security.[24] In the case of the G5, an informal grouping of Interior Ministers initially from 'the five countries with the largest counter-terrorist capability in Europe'[25], this can be seen as a direct response to a less productive EU level of decision making. As a UK Home Office submission notes, such informal gatherings, with their smaller membership, enables 'a freer exchange of views…than would be possible at formal EU meetings involving all twenty five member states'.[26] Taking all of these developments into account, and building on the record at the operational level, where Europol has struggled to fully establish itself as an effective means of information exchange, the tide may actually be turning in the other direction, away from

21 Charlemagne, »In Europe we don't trust,« *The Economist*, 30 September, 2006, 56.
22 For details of the UK position, see House of Lords, *The Criminal Competence of the European Community: Testimony of Richard Plender QC, taken before the Select Committee on the European Union on 3 May 2006* (London: HMSO, 2006).
23 Jorg Monar, »The dynamics of Justice and Home Affairs: Laboratories, Driving Factors and Costs,« *Journal of Common Market Studies* 39, no. 4 (2001).
24 Hugo Brady, »An avant-garde for international security,« *Centre for European Reform Bulletin* 44 (November 2005): 2. For details of the Treaty, see »Prum Convention (Schengen III).« http://www.libertysecurity.org/imprimer.php?id_article=368 (accessed 1 December 2006).
25 House of Lords, *After Madrid: the EU's response to terrorism: Testimony of Jonathan Faull for Fifth Report, taken before the Select Committee on the European Union on 3 November 2004* (London: HMSO, 2004), 37-53. With the inclusion of Poland, its central counter-terrorist focus may be called into question a little more.
26 Home Office cited Lords, *After Madrid*, 129.

formal EU level responses and back towards more informal, bi or multilateral arrangements.

That is not to say that some promising developments have not taken place at the EU level. The 2002 Framework Decision on Combating Terrorism[27] and a similar measure establishing the European Arrest Warrant (EAW)[28] have both proved to be valuable tools in addressing elements of the terrorist challenge. In the case of the former, the EU took a massive step forward by agreeing a formal definition of terrorism. This addressed one of the most problematic elements of the pre-September 11 period, where only seven of the then member states possessed a specific definition of terrorism within their legislative canon.[29] While it did not prove possible to meet the Commission's initial proposal to lay down specific agreed penalties for all of the offences noted in the Framework Decision, this should not undermine the overall achievement of finally agreeing some form of definition. It was also affected by the more traditional problem of missed deadlines and slow implementation, an almost ever-present element of JHA activity. Some have suggested that this was, in part, because the half year timeframe for adoption and implementation, seen as important at the time to demonstrate the EU's renewed commitment, was always going to prove impossible for a number of member states to realistically meet.[30]

The pressing need for speed at that time has also arguably undermined the smooth development of the other major legislative achievement of that period, the development of the EAW. As with the commitment to agree common definitions and penalties for combating terrorism, which was part of the pre-September 11 plans for JHA development, the initial commitment to replace the longer and more complex extradition arrangements with a speedier surrender procedure predates the post September 11 rush. In fact, at the 1999 Tampere European Council, the following conclusion was reached: 'the formal extradition procedure should be abolished among the member states...and replaced by a simple transfer of such persons'.[31] Given the greater impetus to achieve (and be seen to achieve) such objectives, a relatively speedy and truncated decision-making process was undertaken in

---

27 Justice and Home Affairs Council. »Framework Decision on Combating Terrorism.« Brussels. (2002).
28 Justice and Home Affairs Council. »Framework Decision on the European Arrest Warrant and the surrender procedures between member states.« Brussels. (2002).
29 For a more detailed exposition of these arguments, see David Brown, *Unsteady Foundations: The European Union's Counter-Terrorist Framework 1993-2007* (Manchester: Manchester University Press, 2008).
30 Jan Wouters and Frederick Naert, »Terrorist Offences and Extradition deals: An appraisal of the EU's main criminal law against terrorism after 11 September,« *Common Market Law Review* 41, no. 4 (2004): 929.
31 Council of the European Union. »Presidency Conclusions of the Tampere European Council on 15-16 October 1999.« Brussels. (Ocotber 1999).

the aftermath of September 11 (the process lasted less than five months, from proposal by the Commission to final Parliamentary approval, followed by a lengthier implementation phase). Having already failed twice to implement extradition conventions, the fact that a simplified surrender procedure – removing the obstacles of political exception, the bar on nationals being extradited and double criminality as part of a relatively short administrative and judicial arrangement – was achieved is worthy of note. Extending the EAW's remit beyond terrorism, to embrace 32 'European crimes', including murder and rape, the initial take-up by the member states has also been encouraging. It has, on the most up to date European figures available, proved to be a successful arrangement, reducing extradition times from an average of nine months to forty-three days between January and September 2004.[32] In the same period, 2603 warrants were issued, leading to 653 arrests and 104 persons surrendered.[33]

Yet, there was a developing sting in the tail. The speed of the decision-making process led to some noted errors, with the Commission pointing out that eleven of the twenty-five member states had made mistakes in the national legislation ratifying the EAW.[34] While some, such as the UK, have disputed the Commission's interpretation of its implementing legislation, an even greater challenge has emerged to the EAW's longer-term viability. This concerns a series of constitutional challenges, in Cyprus, Germany, Greece and Poland thus far, that, if successful, would call into question one of the central aims of the EAW, namely the removal of the obstacle of surrendering a state's national on request from another competent authority.[35] While the Greek case has been closed, with the central principles of the EAW still intact, and the German government are (at the time of writing) preparing a legislative amendment that would circumvent the current constitutional block, the two 2004 entrants both face longer term challenges, as their Constitutions effectively bar the extradition of their nationals. Although Austria was able to negotiate an exemption from these provisions until 2008, such an arrangement was not available to the accession states at that time, who had to simply accept the EAW in full. As well as potentially undermining one of the perceived practical advantages of moving to the supposedly simpler and speedier system, there is a danger that the already fragile levels of mutual trust that exist between EU partners will be further

---

32 Daniel Keohane, *One Step Forward, Two Steps Back* (London: Centre for European Reform, 2005), 37.
33 »Report from the Commission on the European Arrest Warrant and the surrender procedures between member states.« Brussels. (February 2005), 4.
34 Hugo Brady and Daniel Keohane, *Fighting Terrorism: The EU needs a strategy not a shopping list* (London: Centre for European Reform, 2005), 2.
35 For details, see Zsuzsanna Deen-Racsmany, »The European Arrest Warrant and the surrender of nationals revisited: the lessons of constitutional challenges,« *European Journal of Crime, Criminal Law and Criminal Justice* 14, no. 3 (2006).

weakened. Spain has already decided that, until Germany can resolve its constitutional concerns, it will not surrender Spanish nationals on request, a 'tit for tat' measure that a UK Home Office Minister feared could lead to 'the breakdown of the system'. While, in 2006, the UK was not prepared to endorse similar moves, an ominous warning was given that 'if there was no movement, we would have to review that position'.[36] Additionally, one legal scholar has noted that the 'fact that so far...no constitutional complaints have been lodged against the surrender of nationals in other member states [beyond the four noted above] is not necessarily a reliable indicator' that the EAW is 'considered satisfactory in other jurisdictions'. Poland had successfully extradited nine nationals before facing a legal challenge and an adverse constitutional ruling.[37] Although primarily an intra-EU development, with the US organising separate extradition arrangements both with the individual member states and at an EU level, the breakdown of mutual trust is to no-one's benefit.

Furthermore, a 2005 legal challenge in Belgium, questioning the very appropriateness of a Framework Decision rather than the more cumbersome Convention process of the earlier Third Pillar era, may yet prove to be an even more serious threat. If successful (which was not known at the time of writing), the legal basis on which the EAW was so swiftly adopted would be called into question; given the previous record of extradition conventions within the EU, with two agreed but never implemented, a return to the old ways of doing business would (in the absence of a Constitutionally approved relocation to the First Pillar) entail an even lengthier process of negotiation, with all that this implies, not only for the European level of decision-making, but also wider international co-operation.

One step forward: The implementation gap

Such a move would also have a significant impact on the existing implementation gap. In the pre-September 11 period, only one of the twenty-five agreed conventions ever saw the light of day, leaving behind it a record of unfulfilled legislative promises and incomplete objectives. While Framework Decisions have proved a more successful instrument than its cumbersome predecessor, even here, the record of implementation is not wholly impressive.

---

36 House of Lords, *European Arrest Warrant: Recent Developments: Testimony of Andy Burnham MP for Thirtieth Report, taken before the Select Committee on the European Union on 18 January 2006* (London: HMSO, 2006), 16.
37 Deen-Racsmany, »The European Arrest Warrant and the surrender of nationals revisited: the lessons of constitutional challenges,« 297.

For example, while the initial decision-making processes were successfully truncated, national implementation of both the newly agreed definition of terrorism and the EAW was taken at a more traditional pace. Even though the objectives of both Framework Decisions had actually been on the EU's books in the pre-September 11 era, deadlines were once again missed. For example, in the case of the EAW, not all EU member states had completed the national ratification process by February 2005, with Italy the last to fully ratify in April 2005. The situation with the Framework Decision on Combating Terrorism was even worse, as the Commission could not even get the necessary information to make assessments on the state of ratification in the first place. As they are ultimately dependent on the member states' goodwill to even begin their monitoring responsibilities, the record here makes for uneasy reading. When the initial deadline for ratification – December 31 2002 – was reached, only five of the then EU fifteen had even supplied the Commission with information. After further exhortations and a new deadline, another seven states responded in some fashion, leaving only Greece – providing non-specific information – Luxembourg and the Netherlands (the latter two providing no information at all).[38] While both Framework Decisions were eventually successfully implemented, the combination of a widened membership base that has to implement each measure and a greater sense of removal from the initial trauma of the events of September 11 has led to the noted implementation gap getting wider again in recent times. For example, the three additional Europol Protocols, agreed in 2000, 2002 and 2003 respectively, were not fully implemented at the time of writing, with the 2006 Tampere European Council looking to a successful conclusion in the early part of 2007.[39]

Such delays ultimately undermine the credibility of the EU as an actor in the field of counter-terrorism. It is harder for international partners, such as the US, to fully take the EU seriously, if it is continually seen to commit itself to potentially significant objectives, only for its individual member states to fail to demonstrate the necessary political will and dedication both to ratify and then successfully implement such objectives. A further case in point relates to the sphere of information exchange, which remains Europol's primary function, alongside analytical support. In October 2005, building upon the regular exhortations that had been made for member states to share information more freely, both with each other and with EU agencies, the Commission put forward a proposal to institute the 'principle of availability', which is likely to come into effect 'from the beginning of

---

38 »Report from the Commission on the Council Framework Decision on combating terrorism.« Brussels. (June 2004), 3.
39 See Justice and Home Affairs Council. »Improvement of decision-making in Justice and Home Affairs: Summary of Informal JHA meeting on 20-22 September 2006'.« Helsinki. (September 2006).

2008' (in itself later than the deadline contained within the draft legislation, which notes June 30 2007 'at the latest' as the agreed deadline).[40] The draft Framework Decision 'lays down *an obligation* for the member states to give access or to provide certain types of information available to their authorities to equivalent authorities of other member states' (emphasis added).[41] Highlighting as an 'obstacle' the 'bi and multilateral agreements between member states [which] are either geographically restricted or do not oblige member states to provide information'[42], the shift towards a general commitment to 'availability' is portrayed as a step change in the EU's efforts in this field. In fact, the Commission considers that, once this cornerstone principle has been agreed and implemented, 'the need to maintain numerous bilateral contacts and multilateral networks *will cease to exist*' (emphasis added).[43] Such proposals, to make the European level the primary, or potentially even the only, level of exchange, have echoes in further Commission proposals, such as the suggestion that Europol should consider establishing the intelligence requirements for member states[44], with the first step coming in a December 2005 proposal to permit Europol to receive information on the activities of security and intelligence services.[45]

Leaving aside the question of whether such moves are appropriate for a moment, if successfully implemented, they would constitute a major seachange in the EU's role, not only in counter-terrorism, but within the wider JHA arena. Although there are a number of potential restrictions highlighted in the legislation, both for the limitations to be placed on available information (where three scenarios are envisaged, including not jeopardising an on-going investigation) and the ultimate refusal to provide information (which adds a fourth scenario, namely 'to protect fundamental rights and freedoms of persons whose data are processed under this Framework Decision'[46]), the emphasis is on ensuring as great a European level of in-

---

40 House of Lords, *Behind closed doors: the meeting of the G6 Interior Ministers at Heiligendamm: Fortieth Report, taken before the Select Committee on the European Union on 11 July 2006* (London: HMSO, 2006), 17.
41 Commission of the European Communities. »Proposal for a Council Framework Decision on the exchange of information under the principle of availability.« Brussels. (Ocotber 2005), 12.
42 »Proposal for a Council Framework Decision on the exchange of information under the principle of availability.« 3.
43 »Proposal for a Council Framework Decision on the exchange of information under the principle of availability.« 9.
44 »Strengthening the EU operational police co-operation.« Brussels. (October 2004), 3.
45 European Commission. »Proposal for a Council Decision on the transmission of information resulting from the activities of security and intelligence services with respect to terrorist offences.« Brussels. (December 2005).
46 See Article 14 of Proposal for a Council Framework Decision on the exchange of information under the principle of availability.

formation exchange as possible. In fact, on studying such matters, the UK House of Lords European Union Committee concluded that 'the grounds for declining...are extremely limited'.[47]

Yet, on closer examination, the likelihood of such a shift – from the bilateral to the European level, from the jealously guarded world of national security to the more free-flowing exchange of information presupposed in the Framework Decision draft – is not as high as the Commission suggest. Firstly, given that the legislation highlights the importance of data protection, it is important to note the change in position of the G6 states, who declared in March 2006 that 'the rapid implementation of the availability principle must not depend on the adoption of the Framework Decision on data protection in the Third Pillar'.[48] The EU previously had committed to ensuring that both pieces of legislation would complement each other, with the data protection legislation providing further reassurances that all 'equivalent authorities' involved in data exchange would adhere to the same standards and ensure that the information requested was only used for a clearly stated purpose (after which it would be deleted). Yet, the G6 announcement suggests that data protection is of lesser import than ensuring the increased level of information exchange. The need to increase such co-operation is admirable, but, as with the previous example of the EAW, the EU could be in danger of undermining the longer-term effectiveness of the proposal for the sake of a speedier initial decision-making process. Given that adequate data protection has been explicitly highlighted as a justification, not to limit the provision of information but to refuse the request, it would seem imperative to ensure that sufficient data protection legislation was in place across the board prior to the implementation of the availability principle. It is difficult to argue, as one UK Minister has done, that being 'conscious that you will have to sign up to the Data Protection Framework Decision...at some point'[49] constitutes a sufficient guarantee. With mutual trust already undermined, to create further doubt by failing to implement both the data protection and information exchange principles together may only store up longer-term problems for the EU.

Secondly, the suggested objective of shifting the balance from the bilateral to the European level, leading to the effective elimination of the former, is unlikely to ever be achieved, even if the Framework Decision is implemented in full. As Europol's record demonstrates all too clearly, and the establishment of the G6 reinforces, there remains a lingering suspicion of sharing information too widely. In fact, France's Nicolas Sarkozy has argued that it was unrealistic to expect intelligence sharing between all mem-

---

47 Lords, *Behind closed doors*, 13.
48 Lords, *Behind closed doors*, 15.
49 Baroness Ashton of Upholland cited Lords, *Behind closed doors*, 30-35.

ber states in an enlarged EU.[50] Given the significant problems states have ensuring national police and intelligence agencies share information with each other, a problem not exclusive to the EU by any means, there are even greater difficulties in ensuring a wider European level of exchange. At the end of the day, it runs contrary to the culture and instinct of those that will have to implement such political decisions on the ground, namely the national police and security agencies. As Jurgen Storbeck, former Director of Europol, conceded, 'for a policeman, information about his own case is like property. He is even reluctant to give it to his chief or to another department, let alone giving it to the regional or national services.'[51] It is also significant that, having proposed such a potentially far-reaching objective, the actual terms of the Framework Definition then outline a potential role for bilateral agreements, 'in order to further simplify or facilitate the modalities of the provision of information'.[52] Thirdly, and inherent in all Framework Decisions, there is no enforcement mechanism, to ensure that member states, in the longer term, actually hold to what was agreed. As such, it seems difficult to see how the EU will hold its member states to the obligation they are signing up to. As a result, the implementation gap is likely to remain in place for the longer term.

That said, there are at least some signs of belated recognition that this gap between (at times unrealistic) objective setting and slow and uncommitted national implementation processes cannot be allowed to remain as an unsatisfactory symbol of JHA co-operation. As part of the negotiations over the 2004 Hague Programme, which outlines priorities and programmes for JHA integration over the next five years, Sweden insisted that the 'starting point for the new programme should…be to finalise what remains undone on the Tampere scoreboard'.[53] More recently, this refrain has been taken up by the likes of Ambassador Georg Witschel, Germany's Commissioner for Combating International Terrorism, who argued that the EU's priority must be 'to implement, implement, implement'.[54] Yet, actions speak louder than words. In reality, the EU has yet to grasp this particular nettle, preferring instead to constantly initiate new legislative proposals

---

50 Nicolas Sarkozy cited Mirjam Dittrich, »Facing the global terrorist threat: a European response,« *European Policy Centre Working Paper*, no. 14 (January 2005): 6.
51 Storbeck cited Bares John Bellinger, *Speech by the US State Department Legal Advisor on US-EU Counter-terrorism co-operation on 11 September 2006* (Brussels: United States Mission to the European Union, 2006), 63.
52 See Article 18 of Proposal for a Council Framework Decision on the exchange of information under the principle of availability.
53 For details, see »Memorandum from the Swedish Ministry of Justice on the Commission Communication 'Area of freedom, security and justice: Assessment of the Tampere Programme and future orientations.« Stockholm. (8 September 2004).
54 Ambassador Witschel cited »Protecting Europe: Policies for enhancing security in the EU.« Brussels: Security and Defence Agenda. (2006), 18.

into an already crowded agenda. Ludford has collated the initiatives proposed both by member states and the European institutions between 2001 and 2004, noting fifty-one initiatives from the member states, with an additional thirty-eight Commission proposals in the wider JHA arena. While the pace of activity has not slowed down, even within the context of a substantively widened JHA Council, there is an issue of quality to consider. Ludford's assessment, 'most of these initiatives were designed as press stunts, at the beginning of a Presidency, and have little value'.[55] While quality of legislation is important, the sheer weight of numbers, at a time when deadlines are being missed on pre-existing commitments, is worrying in itself. For the sake of its longer term credibility, the EU needs to restore a sense of realism about the objectives it can achieve and devote significantly more time towards the less glamorous, but potentially more rewarding, area of implementation.

A question of commonality – the rise of Militant Islam

Finally, there is a need to more critically examine the nature of the post September 11 threat within the EU, to consider whether a greater level of commonality has indeed developed, when confronted with the additional threat of militant Islamist terrorism. Given that one of the central pillars of the 2005 Counter-Terrorism Strategy is to 'understand and make collective policy responses to the terrorist threat'[56], it is even more important not to simply accept at face value the assumption of a region-wide, let alone, global threat.

It is worth considering a quantitative chronological development, to give an outline of the level of commonality in the post September 11 era, before fleshing out certain details. In the 2002-03 Europol report, which states that 'no major terrorist attacks occurred within the EU', there is a noted shift of balance within the EU from the pre September 11 era, with eight states registering no incident, as compared to the previous year's total of seven.[57] There is a further shift in 2004, with only five states registering any form of significant terrorist incident. Additionally, three member states – Belgium, Finland and Portugal – did not provide any information.[58] This is de-

---

55 Sarah Ludford, »An EU Justice and Home Affairs policy: What should it comprise?,« in *Justice and Home Affairs in the European Union*, ed. Joanna Apap (Northhampton: Edward Elgar, 2004), 29.
56 »The European Union Counter-Terrorist Strategy.« 3.
57 See »Terrorist Activity in the European Union: Situation and trends report – October 2002-15 October 2003.« The Hague: Europol. (2003).
58 See »Terrorist Activity in the European Union: Situation and trends report – October 2004-October 2005.« The Hague: Europol. (2006).

spite the fact that the threshold for inclusion in the report cannot have been substantial, given that space was allocated to a brief discussion of Hungarian animal rights terrorism, despite the incidence being 'very low'.[59] The situation worsened again in the 2004-05 report, with nine of the 25 member states failing to provide any submission on 'Fundamentalist Jihadist Terrorism'.[60] As with the earlier record regarding the Commission's peer assessment of implementation efforts, the failure to even provide information for what is one of the key assessments of international terrorist trends within the EU ultimately undermines their credibility.

This emphasises the problematic labelling of such issues as 'matters of common concern' still further. With the 2004-05 report accepting that 'the assessment of the threat level varies, depending on the member state, some of which still consider that they are under no direct threat'[61], it is possible to divide the EU into three sub-groups. This gives a more accurate portrayal at least of the quantitative threat posed by militant Islamist terrorism. The first group relates to those that currently do not even provide submissions at all, the aforementioned nine member states. Secondly, there is a group that are not affected to the same extent as the likes of the UK and Spain, but fear that there may be an increased chance of such terrorist activities taking place in their territory in the future. These states – Austria, the Czech Republic, Finland, Ireland, Poland, Slovakia and Sweden (which considers itself as a base for terrorist attacks abroad, rather than a target itself) – help justify the conclusion that 'even those areas of Europe where radicalisation is not a major issue at present or where large Muslim communities do not exist could become targets for extremists'.[62] While it is the case that, theoretically, *any* state within the international system could become a target in due course, there is a need to anchor such assessments in a greater degree of reality. While Austria and Ireland both perceive a developing threat, they offer no evidence to substantiate their fears, with Austria confusingly arguing that 'an increased threat of terrorism has to be assumed' based on the fact that 'there are no indications that extremist Muslims in Austria are used for the purpose of the international jihad'.[63] The Finnish entry in the 2006

---

59 »Terrorist Activity in the European Union: Situation and trends report – October 2004-October 2005.« 18.
60 »Terrorist Activity in the European Union: Situation and trends report – October 2003-October 2004.« The Hague: Europol. (2004), 19-30. In 2006, this group is made up of Estonia, Cyprus, Greece, Hungary, Latvia, Lithuania, Luxembourg, Malta and Slovenia.
61 »Terrorist Activity in the European Union: Situation and trends report – October 2003-October 2004.« 19.
62 »The European Union Strategy for combating radicalisation and recruitment to terrorism.« Brussels. (November 2005), 5.
63 »Terrorist Activity in the European Union: Situation and trends report – October 2004-October 2005.« 18.

report is even more tenuous, concerned primarily with a television programme about Kurdish fundraising.[64]

Finally, there is a substantive core group, which has been – and is likely to continue to be – threatened by the activities of Islamist cells, some of which are linked to the putative Al Qaeda network. This category includes Belgium, Denmark, France, Germany, Italy, the Netherlands, Spain and the UK. France has a longer heritage than some of its counterparts, given its troubled relationship with its former colony in Algeria. However, the more recent targeting of both Spain and the UK, possibly as a reaction to their support for the US intervention in Iraq, has led some commentators to argue that the previously held, although not officially sanctioned, 'covenant of security' – the belief that, if a state did not actively target the various Jihadist groups, they would avoid attack themselves - has come to an end.[65]

It is worth considering this final group in a little more depth, as this is – currently – where the perceived threat lies. Once again, the issue of commonality is called into question. In an interesting study of primarily Sunni Islamist terrorism, Nesser indicated three different levels of motivation – local, diaspora (which relates to the ethnic make-up of the particular activists, who transport their local campaigns to the European mainland) and global level concerns. He examines four specific cases, including the so-called Strasbourg plot and the al Tawhid movement's plan to attack a series of Jewish targets within Germany. While his detailed study offers a number of interesting insights into the differing trigger factors that inspire and motive terrorist groupings, some of which claim to operate under the overall umbrella of 'Al Qaeda', it is his conclusions that are the most intriguing. Summarising overall by noting that all four case studies contained a global dimension, with local factors of significantly less interest, Nesser seems to contradict some of the earlier conclusions made for the individual case studies. In the case of the Strasbourg plot, for example, he notes that it was 'either an attempt indirectly to strike the Algerian regime by deterring France from offering support to the Algerian regime or as a direct attack on France', highlighting the local and diaspora levels as the most important.[66]

This tension between the local and global levels of motivation – in and of itself difficult to discern, but important in, firstly, understanding the nature of the enemy and subsequently addressing the threat directly – can also be seen in the case of the Netherlands, which may be the 'odd man out' of

---

64 »Terrorist Activity in the European Union: Situation and trends report - October 2004-October 2005.« 22.
65 For details, see US Senate, *Islamist Extremism in Europe: Testimony of Professor Mary Habeck in a Hearing before the Committee on Foreign Affairs on 5 April 2006* (Washington DC: US Government Printing Office, 2006).
66 For details, see Peter Nesser, *Jihad in Europe: A survey of the motivations for Sunni Islamist terrorism in post-millennium Europe* (Kjeller: Norwegian Defence Research Institute, 2004).

the core group. Having carried out a number of publicly available assessments on the wider jihadist movement[67], the Dutch intelligence agency has seemed to buck the trend of highlighting international factors in favour of a more localised interpretation of events. Looking at different levels of radicalisation – from foreign influences to first and second generation Dutch Muslims, who have been raised entirely within the context of one of the most liberal societies within the EU – they concluded that, while there was a limited international dimension, it 'plays a less prominent role in jihadism' than in neighbouring states. Instead, the main threat came from 'purely local actions without operational control from international networks'.[68] This contrasts with the motivations of the July 7th bombers in the UK, who were focused primarily on the international dimension, notably the UK's participation in the invasion of Iraq. It also starkly compares with the US, where there does not seem to be the same radicalisation tendencies within the American Muslim community – 'in short, the US has to worry about foreign hit squads, Europe must contend with home-grown terrorists'.[69] While the international actions of the US – and its perceived symbolic role as the epitome of the liberal capitalist economy – continue to make it the primary focus of militant Islamist terrorist activity, the threat is not coming from a discontented national minority.

A reliable partner for the US?

As well as addressing specific problems affecting the credibility of the European side of the 'bridge', there is also a need to consider the wider impact on transatlantic counter-terrorist relations in the post September 11 era. While September 11 may have increased the sense of urgency to at least be seen to do something in the counter-terrorist field, the EU has remained, primarily, wedded to the soft-power, criminal justice model of counter-terrorism. In contrast, the US has shifted closer to a 'war model', accepting that the actions of Al Qaeda and its affiliates constitute a declaration of war and responding with a more consistent and aggressive military assault, both on terrorist training grounds and named state sponsors of terrorism. The attacks on both Afghanistan and Iraq, the shifting position on the use of tor-

---

67 See, for example, Ministry of the Interior and Kingdom Relations. »Violent jihad in the Netherlands: Current trends in the Islamist terrorist threat.« Den Haag. (March 2006).
68 »Violent jihad in the Netherlands: Current trends in the Islamist terrorist threat.« 23-27.
69 Michael Taarnby, *Recruitment of Islamist Terrorists in Europe: Trends and Perspectives: A Research Report funded by the Danish Ministry of Justice* (Aarhus: Centre for Cultural Research, January 2005), 28.

ture, the acceptance of extraordinary rendition and the central focus given to the Pentagon all give some credence to this. For the US, 'September 11 was the day that ended debate about the nature of the threat to the civilized world'[70], whereas the EU, in part because of their more limited involvement in the military and foreign policy field and because of the variegated impact of terrorist activity, seem more resistant to change. As one State Department official noted, 'given the devastation inflicted upon Europe by two world wars...Europeans are understandably reluctant to engage in another war'.[71] Therefore, on the face of it, September 11 does seem to provide a dividing line in transatlantic terrorist co-operation. During the Clinton era, with its greater preference for coalition building and utilising the criminal justice system to combat terrorist threats[72], the two sides of the 'bridge' were most closely aligned. Yet, ironically, this was arguably the time when transatlantic co-operation was needed least (in 1996, for example, the State Department registered only 296 international terrorist incidents, the lowest for over two decades[73]). In the later years, with a changed attitude to formal institutions and coalition building – as indicated by the line that 'the mission dictates the coalition, not the other way round' – and a greater need for 'long duration, complex operations involving the US military...[that] will be waged simultaneously in multiple countries around the world, relying on a combination of direct and indirect approaches'[74], the US government seemed to shift position. In contrast, the EU – and a number of its prominent member states – seemed sceptical of the benefits of a more aggressive response.

This has led some commentators, notably Robert Kagan, to posit a greater drift between the two sides of the transatlantic bridge, with the US as 'Mars' and Europe as 'Venus'.[75] This was based primarily on the perceived power differential between the two sides, affecting how each side interpreted the nature and scale of the various security threats. Yet, there are a number of problems with this forecast of the future. Firstly, as with all

---

70 Bellinger, *Speech by the US State Department Legal Advisor on US-EU Counter-terrorism co-operation on 11 September 2006.*
71 Bellinger, *Speech by the US State Department Legal Advisor on US-EU Counter-terrorism co-operation on 11 September 2006.*
72 See, for example, Loius Freeh, *My FBI: Bringing down the Mafia, Investigating Bill Clinton and Fighting the War on Terror* (London: St. Martin's Press, 2005).
73 For details see US Department of State. »Patterns of Global Terrorism: 1996 report.« http://www.state.gov/www/global/terrorism/1996Report/1996index.html (accessed 1 December 2006).
74 US Department of Defense. »Quadrennial Defence Review Report ». (6 February 2006). http://www.defenselink.mil/qdr/report/Report20060203.pdf (accessed 1 December 2006).
75 See Robert Kagan, *Paradise and Power: America and Europe in the New World Order* (London: Atlantic Books, 2003).

generalisations, it obscures more than it illuminates. By aggregating all of the differing positions of the EU member states under one banner – a temptation which is difficult to avoid, and one that has affected more than Kagan's overarching analysis – it precludes the much needed analysis of differences in both the scale and nature of the threat facing each EU member state, as has been briefly indicated above. While agreed EU positions – in and of themselves normally lowest common denominator agreements between potentially twenty-seven different viewpoints – can be used as a means to measure the differences between the two sides of the bridge, the tendency has been to highlight whatever prominent national view suits the analysis, be it a narrowing gap (where the UK position can be cited as evidence) or a widening one (where the preference is to use 'Old Europe'). Therefore, in the counter-terrorist arena, as with many other areas of transatlantic integration, the situation is more complex than trying to measure the distance between two reasonably fixed points. As a recent survey on the future of transatlantic security has demonstrated, there are a number of EU member states, including the UK, Poland and the Netherlands, who may have more faith in co-operation with the US than with other EU states (a total of 63% mostly agreed with this statement, with 19% strongly agreeing). [76]

Secondly, the characterisations of the US as 'sheriff' and the EU as 'saloon keeper' are also not completely accurate, particularly in relation to the development of the second Bush administration. Changing personnel, notably the shift from the controversial Donald Rumsfeld to Robert Gates at the Department of Defense and the departure of key neo-conservatives, such as Paul Wolfowitz, has led to a more nuanced US approach. While still considering that the overall war model applies, the US is not as 'trigger happy' as the Kagan model suggests, as noted in the less aggressive stance towards Iran, with Secretary of State Rice prepared to meet face-to-face with her Iranian counter-part, if suitable assurances are met regarding the nature of the Iranian nuclear programme. As such, the role of personalities may seem to be as important in determining the nature of the perceived transatlantic 'gap'. The US was considered to be the international system's sole superpower during the Clinton administration; in fact, the potential power differential may have been even greater at this point, given the embryonic nature of the ESDP arrangements. Yet, the belief in a widened transatlantic gap did not gain currency until the rhetorical combat that took place during the build-up to the 2003 Iraq invasion. Also, just as the US is not the wholehearted sheriff of Kagan's model, so the EU's role as 'saloon keeper' needs to be nuanced as well. For example, the EU has formally backed two elements of the US approach to counter-terrorism, although placing significantly less emphasis on them. Firstly, it has accepted a po-

---

76 »Protecting Europe: Policies for enhancing security in the EU.« 46-47.

tential global role, stating that 'it was determined to combat terrorism in every form throughout the world'.[77] Equally, and significantly added in the later, public version of the 2005 Counter-Terrorism Strategy, is an acceptance of a role, however limited, for military action: 'in the event of an incident, there will be a need for...drawing on all available means, including military resources'.[78] Again, whether the EU has the collective political will to actually fulfil that objective remains to be seen.

What is clearer is that the European arena has become a central front in the developing 'war on terror', as 'the significant terrorist attacks we have seen in the past decade have had a European dimension to them'.[79] The prominence of the Hamburg cell in the planning of September 11, the shift in targets away from the US towards its European allies, the greater potential for radicalisation – all of this has placed certain EU member states in the front-line of counter-terrorist activity. The threat seems clear. What is less clear-cut is whether the EU can be a truly reliable partner for the US – and hold up its end of the 'bridge'.

References

Apap, Joanna, and Sergio Carrera. »Progress and obstacles in the area of freedom, security and justice in an enlarging Europe: An overview.« In *Justice and Home Affairs in the European Union*, edited by Joanna Apap. Northhampton: Edward Elgar, 2004.

Archick, Kirstin. *European approaches to Homeland Security and Counter-terrorism.* Washington DC: Congressional Research Service, July 2006.

Badey, Thomas J. »US Anti-terrorism Policy: The Clinton Administration.« *Contemporary Security Policy* 19, no. 2 (1998): 50-70.

Baldwin, Tom. »Blair's bridge between Europe and the US? It's falling down and he is left with nothing.« *The Times*, 30 November, 2006.

Bellinger, John. *Speech by the US State Department Legal Advisor on US-EU Counter-terrorism co-operation on 11 September 2006.* Brussels: United States Mission to the European Union, 2006.

Brady, Hugo. »An avant-garde for international security.« *Centre for European Reform Bulletin* 44 (November 2005).

Brady, Hugo, and Daniel Keohane. *Fighting Terrorism: The EU needs a strategy not a shopping list.* London: Centre for European Reform, 2005.

Brown, David. *Unsteady Foundations: The European Union's Counter-Terrorist Framework 1993-2007.* Manchester: Manchester University Press, 2008.

77 Justice and Home Affairs Council. »Council Decision on the exchange of information and co-operation concerning terrorist offences.« Brussels. (September 2005).
78 »The European Union Counter-Terrorist Strategy.« 15.
79 US House of Representatives, *Islamic Extremism in Europe: Testimony of Peter Bergen in a Hearing before the Subcommittee on Europe and Emerging Threats of the Committee on International Relations on 27 April 2005* (Washington DC: US Government Printing Office, 2005), 5.

Bures, Oldrich. »EU counter-terrorism policy: A paper tiger?« *Terrorism and Political Violence* 18, no. 1 (2006): 57-78.

Charlemagne. »In Europe we don't trust.« *The Economist*, 30 September, 2006.

Commission of the European Communities. »Proposal for a Council Framework Decision on the exchange of information under the principle of availability.« Brussels. (Ocotber 2005).

Cook, Robin. *The Point of Departure*. London: Simon and Schuster, 2003.

Council of the European Union. »Draft Justice and Home Affairs Council Conclusions on the future of Europol on 25 October 2006.« Brussels. (October 2006).

Council of the European Union. »Presidency Conclusions of the Tampere European Council on 15-16 October 1999.« Brussels. (Ocotber 1999).

Deen-Racsmany, Zsuzsanna. »The European Arrest Warrant and the surrender of nationals revisited: the lessons of constitutional challenges.« *European Journal of Crime, Criminal Law and Criminal Justice* 14, no. 3 (2006): 271-306.

Dittrich, Mirjam. »Facing the global terrorist threat: a European response.« *European Policy Centre Working Paper*, no. 14 (January 2005).

»The European Union Strategy for combating radicalisation and recruitment to terrorism.« Brussels. (November 2005).

European Commission. »Biannual update of the Scoreboard to review progress on the creation of an area of freedom, security and justice in the European Union (First Half of 2001).« Brussels. (2001).

European Commission. »Proposal for a Council Decision on the transmission of information resulting from the activities of security and intelligence services with respect to terrorist offences.« Brussels. (December 2005).

»The European Union Counter-Terrorist Strategy.« Brussels. (November 2005).

Freeh, Loius. *My FBI: Bringing down the Mafia, Investigating Bill Clinton and Fighting the War on Terror*. London: St. Martin's Press, 2005.

»Justice and Home Affairs Acquis 1993-2000 ». (2001). http://www.statewatch.org/semdoc/acquis.htm (accessed 1 December 2006).

Justice and Home Affairs Council. »Council Decision on the exchange of information and co-operation concerning terrorist offences.« Brussels. (September 2005).

Justice and Home Affairs Council. »Framework Decision on Combating Terrorism.« Brussels. (2002).

Justice and Home Affairs Council. »Framework Decision on the European Arrest Warrant and the surrender procedures between member states.« Brussels. (2002).

Justice and Home Affairs Council. »Improvement of decision-making in Justice and Home Affairs: Summary of Informal JHA meeting on 20-22 September 2006'.« Helsinki. (September 2006).

Kagan, Robert. *Paradise and Power: America and Europe in the New World Order*. London: Atlantic Books, 2003.

Kaiafa-Gbandi, M. »The Treaty Establishing a Constitution for Europe and challenges for Criminal Law at the commencement of the 21st Century.« *European Journal of Crime, Criminal Law and Criminal Justice* 13, no. 4 (2005): 483-514.

Kaunert, Christian. »The Area of Freedom, Security and Justice: The construction of a 'European Public Order'.« *European Security* 14, no. 4 (2005): 459-483.

Keohane, Daniel. *One Step Forward, Two Steps Back*. London: Centre for European Reform, 2005.

Lords, House of. *After Madrid: the EU's response to terrorism: Testimony of Jonathan Faull for Fifth Report, taken before the Select Committee on the European Union on 3 November 2004*. London: HMSO, 2004.

–. *Behind closed doors: the meeting of the G6 Interior Ministers at Heiligendamm: Fortieth Report, taken before the Select Committee on the European Union on 11 July 2006*. London: HMSO, 2006.

–. *The Criminal Competence of the European Community: Testimony of Richard Plender QC, taken before the Select Committee on the European Union on 3 May 2006*. London: HMSO, 2006.

–. *European Arrest Warrant: Recent Developments: Testimony of Andy Burnham MP for Thirtieth Report, taken before the Select Committee on the European Union on 18 January 2006*. London: HMSO, 2006.

Ludford, Sarah. »An EU Justice and Home Affairs policy: What should it comprise?« In *Justice and Home Affairs in the European Union*, edited by Joanna Apap. Northhampton: Edward Elgar, 2004

«Memorandum from the Swedish Ministry of Justice on the Commission Communication 'Area of freedom, security and justice: Assessment of the Tampere Programme and future orientations.« Stockholm. (8 September 2004).

Ministry of the Interior and Kingdom Relations. »Violent jihad in the Netherlands: Current trends in the Islamist terrorist threat.« Den Haag. (March 2006).

Monar, Jorg. »The dynamics of Justice and Home Affairs: Laboratories, Driving Factors and Costs.« *Journal of Common Market Studies* 39, no. 4 (2001): 747-764.

–. »An emerging regime of European Governance for Freedom, Security and Justice.« *ESRC One Europe or Several? Programme briefing note* 2/99.

Nesser, Peter. *Jihad in Europe: A survey of the motivations for Sunni Islamist terrorism in post-millennium Europe*. Kjeller: Norwegian Defence Research Institute, 2004.

»Protecting Europe: Policies for enhancing security in the EU.« Brussels: Security and Defence Agenda. (2006).

»Prum Convention (Schengen III).« http://www.libertysecurity.org/imprimer.php?id_article=368 (accessed 1 December 2006).

»Report from the Commission on the Council Framework Decision on combating terrorism.« Brussels. (June 2004).

»Report from the Commission on the European Arrest Warrant and the surrender procedures between member states.« Brussels. (February 2005).

Representatives, US House of. *Islamic Extremism in Europe: Testimony of Peter Bergen in a Hearing before the Subcommittee on Europe and Emerging Threats of the Committee on International Relations on 27 April 2005*. Washington DC: US Government Printing Office, 2005.

Senate, US. *Islamist Extremism in Europe: Testimony of Professor Mary Habeck in a Hearing before the Committee on Foreign Affairs on 5 April 2006*. Washington DC: US Government Printing Office, 2006.

US Department of State. »Patterns of Global Terrorism: 1996 report.« http://www.state.gov/www/global/terrorism/1996Report/1996index.html (accessed 1 December 2006).

»Strengthening the EU operational police co-operation.« Brussels. (October 2004).

Suskind, Ron. *The One Percent Doctrine: Deep inside America's pursuit of its enemies since 9.11*. London: Simon and Schuster, 2006.

Taarnby, Michael. *Recruitment of Islamist Terrorists in Europe: Trends and Perspectives: A Research Report funded by the Danish Ministry of Justice*. Aarhus: Centre for Cultural Research, January 2005.

»Terrorist Activity in the European Union: Situation and trends report - October 2002-15 October 2003.« The Hague: Europol. (2003).

»Terrorist Activity in the European Union: Situation and trends report - October 2003-October 2004.« The Hague: Europol. (2004).

»Terrorist Activity in the European Union: Situation and trends report - October 2004-October 2005.« The Hague: Europol. (2006).

»Treaty establishing a Constitution for Europe.« http://europa.eu/constitution/en/lstoc1_en.htm (accessed 1 December 2006).

US Department of Defense. »Quadrennial Defence Review Report ». (6 February 2006). http://www.defenselink.mil/qdr/report/Report20060203.pdf (accessed 1 December 2006).

US Department of State. »Patterns of Global Terrorism 1994-2001.« (1995-2002).

Verbruggen, F. »Bull's Eye? Two remarkable EU Framework Decisions in the fight against terrorism.« In *Legal instruments in the fight against international terrorism: A transatlantic dialogue*, edited by C. et al Fininaut. Leiden: Martinus Nijhoff, 2004, 299-341.

Woodward, Bob. *State of Denial: Bush at War Part III*. London: Simon and Schuster, 2006.

Wouters, Jan, and Frederick Naert. »Terrorist Offences and Extradition deals: An appraisal of the EU's main criminal law against terrorism after 11 September.« *Common Market Law Review* 41, no. 4 (2004): 909-935.

Bridging the Transatlantic Counterterrorism Gap[1]

Jeremy Shapiro and Daniel Byman

Introduction

Rhetorically, the United States and Europe are united in their opposition to terrorism. Governments on each side of the Atlantic frequently assert that counterterrorism cooperation is essential to solving the problem, and they join together to condemn outrages such as the July 7, 2005, attacks in London. In terms of doctrine, the U.S. National Security Strategy of 2002 and European Union Security Strategy of 2003 are remarkably similar in their descriptions of the new threats to national security. Both highlight international terrorism, the proliferation of weapons of mass destruction (WMD), and ungoverned spaces that might foster terrorism as the central security concerns for the future.[2]

Day-to-day cooperation between the United States and most European countries proceeds apace and is often effective. Although officials on each side have complaints, they are generally satisfied. As the Washington Post reported in 2005, the CIA's multinational counterterrorist intelligence center is located in Paris and has been a critical component of at least 12 operations, including the capture of one of Al Qaeda's most important European operatives.[3] Indeed, during the transatlantic crisis regarding Iraq, the practical necessity of counterterrorism cooperation helped preserve U.S. relations with Germany and France.

Yet, counterterrorism cooperation is not purely a day-to-day activity. Sustaining effective cooperation requires an understanding of each side's interests in counterterrorism and a respect for the strategies that follow from those interests. Observed from that type of strategic perspective, the United States and Europe disagree on some basic issues, including the precise na-

---

1 Originally published in *The Washington Quarterly* 29, no. 4 (Autumn 2006): 33-50.
2 See Council of the European Union. »European Security Strategy: A Secure Europe in a Better World.« (December 12, 2003). http://ue.eu.int/uedocs/cmsUpload/78367.pdf (accessed March 1, 2003); The White House. »The National Security Strategy of the United States.« (September 2002). http://www.whitehouse.gov/nsc/nss/2002/nss.pdf (accessed March 1, 2007).
3 Dana Priest, »Foreign Network at Front of CIA's Terror Fight; Joint Facilities in Two Countries Account for Bulk of Agency's Post-9/11 Successes,« *Washington Post*, November 18, 2005, A1; Dana Priest, »Help From France Key in Covert Operations; Paris's 'Alliance Base' Targets Terrorists,« *Washington Post*, July 3, 2005, A1.

ture of the terrorist threat, the best methods for managing this threat, and the root causes of terrorism. Perhaps more importantly, they do not understand or accept each other's positions.

Of course, in the United States and Europe, there are many internal divisions on the appropriate strategies for counterterrorism. In Europe especially, each country has its own threats, its own threat perceptions, and its own approach to terrorism, and there is no central government capable of unifying those strategies. When compared and contrasted with the U.S. approach, however, internal divisions in Europe and the United States fade in significance.

These distinct approaches do not come through in high-level strategy documents or day-to-day operations but can be seen in many of the policy disputes that the United States and Europe have over counterterrorism. European officials and commentators, for example, have criticized the U.S. tendency to resort to the language of war and in particular the use of the neologism »war on terror.«[4] Similarly, Americans and Europeans often disagree about what constitutes a legitimate political or charitable activity and what constitutes support for a terrorist group. Thus, according to Cofer Black, then the Department of State's counterterrorism coordinator, »[d]iffering [U.S. and European] perspectives on the dividing line between legitimate political or charitable activity and support for terrorist groups similarly clouds the picture. The EU as a whole, for example, has been reluctant to take steps to block the assets of charities linked to Hamas and Hizballah, even though these groups engage in deadly terrorist attacks and their 'charitable' activities help draw recruits.«[5] The Europeans are much more hesitant to label such groups, Hizballah in particular, as terrorists because they fear the instability that might result. In February 2005, an EU official summed up this view: »This is a difficult issue because Hizballah has military operations that we deplore, but Hizballah is also a political party in Lebanon ... Can a political party elected by the Lebanese people be put on a terrorist list? Would that really help deal with terrorism?«[6].

Of course, the most dramatic expression of the differences was the distinct views that each side took on the 2003 war in Iraq. For Americans, overthrowing the Ba'ath regime and fostering a democratic Iraq was a crit-

---

4 For examples of these views, see Richard A. Clarke, Barry R. McCaffrey, and C. Richard Nelson. »NATO's Role in Confronting International Terrorism.« The Atlantic Council of the United States. Washington DC. (June 2004) http://www.acus.org/docs/0406-NATO_Role_Confronting_International_Terrorism.pdf (accessed March 1, 2007), 7 (interviews).
5 Cofer Black, »European Cooperation With the United States in the Global War on Terrorism,« testimony before the U.S. Senate Foreign Relations Committee; Subcommittee on European Affairs, March 31, 2004, 1.
6 Weisman, »Allies as U.S. Pushes Terror Label for Hezbollah,« New York Times, 17 February, 2005, 1.

ical component of the struggle to defeat terrorism. It is, in President George W. Bush's words, »the central front in the war on terror.«[7] Europeans tended to believe that the conflict would contribute to the instability and enmity that foster terrorism and possibly bring Islamist terrorism to their doorstep. »People in France and more broadly in Europe,« wrote French ambassador to the United States Jean-David Levitte, »fear that a military intervention could fuel extremism and encourage [Al] Qaeda recruitment.«[8] As French president Jacques Chirac said in a February 2003 interview, war in Iraq risked creating »a large number of little [Osama] bin Ladens.«[9]

The most common explanation for such policy divides between the United States and Europe is that they spring from deep-seated cultural impulses that are then reduced to unhelpful stereotypes. Yet, the good news is that the real reason for U.S.-European strategic differences is far more mundane than the stereotypes imply and much less rooted in immutable cultural differences. They are thus amenable to intelligent policy that can bridge the transatlantic gap. In short, the United States and Europe face different threats from Islamist terrorism, they have different perceptions even of their common threats, and they have different tools in their arsenal for fighting terrorism. Not surprisingly, they also respond differently.

Different Threats: The Near Enemy versus the Far Enemy

The Islamist terrorist threat is not monolithic. There is no single, coherent enemy named Al Qaeda or anything else that is responsible for and capable of a sustained and coherent campaign of terrorist attacks throughout the world. Rather, both the United States and Europe face two interrelated threats. The first stems from a variety of local grievances that in some way pit jihadist groups of greatly varying levels of size, cohesion, and capacities against specific governments, including such groups as Jemaah Islamiya in Indonesia and the Moroccan Islamist Combat Group. Bin Laden's innovation in the 1990s was to convince many of these groups that they had a common foe in the United States, which, he claimed, stood behind and upheld the various repressive governments throughout the Islamic world. Only by defeating this »far enemy« could each local group realize its goal of overthrowing the »near enemy,« the puppet government in question. By attack-

---

7 Office of the Press Secretary - The White House. »President Addresses Nation, Discusses Iraq, war on Terror.« (June 28, 2005). http://www.whitehouse.gov/news/releases/2005/06/20050628-7.html (accessed March 1, 2007), (hereinafter president's 2005 Fort Bragg speech).
8 Jean David Levitte, »A Warning on Iraq, From a Friend,« *New York Times*, February 14, 2003, 31.
9 »France Is Not a Pacifist Country,« *Time*, February 24, 2003, 32.

ing the United States and forcing it to withdraw its support, the near-enemy governments would fall in short order. In this way, bin Laden managed to create a degree of strategic unity, operational cooperation, and priority in the fight against the far enemy. Yet, for all of these groups except the relatively small number of rootless cosmopolitans of Al Qaeda's core, the near enemy remained the primary target.

This observation leads to the essential distinction in the terrorist threat from the point of view of the United States and Europe. The United States faces no group that regards it as the near enemy, but it is the primary target of the Al Qaeda core. Many of the countries of Europe, in contrast, are near enemies for many groups, either because of their implication in specific struggles in the Islamic world through colonial ties, geographic proximity, or their indigenous and poorly integrated Islamic populations. Many of these groups have been inspired by the Islamist rhetoric of Al Qaeda and others and empowered by the example of the September 11 and subsequent attacks, but they are nonetheless focused on a near enemy. With the possible exception of the United Kingdom, European countries are secondary targets of those groups that advocate concentration on the far enemy. They are threatened but in a way that could conceivably be accommodated.

Indeed, in April 2004, the Al Qaeda core offered just such a compromise to Europe: withdraw support for U.S. policies in the Middle East and you can have a truce with Al Qaeda. Europeans immediately rejected this offer but not simply out of solidarity with the United States.[10] They also did so because they understood that Al Qaeda had little ability to carry out its side of the bargain and to constrain the near-enemy-focused groups that threaten Europe. Al Qaeda controls its own members but not local groups such as the perpetrators of the Madrid attacks. Nonetheless, the truce offer demonstrates that Europe could conceivably accommodate the Al Qaeda core.

In short, Washington faces a wounded but global foe, constantly plotting to violate the sanctuary of the American homeland, whereas European states worry more about the Islamist ideology inspiring local groups. Of course, in practice it is often difficult to distinguish between near-enemy– and far-enemy–focused groups. There is a great deal of overlap in their membership and logistics, as well as shared training and information exchanges between them. Groups such as Algeria's Salafist Group for Preaching and Combat have factions that advocate both strategies. Yet, the essential distinction remains: near-enemy groups have as a first priority their struggle against local governments. In contrast, far-enemy groups prioritize the struggle against the United States.

This distinction in the enemy's location leads immediately to a distinction in the type of terrorist attacks that each side can expect. The United

---

10 See Richard Bernstein, »Tape, Probably bin Laden's, Offers 'Truce' to Europe,« *New York Times*, April 16, 2004, 3.

States needs to worry much more about catastrophic terrorism that conceivably makes use of WMD because far-enemy groups tend to be more highly trained and more technical. More importantly, they are more nihilistic and have little interest in accommodation with the enemy. Similarly, they are less attached to any specific social context or constituency, which frees them from the constraints that have typically inhibited WMD use among terrorist groups in the past.

Near-enemy groups, however, have civilian constituencies – potential financiers, recruits, and political supporters – whose opinions they value and whose assistance they need, and they often have more specific political goals that could conceivably be reached through compromise. They would thus benefit less from massive destruction that might fully mobilize their enemies or alienate their base. They also tend to be poorly trained and less capable of sophisticated operations and procurement efforts. These factors help explain why so few terrorist groups, with the notable exception of Al Qaeda, have shown much interest in acquiring or using WMD.[11]

The danger faced from the domestic population, in essence, Muslim residents and citizens of Europe and the United States, also differs strikingly. The U.S. Muslim and Arab population is both small as a percentage of the overall population and scattered throughout the country. In addition, most American Muslims are not Arab, and the majority of Arab-Americans are Christian, not Muslim.[12] These communities, moreover, are prospering; their average incomes are higher than the national average in the United States. Not surprisingly, there is little support for radicalism. Some suspected terrorists, such as the »Lackawanna Six,«[13] have been reported by their own communities.

The contrast with Europe could not be greater. Although individual European countries have their own distinct mix of Arabs and Muslims (in the United Kingdom, for example, most Muslims are from South Asia; in France, most are from the Maghreb; and in Germany, most are from Turkey), all have concentrated communities. Moreover, many residents are both poor and poorly integrated. Youth from these communities often mingle with firebrand preachers, many of whom are recent immigrants to Eu-

---

11 John Parachini, »Putting WMD Terrorism in Perspective,« *The Washington Quarterly* 26, no. 4 (Autumn 2003).
12 See Ishan Bagby, Paul M. Perl, and Bryan T. Froehle. »The Mosque in America: A National Portrait.« Council on American-Islamic Relations. Washington DC. (April 26, 2001) http://www.cair-net.org/mosquereport/Masjid_Study_Project_2000_Report.pdf (accessed March 1, 2007). See also Genieve Abdo, »Islam in America: Seperate but Unequal,« *The Washington Quarterly* 28, no. 4 (Autumn 2005).
13 See Mathew Purdy and Lowell Bergman, »Where the Trail Led: Inside the Lackawanna Terror Case,« *New York Times*, Octobe 12, 2003, 1.

rope. The result is an explosive combination of social unrest and political grievance.

It is tempting to ascribe Europe's integration problems to assimilation policies that, relative to the U.S. melting pot in particular, are ill conceived and ineffective. As Charles Krauthammer wrote, »[T]he real problem [in Europe] is not immigration but assimilation. Anyone can do immigration ... America's genius has always been assimilation, taking immigrants and turning them into Americans.«[14] Krauthammer's critique applies to some European countries, but it fails to capture the diversity of approaches within the EU. Europe has a wide variety of integration policies spanning the entire spectrum, from Dutch multiculturalism to French assimilationism and including a British system not terribly different from that of the United States. The one element that all of these policy experiments have in common is that they have not yet succeeded in integrating a large, socioeconomically disadvantaged Muslim population into their national polity.

Moreover, Europe's Muslim population arguably is in the process of integration. Muslim immigrants have only been present in large numbers in Europe for some 30–40 years and in most countries much less. Under any circumstances, the integration of this type of population would take several generations, but the trajectory of Europe's Muslim population is arguably very much in the direction of integration.[15] At the same time, the process, even if it is working, is clearly painful and long term. In the meantime, European states can expect that some number of their citizens will feel alienated and will occasionally take up the available ideology of radical Islam and the demonstrated technique of terrorism. There is no short-term policy solution to this problem, either in the American or European experience.

This fact, combined with the riots in France, the bombings in London and Madrid, the murder of filmmaker Theo Van Gogh in the Netherlands, and the furor over the Danish cartoons depicting the prophet Muhammad, means that Arab and Muslim integration is becoming perhaps the most important domestic issue in a growing number of European countries. It is implicated in virtually every other issue, from welfare reform to immigration to education, and has already become far more important and more contentious than Hispanic integration in the United States.

Within this panoply of issues, counterterrorism is far from the largest problem that touches on Muslim integration. The United States can pursue

---

14 Charles Krauthammer, »Assimilation Nation,« *Washington Post*, June 17, 2005, A31. See Robert Leiken. »Europe's Mujahideen: Where Mass Immigration Meets Global Terrorism.« Center for Immigration Studies. Washington DC. (April 2005) http://www.cis.org/articles/2005/back405.html (accessed March 1, 2007).

15 For an argument to this effect in the »hard case« of France, see Jonathan Laurence and Justin Vaisse, *Integration Islam: Political and Religious Challenges in Contemporary France* (Washington DC: Brookings Institution Press, 2006).

its counterterrorism objectives in relative isolation from other domestic issues, but in Europe that is simply not possible. This fact often causes the Europeans to perceive the threat in different ways. France's decision, for example, to force Muslim girls to remove their headscarves in school is disastrous from a counterterrorism point of view. France had gained some support from jihadists for its strong anti-U.S. stance during the Iraq war, but the veil issue generated tremendous hostility and was specifically mentioned by groups that kidnapped French journalists in Iraq. For France, however, the ban was part of a broader desire to uphold the principle of the separation of church and state as well as a way of pandering to anti-immigrant voters. For better or for worse, these ideological and political issues trumped counterterrorism.

The Capabilities Gap: The Superpower and the Rest

The United States, beyond facing a more global enemy, also has a much broader range of interests and assets throughout the world than any European country. It thus worries about threats to targets abroad as much as or more than it does about threats at home. Europe obviously has global interests and assets abroad, many of which are threatened (e.g., British targets in Istanbul), but the primary threat is either at home or against a specific number of narrow locations where individual European countries have historical and current ties, particularly in North Africa (e.g., France in Algeria and Spain in Morocco).

The United States spends almost $500 billion on its military and its operations, which is well more than twice as much as all of the EU combined. These raw numbers reflect a huge difference in capabilities. Only the United States can project power in a sustained way far from its borders. Of the European states, only the United Kingdom and France can show up without significant U.S. assistance, and they can only do so in limited numbers and for a limited period of time.

The U.S. intelligence budget alone, at about $44 billion, according to published reports, is more than the entire defense budget of Germany or France and just under that of the United Kingdom.[16] Despite its well-noted weaknesses, U.S. intelligence has a far more significant presence in much of the world compared to the intelligence agencies of any European state. Imagery intelligence and signals intelligence are particular gaps for much of the world, as they require multibillion-dollar systems that few states can afford. The United States is also able to marshal the world's intelligence services behind its counterterrorism campaign. Indeed, prominent Al

---

16 Scott Shane, »Official Reveals Budget for U.S. Intelligence,« *New York Times*, November 8, 2005, A18.

Qaeda leader Ayman al-Zawahiri lamented in December 2002 that, after the September 11 attacks, »the entire world became a CIA office.«[17] Thus, the United States can address many of its terrorism problems by acting in cooperation with governments abroad. This involves both sharing intelligence and rendering suspects to countries, particularly in the Middle East, where their »justice« systems are employed to keep them off the streets and to gain information.

This difference in power leads to divergent perspectives on the world. Much of Europe's modern history has been spent adjusting to the notion that the quarrels between peoples of faraway countries about which Europeans know nothing are not Europe's concern. The United States, in contrast, has a global perspective, in part because it can use force around the world and in part because it faces a global threat. It is the hard facts of geography and capability that lie at the root of the United States' relative reliance on military power rather than any distinct conceptual understanding of the causes of terrorism or the appropriate strategies for countering it. As all of their strategy documents aver, the United States recognizes the need for »root cause« strategies that attempt to win over the hearts and minds of potential terrorists, just as Europeans recognize the utility of military force in battling actual terrorists. Yet, the United States' specific terrorism problem and its unmatched military capabilities lead naturally to a much greater tendency to use force, a tendency that is often mistaken for doctrine. Europeans would point out that possession of a hammer does not make the world into a nail; from the U.S. perspective, having a hammer allows you to make good use of nails.

Perhaps the biggest reflection of this difference in capabilities is Washington's ability to target terrorist sanctuaries abroad. Although modern jihadists are able to exploit the Internet and lax law enforcement to operate from Europe and other advanced Western countries, nothing beats having a sanctuary in which to openly plan, train, recruit, rest, and otherwise sustain the burden of running a major terrorist organization. The United States demonstrated the capability to destroy sanctuaries par excellence when it overthrew the Taliban regime in Afghanistan in 2001. In a matter of months, the United States was able to project force thousands of kilometers away from the sea, gaining bases and access by working with new allies in Central Asia and reinvigorating its alliance with Pakistan, something only a superpower can do with such speed and success. On arriving in Afghanistan, the United States bolstered the long-suffering domestic military opposition to the Taliban with air power and Special Operations forces; within weeks

---

17 Gilles Kepel, *The War for Muslim Minds: Islam and the West* (Cambridge, Mass.: Belknap Press, 2004), 129.

of the initial deployment, the Taliban crumbled.[18] The ease of this overthrow in hindsight obscures the fact that, for any other military, this would have been essentially impossible.

European powers in the past have tried to target sanctuaries abroad, but their efforts were limited to fairly feeble attempts at coercion or diplomatic suasion. An Afghanistan-like option was never really on the table. In the 1980s, France launched a series of raids in Lebanon and even bombed Damascus after a series of Hizballah-linked attacks on French targets in Lebanon and France itself, but these efforts failed. In the 1990s, France tried to stop terrorism emerging from Algeria by pressing the Algerian government, a policy France abandoned when it realized it had little sway in Algiers. In both cases, the problem was not a lack of French will but rather a lack of capabilities.

The contrast between the U.S. experience in Afghanistan and the French failures highlights why the Europeans have made a virtue out of necessity and have concentrated on fighting terrorism at home. Because their militaries are inadequate and their diplomacy weak, they rely more on using law enforcement and intelligence services to fight terrorism on their own soil rather than abroad.

One Nation versus One Union

In addition to being able to act decisively abroad, the United States is also much better able to marshal its power at home. Famously, former secretary of state Henry Kissinger derided the idea of Europe as a diplomatic partner by asking for its phone number. Although European integration has made enormous strides since the 1970s – there is now a »phone number« on issues such as the value of the euro or agricultural price supports – on counterterrorism issues, Kissinger's jibe remains accurate. Almost all operational coordination remains bilateral or, rarely, occurs among a small, ad hoc group of interested countries.

The European Council, Europol, Eurojust, and the other EU institutions range from fledgling to pathetic when it comes to counterterrorism. In interviews conducted in 2005, most officials dismissed these EU institutions out of hand. One senior French intelligence official remarked that these »people talk but they don't act« while a British official dryly noted that the EU does not do much well and that giving it responsibility for counterterrorism would dramatize its many weaknesses. The EU counterterrorism coordinator, appointed with much ceremony after the Madrid attacks in March 2004, has little power to compel cooperation. There are myriad initiatives to

---

18 See Stephen Biddle, »Afghanistan and the Future of Warfare,« *Foreign Affairs* 82, no. 2 (March/April 2003).

strengthen these institutions, but none appear to have the momentum to produce major changes. One German terrorism expert cynically summed up this view, declaring that »European counterterrorism will improve ... after about three more attacks.«[19]

With no European-level coordination, it is difficult for European states to work together to coordinate all of the various information and institutions necessary to prevent terrorist attacks. According to one German intelligence official, »[t]he problem with intelligence in Europe is that we are far too bureaucratic and fragmented across borders ... The extremists also move relatively freely across borders. In this sense, ironically, they are more European than we are.«[20] Two Irish Republican Army suspects under surveillance in France, for example, crossed the unguarded and often unmarked border into Belgium and then traveled on to the Netherlands. To continue surveillance, the French had to work with the Belgians and the Dutch. All had different rules for what constitutes legal surveillance. In addition, Dutch intelligence had no nighttime surveillance capability and lost the trail of the Irish suspects.[21] This problem is even more acute when there is no ongoing surveillance. One German expert told us that if a suspect moves from the United Kingdom or France to Bavaria, they probably would not know, as records are often not exchanged and the rules on such matters are not fixed.

As these examples suggest, Europe is a prisoner to the least motivated and least capable member. Belgium, for example, seemed largely unconcerned about terrorism before the September 11 attacks. Not surprisingly, in the 1990s Belgium became a center for terrorists, where they found a haven, acquired false documents, and obtained financing.[22] In our 2005 interviews, Greece was often singled out for criticism as one of the weaker states in Europe today.

European national agencies fear that handling counterterrorism on a European level risks jeopardizing sensitive information. More prosaically but probably more importantly, there is a widespread perception that working through the EU machinery or coordinating with less-efficient member countries would impede cooperation. Alas, this scorn is well deserved: the EU has neither the bureaucratic competence nor the appropriate sense of urgency to take on these types of vital security tasks.

Creating the necessary sense of urgency is particularly difficult given the disagreement over the terrorist threat within the EU. Because the EU trea-

19 European officials, interviews with authors, May 2005.
20 Tim Golden, Desmond Butler, and Don Van Natta, »As Europe Hunts for Terrorists, the Hunted Press Advantages,« *New York Times*, March 22, 2004, A12.
21 European officials, interviews with authors, May 2004.
22 Elaine Sciolino and Helene Fouquet, »Belgium Is Trying to Unrevel the Threads of a Terror Web,« *New York Times*, October 10, 2005, 1.

ties mandate a common border among much of the EU with the exception of the United Kingdom, Ireland, and the new members, internal security is only as good as its weakest member. It is now just as easy to travel from Helsinki to Paris as it is from Minneapolis to Albany. Finland and France face quite different threats, but no European body exists that forces a common threat assessment and the proper allocation of counterterrorism resources. In the United States, of course, Minnesota and New York also face different threat levels, but the federal government can arbitrate between the two to ensure a unified response. However fraught the U.S. system is with pork-barrel politics or disputes on federalism, its problems pale in comparison with those of Europe.

The U.S. political system makes Washington more prone to play up the threat of terrorism, whereas the European political system tends to lead officials to downplay it. Because the U.S. system is far more open than that of most European states, Congress, the media, and the public have a voice on foreign policy that would be shocking to the well-heeled foreign policy mandarins in Whitehall or the Quai d'Orsay. This more open system can lead politicians to play up threats as a way of gaining the necessary momentum to act. In Europe, however, leaders tend to avoid involving the public, fearing that they will lose control over policy.

Experience has reinforced these different approaches. The United States has experienced a mass-casualty attack, while Europe has experienced numerous low-casualty events. The American mental image of terrorism is of skyscrapers collapsing and thousands dying. Europeans see subway bombings. Both are gruesome, but the scale is quite different. Europeans, even after Madrid and London, quite simply have not wrapped their heads around an attack of the magnitude and symbolic power of the September 11 attacks, and they probably will not unless and until one happens in Europe.

Differences in Strategies

As has been implied, these differing threats and capabilities imply different strategies for counterterrorism. These differences transcend any simplistic »force vs. engagement« dichotomy. U.S. leaders genuinely believe that addressing the root causes of terrorism through a strategy that attempts to win hearts and minds is an important tool in combating terrorism. Indeed, this is the very premise of the democratization strategy that was the centerpiece of Bush's second inaugural address. Similarly, Europeans recognize the utility and, indeed, the necessity of using force against terrorism, as Chirac's threat to retaliate against a terrorist attack with nuclear weapons dramatically illustrated in January 2006. The greater U.S. willingness in recent years to use force flows more from the differences in the threats that the United States and Europe face and in their capabilities than from cultural or ideological differences.

The largest strategic difference comes from the location of the fight. The United States has an externalization strategy, trying to keep terrorists out of its country and fighting them abroad, be it in Iraq, Afghanistan, or elsewhere in the world. As Bush said, »[T]here is only one course of action against [terrorists]: to defeat them abroad before they attack us at home.«[23] In contrast, for Europe the fight begins at home.

This distinction is the source of the U.S. preference for use of the word »war« and the European rejection of that terminology. From a policymaker's perspective, use of the word »war« usefully mobilizes the public, but for a domestic issue, it conjures up images of civil strife and violations of civil liberties. Europeans have often pointed out that waging war against an abstract noun makes little conceptual sense.[24] The phrase »war on terror« therefore condemns us to a permanent state of emergency in a quixotic quest to defeat a technique rather than an enemy. At the March 2004 EU conference on terrorism, Javier Solana, the EU's foreign policy chief, made a point of highlighting this difference by declaring succinctly that »Europe is not at war.«[25]

European objections to the phrase »war on terror« have a solid analytical basis and point out many important flaws or at least pitfalls in U.S. strategy, but they miss the point. Despite those drawbacks, the phrase remains an effective tool for domestic mobilization both in the United States and Europe. That the U.S. government has chosen to make use of this tool and the European governments have not reflects more on the relative value of that tool for their distinct problems and strategies rather than a conceptual difference. Because the United States has an externalization strategy that consciously seeks and even largely is able to separate the foreign from the domestic, use of the word »war« is not only possible but serves to reinforce that distinction. Because the Europeans must fight the war on terrorism at home, the notion of war would conjure images of violations of civil liberties, internal conflict, and domestic chaos rather than a neat separation of the sphere of conflict from the sphere of society. Therefore, the United States thinks globally while Europe acts locally.

The U.S. goals are vast. For example, it seeks to delegitimate the tactic of terrorism under any circumstances and to create a degree of consensus

---

23 President's 2005 Fort Bragg speech.
24 See Gilles Andréani, »The 'War on Terror': Good Cause, Wrong Concept,« *Survival* 46, no. 4 (Winter 2004/2005); Michael Howard, »What's in a Name? How to Fight Terrorism,« *Foreign Affairs* 81, no. 1 (January/February 2002).
25 Tom Regan, »EU, U.S. Differ on How to Fight Terrorism,« *Christian Science Monitor*, March 29, 2004, http://www.csmonitor.com/2004/0329/dailyUpdate.html?s=rel. (accessed March 1, 2007).

regardless of the political context. As with the fight against nazism or communism, terrorism is treated as a cancer that must be extirpated. For the United States, one man's terrorist will never again be another man's freedom fighter.

Europeans seek to manage the danger of terrorism as they do crime. They thus seek more variation; at times they appease terrorists or try to conciliate their »political« wings to cool down the threat at home. Moreover, Europeans can hope to divert the danger, to the United States or another European state for example, while a global enemy is less likely to shift its focus. At the same time, Europeans will act with an iron fist should they feel the need. France's crackdown on radical networks in the mid-1990s involved massive administrative detentions, allegedly included occasional torture, and used domestic surveillance to a degree that would make the most ardent defenders of the USA PATRIOT Act blush. The United States must care far more about a consistent hard line against terrorism, as its policies in one country are being observed by its partners and enemies halfway around the globe.

Different perceptions and capabilities also shape attitudes toward the question of reform abroad. Washington is more comfortable with upsetting the status quo, as it sees the absence of political reform in the Middle East as the source of terrorism for years to come. Simply busting a cell here or killing a terrorist leader there does little to solve the long-term threat, as the jihadists will simply shift their base to another land. The hope of eventual good government, which might dry up the well of terrorist recruits, is worth instability in the short term. Europeans see democracy in the Arab world as far off and hardly a panacea. For them, instability is the enemy. Unrest in one country today may spill over onto their soil tomorrow.

Many of these differences have come to a head in Iraq. The bitter debate preceding the war soured policymakers on each side. Today, however, the United States sees the need to win in Iraq as essential for the war on terrorism, as it will spread the long-term solution of democracy and prevent unrest in a critical region. Europeans, however, worry that Iraq will continue to radicalize their own Muslim population and serve as a training ground for its most radical members, who will then return to their soil in the years to come. Thus, the lesson for Spaniards and indeed for Europeans in general after the March 2004 attack in Madrid was that, as one U.S. commentator said, »they have now been placed on the terrorists' list as a direct consequence of participating in a war that should not have been fought.«[26] American Muslims, in contrast, only go to Iraq as members of the U.S. military. Moreover, although Europe would suffer as much as the United States if unrest spread from Iraq to other oil-rich states in the Persian Gulf, no Euro-

---

26 Robin Niblett, testimony before the U.S. House Committee on Foreign Relations; Subcommittee on European Affairs, March 31, 2004, 3.

pean state sees itself as responsible for ensuring stability there as does the United States.

Cooperation amid Conflict

Many Americans depict Europeans as appeasers, incapable or unwilling to take forceful action and ready to turn a blind eye to terrorists on their soil or even to pay outrageous ransoms that go straight into the bad guys' pockets. In this view, even terrorist outrages such as the March 2004 Madrid bombings or the July 2005 London bombings cannot rouse the Europeans from their stupor. In the words of former U.S. deputy homeland security adviser Richard Falkenrath, »[T]he relatively passive approach of the Spanish – and other Europeans – to the 3-11 attack on Madrid is stunning.«[27]

Similarly, Europeans often seem to view the Americans as trigger-happy simpletons, engaged in a futile quest to protect against every conceivable threat and ready to bomb willy-nilly on the smallest provocation. From this perspective, Americans are losing the fight for the hearts of minds of the Islamic world even as they kill and capture specific terrorists. Even the normally diplomatic EU counterterrorism coordinator Gijs de Vries has asserted that the United States has unnecessarily increased the terrorists' recruitment pool and alienated many of its allies by relying too heavily on a military response and consistently undervaluing the political dimensions of counterterrorism.[28]

Over time, U.S.-European strategic differences and the stereotypes they spawn will have painful policy consequences for the United States. The European continent is perhaps the heart of the struggle against terrorism. Contrary to the popular myth, neither the madrassas of Pakistan nor the slums of Cairo can churn out the shock troops of international terrorism. Rather, these areas produce mostly functional illiterates who are essentially incapable of operating in the United States. Yet, many young, angry Muslims in Europe are being radicalized. They are educated, often speak excellent English, and hold passports valid for visa-free entry into the United States.

---

27 Richard Falkenrath, »Europe's Dangerous Complacency,« *Financial Times*, July 7, 2004, 17.
28 See Charles M. Sennott, »Europe's Terror Fight Quiet, Unrelenting,« *Boston Globe*, Sepember 26, 2004, A1.

As terrorism expert Marc Sageman said, »[I]n terms of the threat to us Americans, the threat comes from Europe.«[29]

An inability of the United States and Europe to cooperate may result either in attacks in the United States or serious disruptions in transatlantic economic links. Commentators such as Reuel Marc Gerecht and members of Congress such as Rep. James Sensenbrenner (R-Wis.) and Sen. Diane Feinstein (D-Calif.) have already pointed to the possibility of suspending the Visa Waiver Program (VWP), which allows about 13 million visa-free visits across the Atlantic each year, unless European countries tighten their internal security procedures.[30] The U.S. Chamber of Commerce estimates that a suspension of the VWP would cost the U.S. economy $66 billion in tourism alone, even before taking into the account the loss of business in other sectors.[31]

Policymakers on each side of the Atlantic must recognize that many problems stem from legitimate differences in the threat faced and relative capabilities, not just politics, European cowardice, or U.S. arrogance. Until this is accepted, current levels of cooperation, however insufficient, are at risk because the cooperation has so little political foundation. Sudden shocks, such as revelations about CIA prisons in Europe or U.S. rendition practices, can threaten the U.S. and European capacity to cooperate in capturing terrorism suspects abroad.

With recognition of differences comes recognition of common interests. Washington should want European states to focus on the internal enemy. If they do not, those radicals will kill Americans in Europe and travel to the United States as well as slaughter the English, French, Spanish, and other Europeans. Similarly, Europeans should cheer on Washington and support it as they can when it confronts terrorists sanctuaries in Afghanistan, Iraq, or elsewhere or renders terrorists to the Middle East. These different approaches at times also allow for a more nuanced treatment of the threat. Algerian jihadists operating from the Maghreb and from France should be

---

29 Peter Bergen, »The Madrassa Scapegoat,« *The Washington Quarterly* 29, no. 2 (Spring 2006); Marc Sageman, remarks at the Saban Center for Middle East Policy symposium »How to Win the War Against Terrorism«, Washington DC, September 22, 2005. http://www.brookings.edu/fp/saban/events/20050922.htm (Panel 1 transcript) (accessed March 1, 2007).

30 See Reuel Marc Gerecht, »Jihad Made in Europe,« *Weekly Standard*, July 25, 2005. http://www.weeklystandard.com/Content/Public/Articles/000/000/005/836esgwz.asp (accessed March 1, 2007); »Senator Feinstein Seeks Major Improvements to the Visa Waiver Program.« (May 13, 2004). http://feinstein.senate.gov/04Releases/r-visawaiver.htm (accessed March 1, 2007).

31 John Letzing, »Cross-Border Security: The Visa Loophole,« *Frontline*, January 25, 2005. http://www.pbs.org/wgbh/pages/frontline/shows/front/special/visa.html (accessed March 1, 2007).

treated differently than Egyptian ones who are part of the Al Qaeda internationale.

Europe and the United States can also pool their resources when it comes to pushing democratization. Every country in the Middle East and many others in the Muslim world need dramatic progress on democratization. That bad news is good news for U.S.-European cooperation. Joint efforts should focus on those countries where democratization has the greatest benefits for counterterrorism and stability, such as Iraq, Afghanistan, and Palestine.

Washington must also recognize that, for counterterrorism, a strong Europe is in its interest. Currently, Washington usually does not care and often does not know whether particular issues are handled by individual member states or by the EU. This is unwise. Stronger European capabilities and more integrated intelligence are necessary to make progress on the mismatch between borders and the reach of European security services, as well as the widely divergent threat perceptions and capacities within Europe. According to Baltazar Garzón, a Spanish investigating magistrate, »[t]here is an enormous amount of information, but much of it gets lost because of the failures of cooperation. We are doing maybe one-third of what we can do within the law in fighting terrorism in Europe. There is a lack of communication, a lack of coordination, and a lack of any broad vision.«[32]

Improving this situation requires accepting a major role for the EU, not just increased bilateral cooperation or a greater role for NATO. Bilateral cooperation between individual countries is necessary, but it enables terrorists to exploit countries in Europe that are lax or that do not work closely with one another. As a multilateral institution, NATO can help address this problem, and years of military cooperation have made it the preferred U.S.-European body for many Americans, particularly defense officials. Yet, NATO's military orientation makes it less suitable for counterterrorism, as most of the issues concern domestic security and law enforcement. Only the EU has the broad mandate to act on domestic and security issues and enjoys the necessary legitimacy within Europe.

Yet, these moves toward understanding and harmony should not mask the need to change some policies on both sides of the Atlantic. Europeans should support U.S. efforts against the recruitment and logistics base of terrorist groups, even when this involves targeting supposedly humanitarian organizations. Europeans should also recognize the risk of catastrophic attacks. This requires more than rhetoric; their counterterrorism procedures and laws must be flexible enough to respond to unprecedented threats. For their part, Americans should support European efforts to integrate counterterrorism into the broader justice and law enforcement system. This does

---

32 Golden, Butler, and Van Natta, »As Europe Hunts for Terrorists, the Hunted Press Advantages,« A12.

not inherently mean a »softer« approach toward counterterrorism. Although rules for counterterrorism can and should be different than those for normal crime, there still must be rules, as well as oversight.

One way to demonstrate this support is to make more information available for trials in Europe. Thus far, Washington has received information from European states to use in legal procedures in the United States while with holding its own information. This is a brilliant diplomatic success but a long-term disaster for counterterrorism. Because European states use their judicial systems to manage terrorism, U.S. efforts to minimize the flow of information for use in trials have created widespread anger. One constant complaint from Europeans is a call for the United States to share more. Because sharing is seen as a one-way street, few European leaders, to say nothing of the general populace, openly support it.

At home, the United States should also work to improve the FBI's ability to liaise with European services. Although European officials noted that they no longer believe that FBI stands for »f***ing bunch of idiots« with regard to counterterrorism, the bureau still has a long way to go with regard to foreign liaison, particularly when compared with the CIA. Washington should also try to soften some of its rhetoric on the war on terror. European officials said that many statements probably meant for domestic audiences in the United States received wide play in European Muslim communities and deepened alienation.

Adopting such a practical approach to work through differences, rather than engaging in simplistic criticisms, will enable the United States and its European allies to meet the challenge of terrorism better. These steps will not end U.S.-European differences, but they will help bridge the gap, strengthening counterterrorism cooperation in ways that will save lives for years to come.

References

Abdo, Genieve. »Islam in America: Seperate but Unequal.« *The Washington Quarterly* 28, no. 4 (Autumn 2005): 7-17.

Andréani, Gilles. »The 'War on Terror': Good Cause, Wrong Concept.« *Survival* 46, no. 4 (Winter 2004/2005): 31-50.

Bagby, Ishan, Paul M. Perl, and Bryan T. Froehle. »The Mosque in America: A National Portrait.« Council on American-Islamic Relations. Washington DC. (April 26, 2001). http://www.cair-net.org/mosquereport/Masjid_Study_Project_2000_Report.pdf (accessed March 1, 2007).

Bergen, Peter. »The Madrassa Scapegoat.« *The Washington Quarterly* 29, no. 2 (Spring 2006): 117-125.

Bernstein, Richard. »Tape, Probably bin Laden's, Offers 'Truce' to Europe.« *New York Times*, April 16, 2004, 3.

Biddle, Stephen. »Afghanistan and the Future of Warfare.« *Foreign Affairs* 82, no. 2 (March/April 2003): 31-46.

Black, Cofer. »European Cooperation With the United States in the Global War on Terrorism.« testimony before the U.S. Senate Foreign Relations Committee; Subcommittee on European Affairs, March 31, 2004.

Clarke, Richard A., Barry R. McCaffrey, and C. Richard Nelson. »NATO's Role in Confronting International Terrorism.« The Atlantic Council of the United States. Washington DC. (June 2004). http://www.acus.org/docs/0406-NATO_Role_Confronting_ International_Terrorism.pdf (accessed March 1, 2007).

Council of the European Union. »European Security Strategy: A Secure Europe in a Better World.« (December 12, 2003). http://ue.eu.int/uedocs/cmsUpload/78367.pdf (accessed March 1, 2003).

Falkenrath, Richard. »Europe's Dangerous Complacency.« *Financial Times*, July 7, 2004.

»France Is Not a Pacifist Country.« *Time*, February 24, 2003.

Gerecht, Reuel Marc. »Jihad Made in Europe.« *Weekly Standard*, July 25, 2005. http:// www.weeklystandard.com/Content/Public/Articles/000/000/005/836esgwz.asp (accessed March 1, 2007).

Golden, Tim, Desmond Butler, and Don Van Natta. »As Europe Hunts for Terrorists, the Hunted Press Advantages.« *New York Times*, March 22, 2004.

Howard, Michael. »What's in a Name? How to Fight Terrorism.« *Foreign Affairs* 81, no. 1 (January/February 2002): 8-13.

Kepel, Gilles. *The War for Muslim Minds: Islam and the West*. Cambridge, Mass.: Belknap Press, 2004.

Krauthammer, Charles. »Assimilation Nation.« *Washington Post*, June 17, 2005.

Laurence, Jonathan, and Justin Vaisse. *Integration Islam: Political and Religious Challenges in Contemporary France*. Washington DC: Brookings Institution Press, 2006.

Leiken, Robert. »Europe's Mujahideen: Where Mass Immigration Meets Global Terrorism.« Center for Immigration Studies. Washington DC. (April 2005). http:// www.cis.org/articles/2005/back405.html (accessed March 1, 2007).

Letzing, John. »Cross-Border Security: The Visa Loophole.« *Frontline*, January 25, 2005. http://www.pbs.org/wgbh/pages/frontline/shows/front/special/visa.html (accessed March 1, 2007).

Levitte, Jean David. »A Warning on Iraq, From a Friend.« *New York Times*, February 14, 2003, 31.

Niblett, Robin. testimony before the U.S. House Committee on Foreign Relations; Subcommittee on European Affairs, March 31, 2004.

Office of the Press Secretary - The White House. »President Addresses Nation, Discusses Iraq, war on Terror.« (June 28, 2005). http://www.whitehouse.gov/news/ releases/2005/06/20050628-7.html (accessed March 1, 2007).

Parachini, John. »Putting WMD Terrorism in Perspective.« *The Washington Quarterly* 26, no. 4 (Autumn 2003): 37-50.

Priest, Dana. »Foreign Network at Front of CIA's Terror Fight; Joint Facilities in Two Countries Account for Bulk of Agency's Post-9/11 Successes.« *Washington Post*, November 18, 2005.

–. »Help From France Key in Covert Operations; Paris's 'Alliance Base' Targets Terrorists.« *Washington Post*, July 3, 2005.

Purdy, Mathew, and Lowell Bergman. »Where the Trail Led: Inside the Lackawanna Terror Case.« *New York Times*, Octobe 12, 2003.

Regan, Tom. »EU, U.S. Differ on How to Fight Terrorism.« *Christian Science Monitor*, March 29, 2004, http://www.csmonitor.com/2004/0329/dailyUpdate.html?s=rel. (accessed March 1, 2007).

Sageman, Marc. remarks at the Saban Center for Middle East Policy symposium »How to Win the War Against Terrorism«. Washington DC, September 22, 2005. http://www.brookings.edu/fp/saban/events/20050922.htm (Panel 1 transcript) (accessed March 1, 2007).

Sciolino, Elaine, and Helene Fouquet. »Belgium Is Trying to Unrevel the Threads of a Terror Web.« *New York Times*, October 10, 2005.

»Senator Feinstein Seeks Major Improvements to the Visa Waiver Program.« (May 13, 2004). http://feinstein.senate.gov/04Releases/r-visawaiver.htm (accessed March 1, 2007).

Sennott, Charles M. »Europe's Terror Fight Quiet, Unrelenting.« *Boston Globe*, September 26, 2004.

Shane, Scott. »Official Reveals Budget for U.S. Intelligence.« *New York Times*, November 8, 2005.

The White House. »The National Security Strategy of the United States.« (September 2002). http://www.whitehouse.gov/nsc/nss/2002/nss.pdf (accessed March 1, 2007).

Weisman. »Allies as U.S. Pushes Terror Label for Hezbollah.« *New York Times*, 17 February, 2005.

Tackling Terror: A Transatlantic Agenda

Daniel S. Hamilton

Introduction

The fight against terrorism has the potential either to drive Europeans and Americans apart or to bring them together. Much depends on leadership. If Europeans and Americans are to be safer than they are today, individual efforts must be aligned with more effective transatlantic cooperation. Neither the framework for the transatlantic relationship nor the way European or North American governments are currently organized adequately address the challenge of catastrophic terrorism. There have been some promising beginnings, but they have been ad hoc achievements rather than integrated elements of a more comprehensive approach.

Individual efforts must now be complemented by a systematic, high profile effort in areas ranging from intelligence, counterterrorism, financial coordination and law enforcement to customs, air and seaport security, biodefense, critical infrastructure protection and other activities.[1]

Four Hurdles

If Europe and the United States are to engage more effectively together, they first need to understand better the different paths each has been on until now. Four hurdles in particular have consistently plagued transatlantic cooperation:

- differences in risk perception;
- the U.S. tendency to treat the issue as one of war and peace, versus European tendencies to treat the issue as one of crime and justice;
- challenges inherent in the U.S. concept of »pushing borders out;« and
- sheer organizational incoherence on both sides.

---

1 This article draws on other work by the author, referenced in additional footnotes, as well as Daniel S. Hamilton, »Transforming Homeland Security: A Road Map for the Transatlantic Alliance,« in *Transforming Homeland Security: U.S. and European Approaches*, ed. Esther Brimmer (Washington DC: Center for Transatlantic Relations, 2006).

Let us review these briefly. The first hurdle is a difference in risk perception. Most Europeans feel significantly less threatened than Americans – despite incontrovertible evidence that Europe is both a base for and a target of international terrorism. Risk perceptions also vary within Europe itself. Many in Europe and not a few in the United States view the 9/11 attacks as isolated incidents. Some in Europe also see terrorism as principally America's problem, one they believe the Bush Administration has exacerbated through its own actions, particularly the war in Iraq. Some see the subsequent Madrid and London attacks through the same perspective – nations were attacked that joined the Americans in the Iraqi war. It is important to note that European governments promptly rejected Osama bin Laden's offer of immunity to any country that would pull its troops out of the Middle East, and that Europe and the United States are working closely to deal with terrorism. But there is still appeal in policies that demonstrate distance from Washington. These divergent risk perceptions tear at both transatlantic partnership and EU solidarity.

A second hurdle is rooted in different approaches to the challenges posed by 21st century terrorism. Whereas U.S. efforts represent a radical break with traditional American approaches to security and reflect a tendency to characterize the issue as one of war and peace, initial European efforts represented an extension of previous efforts to combat terrorism and reflect a tendency to characterize the issue as one of crime and justice.

During the 20th century Americans thought of »national« security as something to be advanced far from American shores. The United States invested massively to project power quickly and decisively to any point on the globe, and invested meagerly to protect Americans at home. September 11 shattered that perspective. Now, Americans share a strange sense that they are both uniquely powerful and uniquely vulnerable. Partisan divisions within the United States are fierce, but they obscure a deeper consensus that the threat of WMD terrorism warrants a reframing of U.S. foreign and domestic policies. Americans disagree intensely whether the U.S. should have invaded Iraq. They disagree over the degree to which public security efforts may intrude on personal liberties. But most agree that America is engaged in a global war on terrorism. And most are willing to project American power abroad to »win« that war.[2] They are far more receptive to radical breaks with traditional thinking, far more inclined to support crash efforts to protect the homeland, and far less concerned with breaking diplomatic crockery along the way.

---

2 For more on these developments, see no author, »One nation after all,« *The Economist*, September 11, 2004, 32; Daniel S. Hamilton, »Transatlantic Societal Security: A new paradigm for a new era,« in *Transatlantic Homeland Security*, ed. Anja Dalgaard-Nielsen and Daniel S. Hamilton (London: Routledge, 2006).

In the name of this »war« on terror the Bush Administration has justified a number of extraordinary actions, including spying on U.S. citizens without court warrants, the practice of rendition, and detaining terrorist suspects as »enemy combatants« beyond the jurisdiction of domestic or international law. These are controversial in the United States as well as abroad, and have hampered international cooperation even with America's closest allies.

Just as Americans have sought to understand the consequences of September 11 within the context of their own national experience, European views have been colored by the kind of domestic terrorism that has confronted them for the past three decades. During that period, more than 5,000 lives were lost to terrorism in Britain, Ireland, and Spain alone. Whereas U.S. officials are suddenly haunted by the prospect of further – and perhaps even more catastrophic – attacks, European officials have long been taunted by domestic terrorists, who have argued that a government's own zeal to apprehend terrorists would lead it to subvert the very rules of the open society it sought to protect. A number of European countries have adopted laws to confront domestic terrorism while preserving civil liberties. Of course, there are differences within Europe as well, which make generalizations difficult. Recent British anti-terror laws, for instance, go even further than some U.S. efforts.

These perspectives influence the way in which each side has addressed the threat. Whereas the U.S. effort has been waged with the rhetoric of war, most European efforts have been viewed largely through the perspective of crime. Most Europeans view terrorism itself as a tactic rather than an enemy. These differing perspectives complicate transatlantic cooperation: American critics charge Europeans with complacency, while European critics accuse Americans of extremism.

A third hurdle has to do with the Bush Administration's initiatives to »push the border out.« Despite the impact of September 11 on the United States, the natural instinct in a nation bounded by two oceans is still to fight one's enemies abroad so one doesn't need to fight them at home. Washington's »forward defense« mentality, which exerts such a pervasive influence over the U.S. military, is also being applied to homeland security. The result has been a series of U.S. efforts to »externalize« the nation's domestic security by »pushing borders out« – essentially to move the focus of the anti-terrorism campaign abroad.

Aspects of this effort are controversial and problematic for transatlantic relations, for instance the Bush Administration's attempts to justify its war in Iraq through its war on terrorism; the notion enshrined in the Patriot Act that non-citizens have fewer rights to privacy and due process than U.S. citizens; or the »Guantanomo« practice of holding non-citizens indefinitely outside the jurisdiction of U.S. courts and without status in either domestic or international law. Tremendous European goodwill towards the U.S. after

9/11 has essentially been squandered by various manifestations of the externalization policy. It is important to note that much of the Guantanamo system remains controversial in the U.S. itself, and is currently under review by the courts.

Other »externalization« initiatives have simply caught European partners flatfooted, since such initiatives either require greater coherence among EU member states than they have been able to muster on such issues as customs, or collide with prevailing European regulations, for instance regarding data privacy.

Despite these difficulties, in select areas »externalization« has formed the basis for practical transatlantic agreements. Such U.S.-led initiatives as the Proliferation Security Initiative, the Container Security Initiative, Operation Safe Commerce or the Customs-Trade Partnership Against Terrorism (C-TPAT)[3] are all examples of »pushing borders out« in ways that have included European partners. The basic premise should be acceptable: it is safer to interdict potentially nasty people or items before they ever reach one's territory rather than trying to find them once they've arrived, even while safeguarding the free flow of people, goods and ideas upon which open societies depend. But »pushing borders out« will require unprecedented international cooperation tied to a major transformation of national customs and immigration agencies into the equivalent of diplomatic services. The resource implications are serious, and as indicated there is potential for abuse – such as conflating anti-terrorist efforts with immigration control efforts in ways that might lead to serious violations of human rights; or paying inadequate attention to the international legal ramifications of ex-

---

3 For details on the Proliferation Security Initiative, see the U.S. Department of State. »Proliferation Security Initiative.« (2006). http://www.state.gov/t/isn/60896.htm (accessed March 1, 2007). For information on C-TPAT see U.S. Customs and Border Protection. »Securing the Global Supply Chain: Customs-Trade Partnership Against Terrorism (C-TPAT) Strategic Plan.« (2004). http://www.customs.treas.gov/linkhandler/cgov/import/commercial_enforcement/ctpat/ctpat_strategicplan.ctt/ctpat_strategicplan.pdf (accessed March 1, 2007). For a description of the Container Security Initiative, see Wikipedia. »Container Security Initiative.« (2007). http://en.wikipedia.org/wiki/Container_Security_Initiative (accessed March 1, 2007). Operation Safe Commerce builds on C-TPAT and CSI by (1) building a greater understanding of vulnerabilities within global supply chains, and (2) ensuring that new technologies and business practices designed to enhance container security are both commercially viable and successful. For a critique of some of these efforts, see Stephen Flynn, »Addressing the Shortcomings of the Customs-Trade Partnership Against Terrorism (C-TPAT) and the Container Security Initiative,« Testimony before a hearing of the Permanent Sub-Committee on Investigations, Committee on Homeland Security and Governmental Affairs, United States Senate, http://www.cfr.org/publication/8141/addressing_the_shortcomings_of_the_customstrade_partnership_against_terrorism_ctpat_and_the_container_security_initiative.html. (accessed March 1, 2007).

traterritorial initiatives.[4] Moreover, such efforts may be self-defeating unless they establish a level playing field for all stakeholders. But the core principle offers important insights into new forms of international collaboration.

A fourth hurdle has been the sheer organizational incoherence of anti-terrorist efforts in the U.S. and in Europe. The Bush Administration's approach has represented little more an aggregation of discrete elements, ranging from counterterrorist intelligence, border security, risk management and cargo screening to health and other issues. The sum is less than the parts, and many parts are still moving to their own beat. For most of these missions, the bipartisan 9/11 Commission in December 2005 gave the Administration failing grades.

U.S. efforts are matched by a byzantine collection of efforts on the other side of the Atlantic. The European Union, having expanded to 25 nations, must now address the domestic security needs of 456 million people, with more to come in the next few years. But preventive and protective efforts still consist of a patchwork of contributions by the EU, its member states, and individual ministries, agencies, and services within those states. Links to non-EU members are uneven. Civil protection remains primarily the preserve of member states, and there are major turf wars between the European Commission and the European Council. There is no European »Minister for Homeland Security« available to the U.S. Secretary of Homeland Security. The EU Coordinator for Counterterrorism, appointed for the first time in the spring of 2004, has neither line authority over Commission bureaucrats or member state agencies, nor a significant budget to promote harmonization of policies, procedures, standards, or equipment, which vary widely across member states. He cannot prescribe; he can only persuade. He reports to the High Representative for Foreign and Security Policy in the European Council, and thus is of a lower level than the U.S. Secretary, and works out of the European Council rather than the European Commission, and so only has a small staff at his disposal. In the meantime, the EU suffers gaps in intelligence sharing, and interoperability between the police, judicial and intelligence services is questionable. SitCen, the center for intelligence in the Council Secretariat, analyzes information, but operational work remains the exclusive competence of the national security and intelligence services. The Union simply has a long way to go, particularly with regard to networked civilian and military capabilities, civil protection and safeguarding critical infrastructure.

In short, both sides face serious organizational challenges. And the interaction between these unwieldy, multi-jurisdictional approaches on each

---

4 For a critique, see Tom Barry, »Pushing Our Borders Out,« *IRC Online*, http://americas.irc-online.org/pdf/briefs/0502immigration.pdf. (accessed March 1, 2007).

side of the Atlantic has complicated efforts to boost transatlantic and broader international cooperation.

Finding Common Ground

Despite these hurdles, much has been done on both sides of the Atlantic to make life safer for ordinary citizens. In recent years a considerable number of cooperative intra-European and transatlantic arrangements have been set in place covering such issues as border security, air transport and container traffic to judicial, law enforcement, and intelligence cooperation.

Within Europe, the EU has created an European Arrest Warrant and started joint investigation teams for criminal investigation. It created a common judicial space, named »Eurojust,« to improve the coordination of member states' law enforcement activities, to help with assistance and extradition requests and to support investigations. The EU has adopted legislation on terrorist financing and beefed up laws against money laundering. Europol is collecting, sharing and analyzing information about international terrorism and assessing EU member state performance. National legislation was tightened by key EU member states. Following the March 11 attacks the EU adopted a solidarity clause that commits member states to help each other to prevent and protect against terrorist attacks and to assist each other in case an attack happens. Moreover, European nations have agreed to develop an integrated threat analysis capability at the EU level. FRONTEX, the European Borders Agency, has become operational.[5]

The U.S. and the EU have also stepped up their cooperation. Mutual legal assistance and extradition agreements have been signed. Intelligence sharing has improved, especially information about specific individuals suspected of ties to terrorism. The U.S. and EU have signed agreements to improve container security, expand customs cooperation, improve public-private partnerships to ensure transportation security, and transfer passenger name record (PNR) data. They have agreed to enhance information exchange to target and interdict maritime threats, work more closely through Interpol to deal with lost and stolen passports and other border issues, incorporate interoperable biometric identifiers into travel documentation, enhance their policy dialogue on border and transport security, and start a dialogue on improving capabilities to respond to terrorist attacks involving chemical, biological, radiological or nuclear weapons.

---

5 The European Council provides six-month updates of its efforts in this area. See Council of the European Union. »Implementation of the Action Plan to Combat Terrorism.« Justice and Home Affairs Council meeting, Brussels. (December 1, 2005). http://ue.eu.int/ueDocs/cms_Data/docs/pressData/en/jha/87254.pdf (accessed March 1, 2007).

A number of these initiatives are also interesting for broader reasons. First, transatlantic efforts have helped to advance deeper European integration. The creation of the European arrest warrant and the formation of Eurojust, for example, would scarcely have come about without intense U.S. pressure.

Second, the U.S. is gradually accepting the EU as a bilateral partner in issues of societal protection. The U.S.- EU mutual extradition and legal assistance treaties represent a significant expansion of traditional bilateral cooperation in law enforcement and modify transatlantic legal assistance in combating transnational crime in 26 countries. They were the first of their kind to be successfully negotiated between the EU and a third party. Given the divergences in European and U.S. legal systems concerning the death penalty, as well as standards in sentencing and for the protection of personal data, these agreements would have been a political impossibility before September 11.

Third, the U.S. is grudgingly accepting EU standards on issues of vital national importance. U.S. cooperation with Europol, for instance, enables the U.S. to share in the EU's growing development of databases and capabilities, based on the EU's own standards for data protection and privacy.

Fourth, transatlantic cooperation on container security, PNR data transfer and biometric passports is very significant because it requires acceptance of mutual constraints on a broad range of state action in the area of border control – one of the defining aspects of territorial sovereignty. The Container Security Initiative, for instance, is reciprocal, meaning not only that U.S. customs officials can operate in such ports as Rotterdam, Le Havre, Hamburg and Algeciras, but European inspectors could be stationed in Boston, Houston, Long Beach or Shreveport. Such a program is perhaps but the harbinger of a coming revolution in border affairs that creates »virtual« borders far from a nation's territory.

Moreover, such efforts are not starting from scratch. Even though terrorism became the overriding focus of transatlantic security discussions after September 11, 2001, a growing substructure of cooperative efforts to combat criminal and financial threats had already developed among the U.S. and the EU, the G-7, and other OECD countries through the 1990's. These initiatives provided a solid platform on which additional counter-terrorism activities could be based.

In short, despite practical, conceptual and political obstacles to deeper transatlantic cooperation in the area of homeland security, both sides have recognized that deeper collaboration is essential if either side of the Atlantic is to be more secure, and are breaking new ground in their efforts to advance their common security. Taken together, the growing array of U.S.-European cooperative ventures provides ample evidence for a rethinking of anti-terrorist efforts to span the transatlantic space. These agreements underscore the resilience of transatlantic partnership even in the face of serious disagreements.

This is important, because there is still much to be done. Compartmentalized approaches to security remain powerful on both sides of the Atlantic. Transatlantic arrangements have largely been ad hoc achievements rather than integrated elements of a more comprehensive approach. Without systematic pan-European and transatlantic coordination, however, each side of the Atlantic is at greater risk of attack. If the transatlantic allies cannot find common ground, there will be little hope for broader global efforts.

A systematic, high-profile effort is necessary, desirable – and now perhaps more possible. A systematic approach could be guided by a few basic propositions.

First, the threat is real – and common. The entire transatlantic space is both a base for and a target of catastrophic terrorism.

Transatlantic squabbles cannot be allowed to distract from a basic fact: the entire transatlantic space is both a base for and a target of international terrorism. Americans are quite focused on this fact. It would be foolhardy to assume that Europe would not be a target of future terrorist attacks. Al-Qaeda and home-grown terrorists inspired by it have directly attacked three European members of NATO – Turkey, Spain and the United Kingdom – and have tried to launch attacks in other parts of Europe as well. Al-Qaeda cells killed European tourists in North Africa. Terrorist cells have been discovered in London, Rotterdam, Milan, Hamburg, and Frankfurt, as have active recruitment efforts by Europe-based radicals in various parts of the world. Plots have been uncovered against the Strasbourg Christmas market, planes using Heathrow airport, the French tourist island La Reunion, the Russian and U.S. embassies in Paris, the U.S. embassies in Rome and Sarajevo, a U.S. military base in Belgium, and U.S. military facilities in Great Britain. Switzerland and other nations are major hubs for financial transactions by letterbox companies linked to al-Qaeda. Moreover, radicals based in London and Lyon managed to manufacture and test toxins like ricin and botulism, presumably for attacks across Europe, before being arrested by the authorities. France, Germany, Turkey, Italy, Bosnia and the UK have all uncovered terrorist activity linked to al-Qaeda. One of the terrorists who crashed into the World Trade Center once flew a precise flight plan over unprotected nuclear installations and key political and economic institutions along the Rhine and Ruhr. The horrific school massacre in Beslan emphatically underscored the potential for spillover of terrorism related to the situation in Chechnya. There is simply no question that international terrorism constitutes an active threat to both Europe and North America.[6]

Second, we must understand that what we must protect is our connectiveness, not just our territory.

Al-Qaeda and related terrorist groupings are lethal networks, often with global reach. Such networks can be flexible and agile, constantly able to reconfigure themselves to address new challenges and seize new opportunities. They are networks that prey on other networks -- the interconnected arteries and nodes of vulnerability that accompany the free flow of people, ideas, goods and services, and the complex interdependent systems on which free societies depend. These range from global electronic financial networks, networked information systems, »just-in-time« food supply chains and business systems, air, sea and land transportation to flows of fossil fuels or nuclear energy. It is our complete reliance on such networks, matched with their susceptibility to catastrophic disruption, that make them such tempting targets for terrorists.[7] In the 21st century, *what we are defending is our connectiveness.*

Globalization is causing a shift in conceptions of power and vulnerability from those that are state-centric and territorial-based to those that are stateless and network-based.[8] A transformative approach to security would supplement the traditional focus on *the security of the territory* with a clearer focus on the *security of critical functions of society.*

Terrorists wielding weapons of mass destruction or mass disruption are less intent on seizing and holding our territory than they are on destroying or disrupting the ability of our societies to function.[9] Antagonists wishing to inflict harm upon a society want to find the key nodes where critical in-

---

6 For other assessments and reports, see the no author, »Die Saudi-Connection,« *Der Spiegel*, no. 14, 2003; Desmond Butler, »3 arrested over ties to Muslim Militants,« *International Herald Tribune*, November 29, 2003; EU. »Non-confidential report on the terrorism situation and trends in Europe.« EU TE-SAT 14280/2/02. 19-27; Jon Henley, »Al-Qaida terror plot foiled, say French policy,« *The Guardian*, January 12, 2004; Joanne Wright, »Terrorism in Europe Since 9/11: Responses and Challenges,« www.cdu.edu.au/cdss2003/papers/Sym3papers/joannewright.pdf.

7 See Stephen Flynn, *America the Vulnerable: How Our Government is Failing to Protect us from Terrorism* (New York: HarperCollins, 2004), 86.

8 See Jean-Marie Guehenno, *The End of the Nation-State* (Minneapolis: University of Minnesota Press, 2000).

9 See Bengt Sundelius, »From National Total Defense to Embedded Societal Security,« in *Protecting the Homeland: European Approaches to Societal Security; Implications for the United States*, ed. Daniel S. Hamilton, Bengt Sundelius, and Jesper Grönvall (Washington DC: Center for Transatlantic Relations, 2005).

frastructures connect. When al-Qaeda destroyed the World Trade Center towers, it engaged simultaneously in attacks on the global securities markets through simultaneous market manipulation, demonstrating that terrorists understand how interconnected, and vulnerable, the world's collective infrastructures are to attack.[10]

Natural disasters, however, may also threaten our connectiveness. Hurricane Katrina, for instance, disrupted key energy supply lines between the Gulf coast states and other regions of the United States. The 2004 Pacific tsunami became a world-class security disaster for distant Sweden because of the major tourist networks Swedish citizens had established in recent decades.

A security system focused on protecting the connective tissue of modern society would seek to protect critical nodes of activity while attacking the critical nodes of those networks that would do us harm. It would integrate security considerations into the design and daily operations of such systems – from oversight of food production to the guarding of airport perimeters to the tracking and checking of ships. It would identify potential vulnerabilities linked to the technological complexity of the modern world and seek to transform them into high reliability systems. In would seek to anticipate and prevent possible »cascading effects« of a breakdown or collapse of any particular node of activity. It would ensure that »connectiveness vulnerabilities« are not built into future systems. It would engage the active participation of the private sector, which actually owns and controls most of these networks.[11]

Under concepts such as »resilience« or »total defense,« countries such as the United Kingdom, Switzerland, Sweden and Finland have advanced efforts at national, regional and local levels to detect, prevent and if necessary handle disruptive challenges. These could range from floods, through outbreaks of human or animal disease, to terrorist attacks.[12] The advantage of these approaches is that they are capacity-based rather than threat-based, and they align efforts to improve internal security with those to promote ex-

---

10 See Jonathan Winer. »The Role of Economic Sanctions in Combating International Terrorism (and Its Place in the Trans-Atlantic Alliance).« American Institute for Contemporary German Studies. Washington DC. (2001) http://www.aicgs.org/documents/winer.pdf (accessed March 1, 2007).

11 Some corporate leaders may resist, but many realize that safety makes sense for the bottom line. The 24-hour manifest rule in the cargo industry, for instance, has actually increased productivity. Remarks by Eugene Pendimonti, Vice President of Maersk Sealand, to the Center for Transatlantic Relations, September 13, 2004.

12 For basic information on UK efforts, see the CCS website, www.ukresilience.info/home.htm. For details and case studies of European national efforts, see Daniel S. Hamilton, Bengt Sundelius, and Jesper Grönvall, eds., *Protecting the Homeland: European Approaches to Societal Security; Implications for the United States* (Washington DC: Center for Transatlantic Relations, 2005).

ternal security. The disadvantage is that for the most part these efforts have been advanced on a national basis and yet, given both the interdependence of complex systems and the nature of contagious disease, effective societal security must also include an international dimension.

Focus on reducing risk rather than perfecting security

Efforts to advance societal security at home and abroad must proceed from the recognition that in an age of catastrophic terrorism there is no such thing as perfect security. It is impossible to stop every potential type of terrorist violence. We cannot protect every possible target, all the time, from every conceivable type of attack. The campaign will never entirely be »won.« Terrorism is a threat that we must constantly combat if we are to reduce it to manageable levels so that we can live normal lives free of fear.[13] Anthony Cordesman summarizes the challenge:

> »Victory cannot be defined in terms of eradicating terrorism or eliminating risk. This war must be defined in much more limited terms. It will consist of reducing the threat of terrorism to acceptable levels – levels that allow us to go on with our lives in spite of the fact that new attacks are possible and that we may well see further and more serious tragedies.«[14]

By focusing on preventing attacks that can cause large casualties, major economic or societal disruption, or severe political damage, nations can approach issues of societal security systematically and with a better chance of preventing future attacks.

Don't destroy what you are trying to protect

Thirty years ago, the Baader-Meinhoff terrorist gang goaded German authorities to hit back at them in ways they believed would break the law and undermine Germany's hard-won democracy. They reasoned that the quickest way to wound the German government would be to force it to break its own rules, corrupt its own nature and generate mistrust between the gov-

---

13 Flynn, *America the Vulnerable*; Bruce Hoffmann. »Presentation to Open Road 2002.« Atlantic Command Transformation. Norfolk VA. (January 2002).
14 Anthony Cordesman, *Biological Warfare and the 'Buffy Paradigm'* (Washington DC: Center for Strategic and International Studies, 2001), 4.

ernment and the governed. German leaders had to find the difficult balance. The anti-terrorist legislation that resulted sought to find this balance.[15]

This challenge is perhaps of even more relevance to democratic governments fighting international terrorism today. A number of the measures introduced to combat terrorism raise serious civil liberties concerns. In addition, abuses at Abu Ghraib and Guantanamo have undermined confidence in the U.S. Administration and international support for the anti-terrorism campaign. If the campaign is not perceived to be legitimate, it is unlikely to be effective. If efforts to protect our societies from catastrophic disruption are not aligned with the freedoms of those societies, we endanger that which we are trying to protect.

At the same time, the U.S. is finding that judicial cooperation is particularly important for dealing with terrorism. The unique nature of terrorism means that maintaining the appearance of justice and democratic legitimacy will be much more important than in normal wars or struggles. Ad-hoc anti-terrorist measures that have little basis in societal values and defined legal procedures provide little long-term bases for the necessary cooperation with other countries.

The U.S. and Europe can each learn from each other's experience with mechanisms that seek to advance security and liberty, such as sunset clauses and provisions for legislative oversight and judicial review. If the U.S. and Europe can help each other live up to their own standards, together they can help set human rights standards for the broader anti-terrorist campaign. On the other hand, if concerns about civil liberties are widespread even in the West's most sophisticated and oldest democracies, how much worse are they likely be in countries without such strong traditions who are also cracking down on suspects? Failure to advance security with liberty has the potential to subvert other key priorities, such as transformation of the Broader Middle East, where the overall trend throughout the Arab world has been a decline in social, political and cultural freedoms in the name of greater security against terrorism.[16]

---

15 For a review of German efforts to confront terrorism then and now, see Oliver Lepsius. »The Relationship between Security and Civil Liberties in the Fedearl Republic of Germany After September 11.« American Institute for Contemporary German Studies. Washington DC. (2001) http://www.aicgs.org/documents/lepsiusenglish.pdf (accessed March 1, 2007).
16 See Alyson Bailes, »Have the Terrorists Already Won?,« Scanbus Conference Speaking Notes, Riga, September 14, 2004.

Recognize that crime and war are merging

The tendency in European to cast the challenge as one of crime and justice and the tendency in America to treat it as one of war and peace are each dangerously myopic. As Catastrophic terrorism has blurred the lines between crime and war, and poses a new threat that requires the orchestration of efforts in both domains. A decade before September 11 military historian Martin van Creveld anticipated these developments:

> »Terrorist organizations and operations will be profoundly affected by information age technologies, which will provide these non-state actors with global reach. Modern communications and transportation technologies will have a profound impact on this new battlefront. There will be no fronts and no distinctions between civilian and military targets. Laws and conventions of war will not constrain terrorists and their state sponsors from seeking innovative means, to include WMD, to attack non-military targets and inflict terrible carnage ... Once the legal monopoly of armed force, long claimed by the state, is wrested out of its hands, existing distinctions between war and crime will break down« [17]

Most of the crucial battles in the campaign against terror around the world are not being fought by the military but by police, judges, border officers, intelligence officers, and financial and banking officials. But military force may be required at times, and in many circumstances military power may indeed need to be considered as an extension of law enforcement. Brian Jenkins suggests that this is likely to lead to new categories of law enforcement and precision warfare and new rules for operations, custody, and possible prosecution where law enforcement and armed conflict overlap.[18]

Tackling Terrorism: A Transatlantic Agenda

During the late 1940s and early 1950s Europeans and American responded together to the challenges facing their generation. The potential of catastrophic terrorism now challenges a new generation of Europeans and North Americans to reshape and reposition existing structures, and to devise new approaches that can help us respond more effectively to current threats. We should not settle for incremental, ad hoc adjustments to a system designed generations ago for a world that no longer exists. Instead, we should supplement traditional efforts, which focused either on territorial security or emergency response, with a third layer of »societal« security as an integral component of our relationship. In the first instance, of course, each nation

---

17 Martin van Creveld, *The Transformation of War* (New York: The Free Press, 1991).
18 See Brian Jenkins, »Intelligence and Homeland Security,« in *Transatlantic Homeland Security*, ed. Anja Dalgaard-Nielsen and Daniel S. Hamilton (London: Routledge, 2006).

must look to improve its own capabilities. But cooperation for societal security has become an urgent addition to the wider transatlantic agenda, and can be advanced on multiple tracks.

National Efforts

Nationally, the U.S. has yet to overcome the artificial distinctions between domestic and national security that continue to plague efforts in this area. The 9/11 Commission has made various proposals in this regard.

Within Europe, national efforts are uneven, given differing traditions. European countries have yet to ratify and implement all UN counterterrorism conventions and protocols. Not all have criminalized material and logistical support for terrorism (and in some cases, terrorism itself). Laws against document fraud need to be strengthened. Not all the ability to freeze terrorist assets. Legal or technical impediments to closer cooperation among countries on intelligence and information exchanges must be removed. Some countries have legal impediments to taking firm judicial action against suspected terrorists, often stemming from asylum laws that afford loopholes, inadequate counterterrorism legislation, or standards of evidence that lack flexibility in permitting law enforcement authorities to rely on classified-source information in holding terrorist suspects. The U.S. is concerned that some European states have at times demonstrated an inability to prosecute successfully or hold terrorists brought before their courts. Moreover, new EU and NATO members have quite uneven capabilities when it comes to societal security. Many need assistance to strengthen their legal framework and develop their capabilities to counter terrorism. [19]

Finally, nations on both sides of the Atlantic need to mainstream societal security and counterterrorism into foreign policy, including through better coordination of development assistance to address root causes of terrorism; pursuing terrorists and those that sponsor them wherever they may be; and cooperating on various efforts at non-proliferation, including significant »internationalization« and expansion of Nunn-Lugar programs.

---

19 The EU has earmarked more than 1 billion euro to continue assisting the new member states in the field of internal security during the period 2004-2006. See Gijs DeVries, European Union Counter-Terrorism Coordinator, to the hearing by the Subcommittee on Europe of the House Committee on International Relations, September 15, 2004. For an official U.S. view of European shortcomings, see the testimony by William Pope, Principal Deputy Coordinator for Counterterrorism, U. S. Department of State, at the same hearing.

Bilateral efforts

Bilateral cooperation between the U.S. and individual European nations will remain important despite more ambitious EU efforts, because even within the EU most of the instruments and competencies in the fight against terrorism remain in the hands of member states. Although the EU can do a lot to help national authorities work together internationally, the hard work of tracking down potential terrorists, preventing attacks and bringing suspects to justice remains the preserve of national authorities. Operational decisions are still national decisions. Even if the EU were to assume more authority in this area, the United States is unlikely to abandon its important bilateral national relationships. Whatever intelligence function would be created at the EU level would most likely coexist with national intelligence services.

Intelligence cooperation against diverse terrorist networks has to be advanced at three levels of »operation:« synchronizing and pooling intelligence products efficiently among different national services; coping with different judicial procedures and legal systems, and managing the risks of intelligence sharing, at both the European and transatlantic level; and global cooperation regarding terrorism and organized crime.[20]

U.S.-EU cooperation

The U.S. can work not only with individual European nations but with at EU level as well. The depth of that cooperation depends in part on the nature of the EU's own competencies in this area. U.S.-EU cooperative mechanisms are likely to evolve as the EU itself evolves. Transatlantic efforts in law enforcement, intelligence and other areas that operate at the member state level need to be coordinated with efforts at infrastructure protection, health security and other areas that are gradually beginning to be coordinated at the Community level. Information sharing will remain a critical yet difficult issue, given different legal regimes and political perspectives. As in so many other fields of policy, the key is to keep each other informed at an early stage of new policy proposals which might have an impact on the other so that potential differences can be resolved before legislation is enacted.

More can be done together, however, not only to protect European and American societies directly, but to help third countries in their fight against terrorism – in essence to »project resilience« to neighboring countries. Eu-

---

20 See Yves Boyer, »Intelligence Cooperation and Homeland Security,« in *Transforming Homeland Security: U.S. and European Approaches*, ed. Esther Brimmer (Washington DC: Center for Transatlantic Relations, 2006).

ropeans and Americans could engage more effectively together in security sector reform in third countries, and better coordinate external assistance to address conditions in which terrorism can grow. A strong homeland security system in one country may mean little if neighboring systems are weak. Terrorists in Europe, for example, have shown themselves to be far more pan-European than most of Europe's security agencies. They plan attacks in one country and execute them in the next.[21] Health issues, to take another example, have become integral elements of national security in a world of potentially catastrophic bioterrorist threats. In this regard, developed countries are only as secure as the world's weakest public health system.

NATO and its Partners

In past years NATO reforms have focused on projecting force and coping with threats beyond the NATO area. But NATO's nations – and their partners – must be prepared not only to project power beyond Europe but also to prevent, deter and, if necessary, cope with the consequences of WMD attacks on their societies – from any source. Territorial defense in the Cold War sense of protecting sealanes from Soviet submarines or guarding the Fulda Gap from Soviet tanks must give way to a new common conception of societal protection from WMD attacks from any source. If Alliance governments fail to defend their societies from a major terrorist attack, potentially involving weapons of mass destruction, the Alliance will have failed in its most fundamental task. It will be marginalized and the security of Europe and North America will be further diminished.[22]

In most countries these issues are primarily civilian, national and local priorities. But NATO has a role to play, particularly in civil-military planning capabilities, security sector reform, intelligence-sharing, political consultations and consideration of missile defense. NATO's civilian disaster response efforts are still largely geared to natural disasters rather than intentional attacks, and remain very low priority. It is time to ramp up these efforts to address intentional WMD attacks on NATO territory, to develop more serious transatlantic efforts to protect critical infrastructure, to work with partners such as Russia to develop new capabilities and procedures for

---

21 See John L. Clarke, »European Homeland Security: Promises, Progress and Pitfalls,« in *Securing the European Homeland: The EU terrorism and homeland security*, ed. Bertelsmann Stiftung (Gütersloh: August 2005).

22 See Daniel S. Hamilton, »Renewing Transatlantic Partnership: Why and How,« European Subcommittee Testimony to the House Committee on International Relations, June 11, 2003; Daniel S. Hamilton, ed., *Transatlantic transformations: Equipping NATO for the 21st century* (Washington DC: Center for Transatlantic Relations, 2004).

collaboration with civilian authorities, and to tap the expertise of partners who have had decades of experience with »total defense.«

In fact, the area of »transatlantic societal security« could be an attractive new mission for a rejuvenated Partnership for Peace and its political umbrella, the Euro-Atlantic Partnership Council. A bioterrorist attack of contagious disease, for instance, will not distinguish between »allies« and »partners,« and a number of partners have more experience mobilizing for societal security than do many allies. Following the last round of NATO enlargement the Partnership for Peace is a strange mix of prosperous, non-aligned Western countries such as Sweden, Finland, Austria, Ireland and Switzerland, and a number of Central Asian nations. It is precisely some of these non-aligned countries, however, which have decades of experience with approaches to societal defense, and it is precisely the area of Central Asia in which forward defense, security sector reform and preventive efforts against WMD threats are critical. NATO's special partnerships with Russia and Ukraine could also be utilized to good effect in this area.

Joint work on societal security could also infuse NATO-EU relations with a new sense of common purpose and lend substance to the »strategic partnership« each has declared yet neither has achieved. While both organizations are exploring how to strengthen their cooperation, they have little to show for it except for some successes in the Balkans. A joint focus on societal security, including consequence management, could inject new energy into their efforts, and both organizations have tools to offer.

Transatlantic efforts can be the motor of effective global efforts

Given the nature and scope of the threat, many solutions will ultimately have to be global. There is some recognition of this on both sides of the Atlantic. The 9/11 Commission reports that America's homeland is, in fact, »the planet.« Javier Solana speaks of »global homeland security.«[23] And yet any »global« solution must be built by a coalition of nations committed to the effort, and the core to any effective global coalition is most often the transatlantic community. Close transatlantic cooperation is thus likely to provide the backbone to any effective multilateral action.[24] Jonathan Winer

---

23 On November 4, 2002, during a visit to Brussels, DHS Secretary Ridge stated '[o]ne of the conclusions we drew early on – and I think it's one that our friends in Europe concluded, perhaps before much of the world – was that the reach of terrorism is global, that targets are global in nature, and that at the end of the day the 21st century world needs to find global solutions to global vulnerabilities.' 'Homeland Security Advisor Ridge in Brussels for EU, NATO meetings – November 4 2002' accessed via http://www.useu.be/Terrorism/EUResponse/.

24 See Hamilton, »Renewing Transatlantic Partnership: Why and How.«

and Ann Richard provide a good example of how the Financial Action Task Force has advanced universal and global adoption of standards that were derived from cooperation between Europe and North America.[25] There are many other such examples in many different fields. More often than not, transatlantic cooperation is a stepping stone, not an alternative, to broader global cooperation, not only in the UN Security Council but in such specialized fora as the World Customs Organization or the International Civil Aviation Organization. Moreover, multilateral agreements and global standardization may take considerable time to achieve. Deeper transatlantic cooperation allows for quicker action while providing an important means to set the stage for broader global cooperation.

It takes a network to beat a network

Repositioning existing structures will be important. But traditional alliance mechanisms or government-to-government relationships are inadequate to the challenge of globally networked terrorism. It will take a network to beat a network. A key premise of the anti-terrorist campaign must be networked defense: traditional structures must be supplemented by an overlay of informal networks that offer a denser web of preventive efforts. Since most of the critical infrastructures that terrorists might want to destroy or disrupt are linked to global networks, it is vital to include citizens and companies in any new regime.[26] This will require governments to define national security more in societal than statist terms and to move beyond traditional »public diplomacy« and »outreach« activities for NGOs toward more effective public-private networks. Traditional alliance mechanisms may be the densest weave in the web, but other connections will be needed to make the overall effort more effective.

During the 1980s and 1990s, military planners moved defense establishments into network-centric warfare, while business executives moved away from vertical hierarchies to flat structures and networked operations. Foreign ministries and other agencies of government, however, remain caught in state-centric approaches and organizational stovepipes. They need to undergo the same type of network-centric reforms. The 9/11 Commission has proposed unifying the many participants in the U.S. domestic counterterrorism effort and their knowledge in a network-based information-sharing

---

25 See Ann Richard, *Fighting Terrorist Financing: Transatlantic Cooperation and International Institutions* (Washington DC: Center for Transatlantic Relations, 2006); Jonathan Winer, »Cops across borders: the evolution of transatlantic law enforcement and judicial cooperation,« in *Transatlantic Homeland Security*, ed. Anja Dalgaard-Nielsen and Daniel S. Hamilton (London: Routledge, 2006).

26 Flynn provides a variety of proposals, see Flynn, *America the Vulnerable*, 166.

system that transcends traditional bureaucratic boundaries. An international dimension to such an effort would also be essential, and if it were to be launched it would most likely begin with America's closest allies.

Of course, governments are not starting from scratch. In a number of areas relevant to societal security the rigid trappings of state-to-state diplomacy have been giving way, gradually and unevenly, to new forms of interaction among state and non-state actors. Beyond the media glare on transatlantic squabbles the United States and its European allies have been forming their own complex, almost invisible and somewhat unconventional networks of cooperation that have become the foundation of joint efforts to freeze terrorist funds, toughen financial transparency measures, and bring aggressive threats of sanctions to those not cooperating. National governments are linking with their regulatory counterparts and the private sector across the globe to tackle thorny transnational issues such as money laundering, securities fraud, and drug trafficking. Governments are finding that such networks can be fast, flexible, cheap, and effective. They can lower the cost of collective action and enable large and disparate groups to organize and influence events faster and better than before. They can build capacities without building bureaucracies.

Effective anti-terrorism efforts will depend increasingly upon new forms of cooperation among state and non-state actors. In the international sphere, such efforts have been led almost entirely by institutions that are neither nation states, regional unions, multilateral organizations, or international organizations, but rather informal networks of law enforcement agencies, regulators, and the private sector. Such »international non-organizations« such as the Financial Action Task Force (FATF), the Egmont group or the Lyon Group can make a difference by setting standards and attacking nodes of terrorist or criminal activity. These structures developed in response to particular crises in the global financial system, as stakeholders came to realize from painful experience that transborder financial crime, including money laundering, terrorist finance, the theft and sequestration of national patrimonies by corrupt officials, stock market and investment fraud, contributed to such serious domestic problems as drug trafficking, immigrant smuggling, insurance crime and terrorism. By naming and shaming miscreants and threatening to block their access to the world's two most important markets, the Europeans and North Americans at the core of such networks began to produce practical results.[27] Such groups might offer models for similar networked cooperation in related fields.

Such networks aim to protect the critical nodes of activity that connect modern societies while attacking the critical nodes of those networks that would do us harm. Nodal strategies give higher priority to creating an en-

---

27 See Winer, »Cops across borders: the evolution of transatlantic law enforcement and judicial cooperation,« 106-125.

vironment hostile to all antagonists than to invest inordinate resources in chasing any particular offender. In each relevant sector the ultimate objective must be to create a loose, agile but muscular public-private network capable of responding to the terrorists' own transnational networks.

Needed: New mechanisms and new approaches

The world is on the cusp of exponential change in challenges posed by pathogens and their accessibility to state and non-state actors. These challenges require actions beyond piecemeal extensions of current policies. They require something more holistic than disease-specific stockpiles of medicines or vaccine. They require us to integrate public health and national security communities in ways that allow us to deal with an unprecedented challenge. Key multilateral frameworks such as NATO and the EU are limited in their ability to cope with the unique challenges posed by a bioweapon-induced spread of epidemic disease. Would a bioweapon attack that threatens a nation's health rather than its territory warrant a collective response under NATO's mutual defense clause or the EU's »solidarity clause?« What might such a response entail, and is either institution equipped for such action? Joint planning for traditional international security contingencies has occurred in NATO for decades. Planning with that degree of rigor and strategic and operational detail, but now for international response to epidemics, is but one example of what is needed to cope with potential threats to the European or North American homelands.

Conclusion

Europeans and Americans again face a new era. The open question is whether we are prepared to face it together. Our economies and our societies are too deeply intertwined to allow transatlantic divorce, but we do face the very real possibility of transatlantic dysfunction in the face of terrorist dangers that blur the lines between domestic and international security and between crime and war, and that neither Europeans nor Americans will be able to tackle alone.

Separate or competitive approaches will prove inadequate to the common challenge of catastrophic terrorism. A broad transatlantic campaign to confront this threat will require comprehensive cooperation among intelligence officials, police, diplomats, military, medical doctors, public health authorities and first responders, customs and financial institutions, the private sector and individual citizens. It will force us to understand more clearly where and why we agree and where – due to different national experiences and perspectives – our approaches may need to be reconciled. It will mean aligning Europe's grand yet difficult experiment of integration with a reorientation and strategic transformation of transatlantic relations to create new models of Atlantic partnership. Victory will be piecemeal and incremental. In President Bush's words, it will require a »patient accumulation of success.« The alternative could be tragedy on a scale exceeding even the horrors of the bloody century we left behind.

References

author, no. »Die Saudi-Connection.« *Der Spiegel*, no. 14, 2003, 70-72.

–. »One nation after all.« *The Economist*, September 11, 2004.

Bailes, Alyson. »Have the Terrorists Already Won?« Scanbus Conference Speaking Notes, Riga, September 14, 2004.

Barry, Tom. »Pushing Our Borders Out.« *IRC Online*, http://americas.irc-online.org/pdf/briefs/0502immigration.pdf. (accessed March 1, 2007).

Boyer, Yves. »Intelligence Cooperation and Homeland Security.« In *Transforming Homeland Security: U.S. and European Approaches*, edited by Esther Brimmer. Washington DC: Center for Transatlantic Relations, 2006, 155-164.

Butler, Desmond. »3 arrested over ties to Muslim Militants.« *International Herald Tribune*, November 29, 2003.

Clarke, John L. »European Homeland Security: Promises, Progress and Pitfalls.« In *Securing the European Homeland: The EU terrorism and homeland security*, edited by Bertelsmann Stiftung. Gütersloh, August 2005

Cordesman, Anthony. *Biological Warfare and the 'Buffy Paradigm'*. Washington DC: Center for Strategic and International Studies, 2001.

Council of the European Union. »Implementation of the Action Plan to Combat Terrorism.« Justice and Home Affairs Council meeting, Brussels. (December 1, 2005). http://ue.eu.int/ueDocs/cms_Data/docs/pressData/en/jha/87254.pdf (accessed March 1, 2007).

Creveld, Martin van. *The Transformation of War*. New York: The Free Press, 1991.

EU. »Non-confidential report on the terrorism situation and trends in Europe.« EU TE-SAT 14280/2/02.

Flynn, Stephen. »Addressing the Shortcomings of the Customs-Trade Partnership Against Terrorism (C-TPAT) and the Container Security Initiative.« Testimony before a hearing of the Permanent Sub-Committee on Investigations, Committee on Homeland Security and Governmental Affairs, United States Senate, http://www.cfr.org/publication/8141/addressing_the_shortcomings_of_the_customstrade_partnership_against_terrorism_ctpat_and_the_container_security_initiative.html. (accessed March 1, 2007).

–. *America the Vulnerable: How Our Government is Failing to Protect us from Terrorism*. New York: HarperCollins, 2004.

Guehenno, Jean-Marie. *The End of the Nation-State*. Minneapolis: University of Minnesota Press, 2000.

Hamilton, Daniel S. »Renewing Transatlantic Partnership: Why and How.« European Subcommittee Testimony to the House Committee on International Relations, June 11, 2003.

–. »Transatlantic Societal Security: A new paradigm for a new era.« In *Transatlantic Homeland Security*, edited by Anja Dalgaard-Nielsen and Daniel S. Hamilton. London: Routledge, 2006, 172-196.

–. »Transforming Homeland Security: A Road Map for the Transatlantic Alliance.« In *Transforming Homeland Security: U.S. and European Approaches*, edited by Esther Brimmer. Washington DC: Center for Transatlantic Relations, 2006, ix-xxxvi.

–, ed. *Transatlantic transformations: Equipping NATO for the 21st century*. Washington DC: Center for Transatlantic Relations, 2004.

Hamilton, Daniel S., Bengt Sundelius, and Jesper Grönvall, eds. *Protecting the Homeland: European Approaches to Societal Security; Implications for the United States*. Washington DC: Center for Transatlantic Relations, 2005.

Henley, Jon. »Al-Qaida terror plot foiled, say French policy.« *The Guardian*, January 12, 2004.

Hoffmann, Bruce. »Presentation to Open Road 2002.« Atlantic Command Transformation. Norfolk VA. (January 2002).

Jenkins, Brian. »Intelligence and Homeland Security.« In *Transatlantic Homeland Security*, edited by Anja Dalgaard-Nielsen and Daniel S. Hamilton. London: Routledge, 2006.

Lepsius, Oliver. »The Relationship between Security and Civil Liberties in the Fedearl Republic of Germany After September 11.« American Institute for Contemporary German Studies. Washington DC. (2001). http://www.aicgs.org/documents/lepsiusenglish.pdf (accessed March 1, 2007).

Richard, Ann. *Fighting Terrorist Financing: Transatlantic Cooperation and International Institutions*. Washington DC: Center for Transatlantic Relations, 2006.

Sundelius, Bengt. »From National Total Defense to Embedded Societal Security.« In *Protecting the Homeland: European Approaches to Societal Security; Implications for the United States*, edited by Daniel S. Hamilton, Bengt Sundelius and Jesper Grönvall. Washington DC: Center for Transatlantic Relations, 2005.

U.S. Customs and Border Protection. »Securing the Global Supply Chain: Customs-Trade Partnership Against Terrorism (C-TPAT) Strategic Plan.« (2004). http://www.customs.treas.gov/linkhandler/cgov/import/commercial_enforcement/ctpat/ctpat_strategicplan.ctt/ctpat_strategicplan.pdf (accessed March 1, 2007).

U.S. Department of State. »Proliferation Security Initiative.« (2006). http://www.state.gov/t/isn/60896.htm (accessed March 1, 2007).

Wikipedia. »Container Security Initiative.« (2007). http://en.wikipedia.org/wiki/Container_Security_Initiative (accessed March 1, 2007).

Winer, Jonathan. »Cops across borders: the evolution of transatlantic law enforcement and judicial cooperation.« In *Transatlantic Homeland Security*, edited by Anja Dalgaard-Nielsen and Daniel S. Hamilton. London: Routledge, 2006.

–. »The Role of Economic Sanctions in Combating International Terrorism (and Its Place in the Trans-Atlantic Alliance).« American Institute for Contemporary German Studies. Washington DC. (2001). http://www.aicgs.org/documents/winer.pdf (accessed March 1, 2007).

Wright, Joanne. »Terrorism in Europe Since 9/11: Responses and Challenges.« www.cdu.edu.au/cdss2003/papers/Sym3papers/joannewright.pdf.

The European Union and Conflict Prevention

Fraser Cameron

Introduction

The early warning of conflicts is a complex issue, requiring analysis of the interaction of a wide range of political, economic, military, environmental and social factors. In recent years, largely as a result of events in the Balkans and Africa, the EU has paid increasing attention to conflict prevention even though the development of effective early warning systems and the utility of early warning are problematic. Early warning is of little value unless it is linked to policy formulation and results in timely and effective action. Many conflicts have been widely predicted and the failure to prevent them has lain not so much in the lack of early warning but rather in the absence of political will to take effective action – Rwanda, Kosovo and Dafur being only a few of the most recent and obvious examples. In the EU, there has been a growing recognition that effective conflict prevention requires a more comprehensive approach addressing the underlying causes of instability and conflict, not simply the more immediate causes or symptoms of violence. The EU is now involved in conflict prevention and crisis management in many different parts of the world ranging from Aceh to Kosovo, both under the supervision of the former Finnish President, Mr Martti Ahtisaari.

This chapter provides an overview and assessment of the European Union (EU)'s gradual involvement in conflict prevention. It specifically considers what progress has been made since the 2001 Gothenburg European Council; assesses to what extent the EU's conflict prevention tools and policies are complimentary and coherent to other EU policies; discusses the likely impact of the European Security Strategy (ESS) and human security doctrine on future EU approaches to conflict prevention; and examines the impact of the delay to the proposed new position of EU Foreign Minister and new EU External Action Service on the EU's conflict prevention capacity.

The EU's Growing Role in Conflict Prevention

Set against the background of modern European history, the EU may be described as the best example of conflict prevention. One of the main motives of the Founding Fathers in the early 1950s in establishing the EU was the desire to prevent any further recurrence of conflict by creating a security community. The recent and continuing enlargement of the Union may also be seen in this context, namely as a massive conflict prevention programme designed to spread the Union's values relating to democracy and the rule of law throughout the entire continent. By imposing strict conditions (Copenhagen criteria) for membership, the EU has been able to use its mix of carrots and sticks (essentially financial and technical assistance, trade concessions and political cooperation) to extend the Western European zone of peace, prosperity and stability towards the East. Rarely has there been such voluntary interference in the domestic affairs of individual countries as in the central and eastern European countries preparing for EU membership.[1]

The EU's more traditional role in conflict prevention emerged parallel to the EU's growing international role. But the EU's political ambitions never matched its economic stature, hence the unkind description of »an economic giant and political dwarf.' The EU was quite unprepared for the challenges emerging as a result of the ending of the Cold War and the statement of Luxembourg Foreign Minister Jacques Poos in the summer of 1991 in regard to the onset of the Yugoslav crisis that this would be »the hour of Europe« was greatly misplaced. But the successive foreign policy crises of the 1990s brought a rapid maturing of the EU in terms of foreign and security policy. The EU came to accept that its external policies should be tied to the promotion of democracy, the rule of law and respect for human and minority rights. A number of treaty changes boosted the common foreign and security policy (CFSP) and paved the way for a military component (ESDP). Since the 2001 Swedish Presidency, there has been a major increase in the EU's awareness of the importance of conflict prevention and on the need to develop policies that tackle the root causes of violent conflict. The 2001 Gothenburg *Programme for the Prevention of Violent Conflict* was a key landmark in this process as was the 2003 European Security Strategy (ESS).

---

1 The new members included Estonia, Lithuania, Latvia, Poland, Czech Republic, Slovakia, Hungary, Slovenia, plus Malta and Cyprus. Bulgaria and Romania joined on 1 January 2007. Turkey and Croatia opened accession negotiations in October 2005 while the Western Balkans have a road map for eventual membership.

The Gothenburg Programme

At the Gothenburg European Council in 2001, the EU agreed an ambitious *Programme for the Prevention of Violent Conflicts* with four key priorities. The EU should –

Set clear political priorities for preventive actions. The Commission and the Council should cooperate more closely on conflict prevention: the Commission should provide assistance for the monitoring of potential conflict issues at the beginning of each Presidency and should also strengthen the conflict prevention content of its Country Strategy Papers. One of the main problems is the division of responsibilities (competences in EU jargon) between the Council and Commission. Broadly speaking the Council leads on the more political-security issues. It has far fewer resources (human and financial) than the Commission but it clearly feels in the ascendancy as a result of the High Representative for CFSP, Javier Solana's high profile and the overall trend towards greater inter-governmentalism in the Union. The Commission has the resources and most of the instruments useful for conflict prevention but finds itself on the defensive as a result of Member States reluctance to grant the Commission any powers in foreign and security policy. Indeed under the proposed new Constitutional treaty the Commission would have lost its automatic (shared) right of initiative. It would only have been able to put forward proposals under the aegis of the double-hatted Foreign Minister. The on-going tension between the Council and Commission was often hidden because of the good personal relations between the Javier Solana and the Commissioner for external relations (Chris Patten until late 2004 and now Benita Ferrero-Waldner). This is not to say that cooperation does not proceed, rather that it often relies more on informal contacts and relationships than agreed structures.

Within the Commission, DG Relex and DG Development are the two most important DGs in terms of conflict prevention. The Conflict Prevention and Crisis Management Unit in DG Relex is responsible for coordinating Commission conflict prevention activities. It provides expertise and training to headquarters and field staff and promotes conflict assessment methodologies within the Commission. Despite its extensive mandate, the Unit which was established only in 2001 has a very small staff. In close cooperation with the Council Secretariat and the Joint Situation Centre, the unit provides the Council with a watch-list of potential crisis states on which the EU should focus. This is given to each Presidency and periodically reviewed. However, despite their recent creation, the Commission and Council have been criticized for overly stressing the economic and financial issues contained in the *check list*, while only superficially covering the questions on the existence of a civil society or the political legitimacy of the regime in place. An early report – »One Year On«[2] – indicated the Unit has had some success in coordinating EU instruments and increasing the efficiency of actions that target so-called cross-cutting issues. The Unit has also done well to push for integrating conflict prevention concerns into Commission policies, particularly the programming of external assistance. This appears to have led to the progressive inclusion of conflict prevention indicators[3] in the Country Strategy Papers, which the Council welcomed as a »significant contribution to achieving the objective of giving multi-annual programming greater substance, increasing the effectiveness and quality of EU external assistance«.[4]

Improve its early warning, action and policy coherence. To help achieve this aim the Union agreed that there should be greater input (intelligence, assessments, political reporting) from Member States into the institutions. Coherence among the different EU policy areas should continue to be ensured by Coreper, while the Political and Security Committee (PSC)'s role in supervising the EU's activities on the front of conflict prevention should be reinforced.

There has been a steady increase in material flowing from Member States but it is patchy and sometimes provided with caveats. There is perhaps at least as much information provided informally to national diplomats serving temporarily in the Policy Planning Unit of the Council. More use could be made of open source intelligence including satellite imagery. Language is another factor that inhibits free circulation of material. The establishment in 2005 of the new civilian-military cell could also improve coherence as it is mandated to conduct integrated civ-mil strategic planning. It is worth noting that similar considerations lay behind the High Level-panel proposals for a UN Peacebuilding Commission. EU support will be crucial in the successful establishment of this body.

Some progress has been made in terms of action, mainly through the 2001 *Rapid Reaction Mechanism* (RRM). This is a flexible instrument and has been deployed usefully on numerous occasions (18 operations in 2002). The Rapid Reaction Mechanism (RRM) has helped make EU assistance more responsive and is run by the Conflict Prevention Unit in DG Relex. Its budget for 2003 was €27.5 million, to be spent on projects lasting no longer than six months. The RRM is intended to allow more flexible and rapid funding in crisis situations for primarily civilian initiatives. It has

---

2 See DG Extermal Relations. »One Year On: the Commission's Conflict Prevention Policy.« (2002). http://ec.europa.eu/comm/external_relations/cfsp/cpcm/cp/rep.htm (accessed February 15, 2007).
3 See Commission check list for root-causes of conflict/early warning indicators elaborated by the Conflict Prevention Unit. See DG External Relations. »European Commission Check-list for Root Causes of Conflict.« http://ec.europa.eu/comm/external_relations/cfsp/cpcm/cp/list.htm (accessed February 15, 2007).
4 GAERC meeting, 18 March 2003.

been used in Afghanistan, Macedonia, Nepal, Sri Lanka, Sudan, Somalia, Aceh, DRC and elsewhere. In June 2003, at the request of ECOWAS, RRM funded the roundtable that brought together in Ghana the parties who reached an agreement on ending the Liberian conflict

Election observation is a significant component of the EU's policy of promoting human rights and democratisation throughout the world, and thus, part of its overall conflict prevention strategy. This is an area where the Commission has asserted leadership.[5]

Enhance its instruments for long- and short-term prevention. Gothenburg proposed that all relevant EU institutions should mainstream conflict prevention in their areas of competence. The instruments for disarmament, non-proliferation and arms control, it was noted, should also play a vital role in the EU's conflict prevention policy.

Although the EU has managed to introduce the concept of conflict prevention into all its institutions, a strong discrepancy persists between long-term (structural) policy aimed at addressing the root causes of conflict, and medium/short-term early warning and crisis management. Development issues have been effectively separated from external relations policy in the Commission. In *DG Relex*, attention to the root causes of a conflict is very limited and hinges largely on the geopolitical significance of the country considered. There is also very little attention paid to development issues at the Council level, which de facto undermines the coordination of ESDP/CFSP policy with longer-term conflict prevention. Another type of discrepancy affects the allocation of funds between civilian and military crisis management. Operations with a military component are more easily funded, as they are directly charged to Member States. The financing of civilian operations is more intricate, as some operations can be financed through the Community budget and others through the CFSP budget. These differentiated financing constraints logically result in clear imbalances between military and civilian crisis management staff at EU level, to the advantage of the former.

The institutional problems noted above also affect attempts to ensure the benefits of conflict-prevention mainstreaming in most EU policy areas. In addition to the problems between the 'first' and 'second' pillars an additional complexity arises when policing is involved as this requires activation of the 'third' pillar. The different procedures under the pillar system thus serve to complicate matters and often delay decisions. The Commission has a relatively unchallenged role in trade, development cooperation and humanitarian assistance but a much more modest one in CFSP, which

---

5 The legal basis for EU Election Observation Missions consists of Council Regulations 975/99 and 976/99. The decision to provide electoral assistance and to send EU observers must be taken on the basis of a Commission proposal.

is the domain of intergovernmentalism.⁶ Still, its management of the CFSP budget gives it influence. Its comparative advantage in conflict prevention and management lies in areas closely linked to long-term structural issues or immediate humanitarian needs. It controls many of the resources for EU action and has numerous instruments at its disposal, from election monitoring to its rapid reaction mechanism (RRM). This contrasts with the Council and the High Representative, who deal with a wider range of security issues but have many political constraints and fewer instruments they can use to influence situations. The Commission will continue to be the main, sometimes exclusive, purveyor of EU foreign policy in those regions of the world member states do not consider strategic priorities.

Build effective partnerships for prevention. The EU should intensify its cooperation and exchange of information with the other relevant global institutions (UN, OSCE, NATO), as well as with the regional organizations competent for the regions of concern.

With conflict prevention an increasingly visible external objective, the EU has expanded its contacts with and operational dealings with a number of international partners. The EU institutions are in regular contacts with the UN, the OSCE, NATO and several relevant regional organizations such as the African Union (AU). In the Western Balkans, and especially in Macedonia, cooperation between the EU and other multilateral organizations, primarily NATO, but also the OSCE and the World Bank, was decisive during the critical phase of the conflict. This concerted and successful action was underpinned by a common assessment of the situation and a consensus on the goals. The EU has also proved to be an influential actor in the building of international regimes, such as small arms control (1988 code of Conduct and 1999 Joint Action). The EU continues to seek to work with as many relevant international actors as possible. First and foremost this means the UN and the December 2003 European Council welcomed the EU-UN »Declaration on Cooperation in Crisis Management.« Clearly, one of the goals of the effort to develop standardised ESDP training mechanisms is to allow EU forces to make meaningful and efficient contributions to UN operations.

Relations with the UN have developed rapidly in the past few years and need to be further strengthened. The EU also plays an active if sometimes incoherent role in the OSCE and the Council of Europe as well as the international financial institutions, notably the IMF and World Bank, both key actors in conflict prevention. It has also tried to strengthen other international frameworks such as the UN Convention against Corruption (UN-

---

6 The Commission, which has exclusive right to initiate EU policy measures in Pillar One, shares this right with member states in CFSP (Pillar Two).

CAC), the Financial Action Task Force (FATF) and the Extractive Industries Transparency Initiative (EITI).

Perhaps the EU's most ambitious support initiative for a regional organisation is its African Peace Facility (APF), established on 19 April 2004 in response to a request from the AU's Maputo Summit. It makes _250 million available from the European Development Fund (EDF) to promote African solutions to African crises by giving the AU financial muscle to back up its political resolve. This money will help pay for African-led, operated and staffed peacekeeping initiatives, though these need not be exclusively military; indeed APF money cannot be used to buy arms. The latest Common Position on conflict prevention, management and resolution in Africa[7] identifies a need for a longer term, more integrated approach to conflict prevention. It stresses mainstreaming conflict prevention perspectives in particular within development and trade policies to reduce the risk of fuelling conflicts and to maximise impact on peacebuilding.

The necessity to support other international peacebuilding regimes and organisations has been recognised for some time. The EU has a strong interest in promoting these at both the regional and sub-regional level, such as ASEAN, the OAS, the Community of Andean Nations, and Mercosur. In addition to the previously cited support for the African Union, the EU also works on that continent with ECOWAS (West Africa), SADC (Southern Africa) and IGAD (the Horn).[8]

Gothenburg Assessment

The Irish Presidency in 2004 reported positively on the implementation of the Gothenburg Programme, and its conclusions were endorsed at the European Council in June of that year. The reform of EU external assistance that began in 2000 aimed to establish a closer match between development cooperation and the political commitment to address the root causes of conflict, while ensuring high quality standards were met. A main focus of the reform is the actual programming of assistance, which is supposed to lead

---

7 Council of the European Union. »Council Common Position 2004/85/CFSP of 26 January 2004 concerning conflict prevention, management and resolution in Africa and repealing Common Position 2001/374/CFSP.« (2004). http://www.eur-lex.europa.eu/LexUriServ/LexUriServ.do?uri=OJ:L:2004:021:0025:0029:EN:PDF (accessed February 15, 2007).

8 See also the latest communication from the Commission on an EU-Africa partnership October 12, 2005: Commission of the European Communities. »Communication from the Commission to the Council and the European Parliament: EU Strategy for Action on the Crisis in Human Resources for Health in Developing Countries.« (2005). http://eur-lex.europa.eu/LexUriServ/LexUriServ.do?uri=COM:2005:0642:FIN:EN:PDF (accessed Feburary 15, 2007).

to greater coherence between the EU's strategic priorities and to the right 'policy mix' for each country or region. As early as March 2002, the Commission claimed that it »has delivered« on its commitment,[9] a judgment with which several significant external observers have agreed.[10]

Complementarities between Conflict Prevention and Development Policies

There is an emerging consensus that development and security are interlinked. Without development there can be no security and without security there can be no development. The reorganization of the Commission Directorate Generals in 1999 and the transfer of conflict prevention competences from DG Dev to DG Relex was regarded by some as limiting the EU's capabilities in terms of long-term conflict prevention policy. There is little inter-action between the two DGs apart from preparation of the Country Papers which are meant to help the desk officers and delegations of the Commission to better target the Community aid, by increasing their awareness and knowledge of the root causes of conflicts. A more substantive issue is the need to assess the match between development cooperation and conflict prevention objectives. There is no in-house system for reviewing the overall impact of EU assistance on local and regional conflicts.

An additional difficulty is represented by the internal fragmentation of competences within DG Dev, as EuropeAid handles the planning, management and implementation of EC aid, while the responsibilities of DG Dev are further downsized by the decentralization of aid management, gradually transferred to the EC delegations in the developing countries. This internal fragmentation of DG Dev has not helped raise the profile of development considerations in EU conflict prevention policies. Partly because of the transfer of competence, development and conflict prevention policy tend to mutually ignore each other. The website of DG Dev devotes little space to conflict prevention and speeches by the Commissioner have paid little more than lip service to the concept. It seems that DG Dev is still groping for a clearer articulation between development and conflict prevention objectives as evidenced by the latest issues paper from DG Dev, »Consultation on the future of EU development policy« of 7 January 2005. It is of course true that development and conflict prevention do not always go hand in hand. Strategies to reduce poverty for instance will not necessarily contribute to strengthening democracy and preventing conflict. Economic and social development meant to alleviate poverty may fuel conflict in communi-

---

9 »One Year On: the Commission's Conflict Prevention Policy.«
10 See, for example, OECD. »Report of the OECD Development Assistance Committee (DAC) High Level Meeting.« (15-16 April 2004); UK House of Lords European Union Committee. »EU Development Aid in Transition.« (April 29, 2004).«

ties, depending on which social, sectoral or ethnic groups are the beneficiaries of this aid. Further reflection on these problems, perhaps with the World Bank and UN, might be fruitful in terms of better coordination of the EU development and conflict prevention policies.

The majority of EU external assistance is delivered through long-term instruments and intended to support structural conflict prevention and peaceful resolution of disputes through targeted programs that promote the rule of law, good governance and poverty reduction.[11] Humanitarian aid delivered through ECHO can also help mitigate crises or prevent conflicts as witness efforts in the Congo (DRC), Liberia and Sudan. As best it can, ECHO seeks to insulate its humanitarian mission from the political decisions and policies pursued by other elements of the EU and by its member states. The Commission has recently proposed a new Stability Instrument that would be useful for conflict prevention but the proposal will have to await agreement on the new financial perspectives for the EU. Critics have suggested that highly developed participants in the global economy such as the EU and the U.S. could provide substantially more benefits to many underdeveloped countries by eliminating trade subsidies, particularly in agriculture, than they do through foreign aid. This debate will intensify in the run up to the Doha development round ministerial in Hong Kong in December 2005.

The European Security Strategy

The European security strategy (ESS) offers a number of guidelines of direct concern to conflict prevention.[12] The emphasis is on extending the zone of security on the EU's periphery, supporting multilateral institutions (specifically the UN and regional organisations) and seeking a comprehensive approach to old and new security threats. The ESS stresses that priority security objectives (WMD proliferation and international terrorism) should be addressed through »effective multilateralism«. In other words, by supporting the UN system, strengthening national responses through EU synergies and by addressing root causes such as poverty and weak governance by drawing upon community instruments and regional dialogue. These characteristics, along with an emphasis upon »preventive engagement« rather than »pre-emption«, are generally acknowledged to make the ESS stand apart from the US National Security Strategy. Yet, the ESS recog-

---

11 These are the Cotonou Agreement for the ACP countries, ALA for Asia and Latin America, TACIS for Eastern Europe and Central Asia, MEDA for the countries of the Mediterranean and CARDS for South Eastern Europe.
12 Javier Solana. »European Security Strategy: A Secure Europe in a Better World.« ISS-EU. Paris. (2003) http://www.iss-eu.org/solana/solanae.pdf (accessed February 15, 2007).

nises that the first line of defence lies beyond EU frontiers; acknowledging that inaction is not an option; understanding that a military response is not always appropriate but might form one element of a combined response. In this way, the EU can engage in the systematic political engagement of »prevention«. The ESS also stresses that Europeans generate inadequate capability from their considerable defence spending. Member States must make better use of the €160 billion devoted annually to defence (the US spends around €340 billion).[13]

The Human Security Doctrine

While much attention has been paid on the need for the EU to improve its military capabilities there has been a parallel pressure to improve its civilian capabilities and to ensure more attention for human security. Solana has taken a strong interest in the whole human security agenda and commissioned a report in 2004 that urged greater EU resources to deal with conflict prevention and crisis management. The report urged more attention to be paid to human rights and proposed a mainly civilian, 15,000 strong, Human Security Response Force.[14]

The EU had already sought to increase its civilian capabilities when Member States agreed at the Feira European Council in June 2000 to provide by 2003:

- policing: a minimum of 5,000 officers, 1,000 of whom can be deployed within 30 days;
- rule of law: 200 experts, including prosecutors, lawyers and judges and a rapid response group capable of deployment within 30 days;
- civilian administration: a pool of experts; and
- civil protection: two or three assessment teams of ten experts each, capable of dispatch within hours of a disaster, with a 2,000-strong civil protection intervention contingent available for later deployment.

The EU has done a fair job in meeting these goals, at least in principle. The Civilian Capabilities Commitment Conference on 22 November 2004 de-

13 The Solana Paper uses the figure €160 billion, slightly different figures can be calculated from the figure drawing on SIPRI and IISS, which may be due to exchange rate differences (usually occurring when drawing upon NATO figures which are in dollars).
14 Group on Europe's Security Capabilities Study. »A Human Security Doctrine for Europe: The Barcelona Report of the Study Group on Europe's Security Capabilities.« Barcelona. (September 15, 2004) http://www.lse.ac.uk/Depts/global/Publications/HumanSecurityDoctrine.pdf (accessed February 15, 2007).

clared that member states have volunteered 5,761 police, 631 rule of law specialists, 562 civilian administrators and 4,988 civil protection personnel.[15] Proxima in Macedonia and the EUPM in Bosnia were police missions as was the EUPOL mission to the Democratic Republic of Congo («Kinshasa»);[16] and in response to an invitation from Georgia, decided in June 2004[17] to send the EU's first ever ESDP Rule of Law Mission (Themis) to Tbilisi for one year. In December 2004, the European Council asked the incoming Luxembourg Presidency and Solana to prepare for the possibility of an integrated police, rule of law and civilian administration mission for Iraq but while preparations continue no date for deployment has been announced.[18] The EU has also agreed a new Civilian Headline Goal (2008) that runs parallel to the military headline goal (2010). The aim of the new CHG is to improve the EU's capacity to act both in terms of quantity and quality of resources. There is a need to have a roster of experts with language skills and areas of expertise and have them trained with other nationalities. There is also likely to be a demand for increased integrated packages involving rapidly deployable civilian response teams.

In the longer term, the EU's added value in conflict management should be its ability to deploy mixed civilian and military missions rapidly. But just as this requires new thinking about the function of armed forces, it also requires new seriousness about civilian capabilities as, in many situations, at least an equal complement to military capabilities. To date, the EU has trained over 200 people for possible civilian deployment. As this has been mainly done at the national level, it is crucial to ensure more coherence in national training programs, so that personnel deployed from different member states can work together effectively from day one. There is currently no link between training courses and deployment, and mechanisms need to be introduced to ensure that those trained are also willing and able to take part in EU operations.[19] Recruitment – the responsibility of member states – is

15 Council of the European Union. »Civilian Capabilities Commitment Conference: Ministerial Declaration.« (November 22, 2004). http://ue.eu.int/ueDocs/cms_Data/docs/pressData/en/misc/82760.pdf (accessed February 15, 2007).
16 Council of the European Union. »Council Joint Action on the European Union Police Mission in Kinshasa (DRC) regarding the Integrated Police Unit (EUPOL »KINSHASA«) (15070/04).« (December 6, 2004). http://register.consilium.europa.eu/pdf/en/04/st15/st15070.en04.pdf (accessed February 15, 2007).
17 By Council of the European Union. »Council Joint Action 2004/523/CFSP of 28 June 2004 on the European Union Rule of Law Mission in Georgia, EUJUST THEMIS.« (June 28, 2004). http://www.eur-lex.europa.eu/pri/en/oj/dat/2004/l_228/l_22820040629en00210024.pdf (accessed February 15, 2007).
18 Council of the European Union. »Presidency Conclusions.« (16-17 December, 2004). http://www.consilium.europa.eu/ueDocs/cms_Data/docs/pressData/en/ec/83201.pdf (accessed February 15, 2007).
19 Malin Tappert, »Developing Civilian Crisis Management Capabilities,« *European Security Review*, no. 20 (2006).

procedurally diverse, which makes it quite difficult to identify qualified personnel to deploy at short notice. Indeed in late 2005 the EU faced some problems in obtaining less than a hundred personnel to man border and customs posts in Gaza.[20] The newly adopted standard EU training concept in ESDP has the potential to improve interoperability between civilian officials from different member states and spread a common ESDP culture based on lessons learned from past operations.

However, it is clear that EU civilian capabilities have not yet come near their potential. The problem is one of coordination between both political priorities and Council and Commission competencies. There has been pressure from some NGOs to create a European Peacebuilding Agency while others have proposed a European Civil Peace Corps (ECPC) but Member States are yet to be persuaded of the viability or desirability of these proposals.

Will there be a EU Foreign Minister?

The rejection of the Constitutional treaty by France and the Netherlands has left the fate of the treaty in the balance. The Union is currently engaged in a »period of reflection« trying to establish how best to connect with its citizens and gain support for further integration. One of the most innovative proposals in the Constitutional treaty was the new position EU Foreign Minister who would largely replace the traditional rotating Presidency. Partly to deal with this discontinuity, the Constitutional treaty instituted a two-and-half-year term for a Chairman of the European Council. Even now there are attempts to put forward joint programmes spanning two or three Presidencies to try and achieve more coherence. The joint Irish-Dutch Presidencies »Operational Programme of the Council for 2004« declared conflict prevention to be »a major crosscutting priority for the Union« and pledged to improve cooperation with the UN in conflict management. It identified as regional priorities strengthening AU-led African initiatives in conflict prevention, support of the political process in Kosovo in anticipation of discussions on final status in 2005, implementation of the Road Map for the Middle East Peace Process, and stabilisation of Afghanistan

The new EU Foreign Minister foreseen in the Constitutional treaty should have been in a powerful position to ensure greater coherence in the EU's efforts in conflict prevention. He (it was already foreseen that the first occupant would be Javier Solana) would have been 'double-hatted' i.e. he would simultaneously have chaired the Foreign Affairs Council and have been a Vice President of the European Commission. This would have al-

---

20 Conversation with Marc Otte, EU special representative.

lowed him to play a major role in bringing together all the various EU instruments available in external relations. The Foreign Minister would of course have needed to ensure that he enjoyed a good working relationship with the President of the Commission and the new Chairman of the European Council, both of whom would have had their own foreign policy responsibilities.

As Vice President of the Commission, the EU Foreign Minister would have chaired meetings of the Relex Commissioners (Trade, Development, Enlargement) and thus have been able to steer Community action towards supporting overall EU foreign policy goals. He would have been supported by an EU Foreign Service or EU External Action Service. The precise size and location of this new service was an open issue but it was likely to be sui generis and include the current 129 Commission delegations, that were foreseen to become EU missions. These missions would have had a greater political reporting responsibility, including assessment of important indicators for conflict prevention purposes.[21] The evolution of Commission delegations toward true EU embassies could improve the Union's ability to pursue timely conflict prevention since it would have given it greater capacity to develop more of its own internal assessments rather than being forced to rely on member states to contribute theirs. EU missions also should be competent to implement specific policies in a range of fields – CFSP as well as justice and home affairs cooperation – that hitherto have been mostly beyond the scope of the delegations.

It is difficult to assess the likely impact of the delay in establishing the new post of EU Foreign Minister and the external service. Foreign and security policy remains a very sensitive area for the Member States and there is a general reluctance to cede powers to the EU institutions in this area. At present, Solana only has a very limited role on paper »to assist the Presidency« but due to his experience and connections he has carved out a role where he is now routinely described as »the EU's foreign policy chief.« The new constitutional treaty would have granted him considerable increased powers but he would still be dependent ultimately on the goodwill and support of the Member States, especially the larger ones. Solana has always recognised the importance of conflict prevention and the new position would have enabled him to wield more clout both within the institutional set up in Brussels and with Ministers in the Foreign Affairs Council over which he would have presided. But although the pillars were to have been abolished under the new constitutional treaty the old procedures would have remained in place.

Whatever structure is agreed in future, the Commission will continue to hold considerable competences in the external field as well as managing the

---

21 See Giovanni Grevi and Fraser Cameron, »Towards an EU Foreign Service,« *EPC Issue Paper*, no. 20 (2005).

sizeable external budget. The proposals for an EU Foreign Minister and an external action service were not controversial and, according to Eurobarometer, enjoyed wide public support. There are those who believe that it would be possible to 'cherry-pick' these (and other) parts of the Constitution. But it is unlikely that there will be the necessary political will to undertake such a move until there is some clarity about the fate of the treaty. The new structures should have led to greater harmony and less bureaucratic turf wars. The delay in ratifying the treaty means that there is a danger of continuing Brussels in-fighting and, perhaps more serious, a danger of the larger member states moving to form a directoire in foreign policy.

The Development of ESDP

Conflict prevention and crisis management sometime requires properly trained and equipped armed forces to intervene at crucial junctures. The acceptance in 1997 of the Petersberg Tasks (»humanitarian and rescue tasks, peacekeeping tasks, and tasks of combat forces in crisis management, including peacemaking«) was recognition of the EU's willingness to engage militarily when necessary. But fulfilment of these tasks was handicapped by the structure and poor capabilities of the defence forces in most member states. There was also a perennial dispute between the UK and France about the degree of autonomy of such an EU force vis-à-vis NATO. At St. Malo in December 1998 London and Paris initiated a new bi-lateral push on EU defence efforts with a declaration stating that the EU should develop »… the capacity for autonomous action, backed up by credible military forces, the means to decide to use them, and a readiness to do so, in order to respond to international crises«[22].

Since then the European Council has developed ESDP further. First, by its 1999 Helsinki Headline Goal (HHG) where the Member States agreed that in »cooperating voluntarily in EU-led operations, Member States must be able by 2003, to deploy within 60 days and sustain for at least one year military forces of up to 50,000-60,000 persons capable of the full range of Petersberg Tasks«. Second, by its 2000 decision at Nice to establish the permanent structures of the Political and Security Committee, Military Committee and EU Military Staff. Third, by agreeing the financing of military

---

22 For a review of the defence policy and economics of the evolution of ESDP since St. Malo see: Jocelyn Mawdsley and Gerrard Quille. »The EU Security Strategy: A new framework for ESDP and equipping the EU Rapid Report Reaction Force.« ISIS Report. (December 2003) http://www.isis-europe.org/ftp/download/reportdefence.pdf (accessed February 15, 2007). See also Maartje Rutten. »From St. Malo to Nice: European defence, core documents.« ISS. Chaillot Papers no. 47. Brussels. (2001).

crisis management operations in 2002. Four, by its 2002 decision approving the European Capability Action Plan (ECAP) that called on Member States to »mobilise voluntarily all efforts, investments, developments and coordination measures, both nationally and multinationally, in order to improve existing resources and progressively develop the capabilities needed for the Union's crisis-management actions.«[23] The Berlin Plus arrangements with NATO whereby the EU could draw on NATO assets were also an important step forward. Finally, the Union began its first actual military operations under ESDP (Concordia[24] and Artemis[25]) in April and June 2003 and is now in the process of establishing Battle Groups that could be used for UN-sponsored conflict prevention and peacekeeping activities.

Conditionality

Conditionality entails the EU linking perceived benefits to another state, such as financial assistance, trade concessions, co-operation agreements, political contacts or even membership, to the fulfillment of certain conditions. These normally relate to the protection of human and minority rights, the advancement of democratic principles and, in some cases, willingness to engage in regional co-operation. Negative conditionality would lead to the withholding or withdrawal of such benefits. Conditionality, however, is not an easy instrument to use. There are no scientific rules covering democracy and there remain different interpretations of human rights. In December 1991 Croatia was recognized even though it had not met the (Badinter) conditions[26] whilst recognition of Macedonia was withheld even though it had met the conditions. In 1992 the EU turned a blind eye as the military intervened after the first round of voting in the Algerian election. Indeed the

---

23 European Parliament. »European Parliament Fact Sheets.« (2006). http://www.europarl.europa.eu/facts/6_1_3_en.htm (accessed February 15, 2007).
24 The European Union launched a military operation (Concordia) in the Former Yugoslav Republic of Macedonia (FYROM) on 31 March 2003. The core aim of the operation , at the explicit request of the FYROM government, was to contribute further to a stable secure environment to allow the implementation of the August 2001 Ohrid Framework Agreement.
25 The European Union (EU) launched a Military Operation in the Democratic Republic of Congo (DRC) in June 2003. The operation was code-named *ARTEMIS*. The European military force worked in close co-ordination with the United Nations Mission in DRC (MONUC). It was aimed, inter alia, at contributing to the stabilization of the security conditions and the improvement of the humanitarian situation in Bunia.
26 The French constitutional judge, Robert Badinter, was asked by the EU in 1991 to produce a number of criteria on which to base recognition of states. These included control of territory, and respect for human and minority rights.

EU has never invoked the articles allowing for suspension in the Association Agreements with the Mediterranean partners if there is evidence of human rights abuses. Although the use of conditionality by the EU has increased steadily in recent years it is difficult to assess its effectiveness. A preliminary conclusion may be that the higher the EU carrot on offer, the greater the likelihood of EU pressure bringing results. There is little doubt that the carrot of EU membership has acted as an incentive to all central and eastern European countries to improve their democratic structures. There is also some evidence that geographical proximity to the EU is an important factor as is the size of the country. It is easier to influence Albania than China or Russia.

Recent Developments

In 2005-06 the EU engaged in a number of activities to try and ease conflict situations. One successful operation was the financial support for President Ahtisaari's peace negotiations in Aceh followed by an EU-led Monitoring Mission to monitor compliance with the Peace Agreement. At the same time the EU launched a package of long term measures to support the peace process including: reintegration of combatants and prisoners; reforms of the local administration and promoting the rule of law, human rights and democracy.

The EU also used the RRM to respond quickly to a political opening between Moldova and Ukraine and mobilised a monitoring mission to their border in late 2005. By helping prevent trafficking of people, smuggling of goods, proliferation of weapons and customs fraud it is hoped that the mission will contribute to a peaceful resolution of the Transnistrian conflict.

In the Democratic Republic of Congo the EU financed projects covering security sector reform, demobilisation and reintegration of former combatants and election monitoring. Additional projects covered community outreach projects in Kinshasa, judicial reform and sustainable governance. Another important element of EU conflict prevention activities of direct relevance to DRC is the focus on the role natural resources play in igniting and sustaining conflict. The EU has been a strong supporter of the Kimberley Process on conflict diamonds, and will take over the Chairmanship of the Process in 2007. The EU is also working on conflict timber and implementing the EU action plan for Forest Law Enforcement, Governance and Trade in a number of countries. The EU is also supporting better regional management of shared water resources and giving more attention to gender issues..

The European Neighbourhood Policy (ENP) also contains proposals in several of the Action Plans that relate to specific conflict prevention activities. Apart from the emphasis on governance issues, including security sector reform, there are detailed references to proposals which could contribute to conflict prevention in Moldova, the South Caucasus, and around the Mediterranean.

Conclusion

In the past four years there has been a step change in the EU's approach to conflict prevention and crisis management. It is more active and had developed significant new capabilities. The EU has had a number of modest achievements but paradoxically this has raised new questions on the limits of its role. Had Macedonia been devoid of any hope of future EU membership, could the EU still have been successful in its intervention? Is it likely that the institutional constraints inherent to the EU conflict prevention policy (pillarization, dispersal of bodies and complexity of decision making) condemn it to a more modest policy agenda, covering only crises in regional proximity and horizontal issues of a limited range. international crime, the diamond trade, drug trafficking, child soldiers? Or could it overcome these barriers and draw on its entire range of instruments - trade policy and trade and co-operation agreements, or tools derived from areas such as justice and home affairs, migration, social or environmental policy? A coherent preventive approach to conflict and crisis depends on three factors: a clear definition of objectives, capacity to act, and the political will to act

It is clear that mainstreaming – the process of establishing an in-house culture of prevention   has become more and more embedded in EU bodies. But it is not an easy task to assess its strengths and weaknesses at this stage. Although the EU has moved steadily into the field of conflict prevention there are a number of ways in which it might expand and enhance its role. There is a continuing need to develop ways in which conflict prevention is integrated, including gender sensitivity and awareness, more fully into existing programmes and policies; and to develop new frameworks through which women's conflict prevention and peace-building activities are supported. More sophisticated Conflict Impact Assessments could assist in the development of a strategic framework. The Union also needs to have clearer guidelines as regards financing for its external actions in order to avoid confusion and delays. It should also reflect more on how to maximize use of its growing array of Special Representatives.[27]

27 There are currently seven EU Special Representatives, with a wide range of responsibilities. The experience with Special Representatives has generally been positive but success depends considerably on the personality and political weight of the individual and his or her ability to gain the respect of diplomatic peers and the parties in the crisis area.

Perhaps the major obstacle facing the EU and other international actors is the lack of political will to take effective action at an early enough stage in the process. But what does 'political will' really entail? Much depends on the building of a political consensus to act as well as ensuring the necessary capabilities. There are sometimes differences between the 25 EU member states on the use of instruments to deal with potential conflicts and some may also have specific interests in a region. There are also the oft-cited rivalries between those responsible for Community instruments and those for CFSP/ESDP. It is thus not always easy to secure a common vision of the desired outcome of a crisis and there are limitations on the EU's use of its well-stocked toolbox. Another problem is the necessity of securing international support for EU objectives. Here the attitude of the US is often critical. Washington has sought to undermine EU efforts to establish the international criminal court (ICC) and has refused to sign up to several arms control agreements, including a code of conduct on small arms. The funding the EU devotes to external affairs overall and conflict prevention and crisis management in particular leaves much to be desired. Practitioners need to recognize that these constraints are likely to inhibit the EU's potential in conflict prevention for some considerable time.

References

Commission of the European Communities. »Communication from the Commission to the Council and the European Parliament: EU Strategy for Action on the Crisis in Human Resources for Health in Developing Countries.« (2005). http://eur-lex.europa.eu/LexUriServ/LexUriServ.do?uri=COM:2005:0642:FIN:EN:PDF (accessed Feburary 15, 2007).

Council of the European Union. »Civilian Capabilities Commitment Conference: Ministerial Declaration.« (November 22, 2004). http://ue.eu.int/ueDocs/cms_Data/docs/pressData/en/misc/82760.pdf (accessed February 15, 2007).

Council of the European Union. »Council Common Position 2004/85/CFSP of 26 January 2004 concerning conflict prevention, management and resolution in Africa and repealing Common Position 2001/374/CFSP.« (2004). http://www.eur-lex.europa.eu/LexUriServ/LexUriServ.do?uri=OJ:L:2004:021:0025:0029:EN:PDF (accessed February 15, 2007).

Council of the European Union. »Council Joint Action 2004/523/CFSP of 28 June 2004 on the European Union Rule of Law Mission in Georgia, EUJUST THEMIS.« (June 28, 2004). http://www.eur-lex.europa.eu/pri/en/oj/dat/2004/l_228/l_22820040629en00210024.pdf (accessed February 15, 2007).

Council of the European Union. »Council Joint Action on the European Union Police Mission in Kinshasa (DRC) regarding the Integrated Police Unit (EUPOL »KINSHASA«) (15070/04).« (December 6, 2004). http://register.consilium.europa.eu/pdf/en/04/st15/st15070.en04.pdf (accessed February 15, 2007).

Council of the European Union. »Presidency Conclusions.« (16-17 December, 2004). http://www.consilium.europa.eu/ueDocs/cms_Data/docs/pressData/en/ec/83201.pdf (accessed February 15, 2007).

DG External Relations. »European Commission Check-list for Root Causes of Conflict.« http://ec.europa.eu/comm/external_relations/cfsp/cpcm/cp/list.htm (accessed February 15, 2007).

DG External Relations. »One Year On: the Commission's Conflict Prevention Policy.« (2002). http://ec.europa.eu/comm/external_relations/cfsp/cpcm/cp/rep.htm (accessed February 15, 2007).

European Parliament. »European Parliament Fact Sheets.« (2006). http://www.europarl.europa.eu/facts/6_1_3_en.htm (accessed February 15, 2007).

Grevi, Giovanni, and Fraser Cameron. »Towards an EU Foreign Service.« *EPC Issue Paper*, no. 20 (2005).

Mawdsley, Jocelyn, and Gerrard Quille. »The EU Security Strategy: A new framework for ESDP and equipping the EU Rapid Report Reaction Force.« ISIS Report (December 2003). http://www.isis-europe.org/ftp/download/reportdefence.pdf (accessed February 15, 2007).

OECD. »Report of the OECD Development Assistance Committee (DAC) High Level Meeting.« (15-16 April 2004).

Rutten, Maartje. »From St. Malo to Nice: European defence, core documents.« ISS. Chaillot Papers no. 47. Brussels. (2001).

Solana, Javier. »European Security Strategy: A Secure Europe in a Better World.« ISS-EU. Paris. (2003). http://www.iss-eu.org/solana/solanae.pdf (accessed February 15, 2007).

Study, Group on Europe's Security Capabilities. »A Human Security Doctrine for Europe: The Barcelona Report of the Study Group on Europe's Security Capabilities.« Barcelona. (September 15, 2004). http://www.lse.ac.uk/Depts/global/Publications/HumanSecurityDoctrine.pdf (accessed February 15, 2007).

Tappert, Malin. »Developing Civilian Crisis Management Capabilities.« *European Security Review*, no. 20 (2006).

UK House of Lords European Union Committee. »EU Development Aid in Transition.« (April 29, 2004).

The EU's Preference for Prevention
– Burden or Boost for the Transatlantic Security Partnership?

Reinhardt Rummel

Abstract

The EU expresses its preference for prevention in many ways: in its declaratory policy, its operational structures, the resources attributed to the issue and the techniques developed to deal with violent conflict. Despite some achievements on the ground as well as some experience gathered, Brussels continues to operate intensively in a sphere of learning with only a few convincing practical show cases of success. Yet, there is hardly any alternative for Europe to try and substantiate its contribution to an effective global crisis management as well as a balanced transatlantic security partnership. While Europe's preventive efforts are somewhat recognized by large parts of the international community, this is still not the case in the US. A reassessment could be useful for both, Brussels and Washington.

Introduction

The very idea of prevention has been, and continues to be, at the heart of the European unification process itself. The EU's enlargement policy inherently represents a preventive security concept. This concept of »security via unification« remains, however, limited to member states of the Union or candidates thereof. Non-European neighboring states are not covered by this formula and the recent attempt to create security via a specific European Neighbourhood Policy (ENP) is a proof of this fact.[1] Likewise, to create security (in the sense of preventing violent conflict) outside of Europe and beyond the neighboring states of the EU requires to develop a concept of its own and to widen the EU's responsibility accordingly.

---

1 Fraser Cameron and Rosa Balfour, »The European Neighbourhood Policy as a conflict prevention tool,« *EPC Issue Paper*, no. 47 (June 2006). The study concludes that although the ENP was not designed with conflict prevention in mind, it has the potential to be an important instrument to stabilise and resolve conflicts in the wider Europe.

In this regard the EU's enlargement to 27 members, the initiated negotiations with Turkey and the membership perspective opened up to countries of the Western Balkans are significant. They all extend the EU toward a rather unstable neighborhood. This has helped EU policy makers to become more immediately aware of risks and dangers at the Union's new borders. They also helped – and this is the relevant factor here – to develop a better European understanding of instabilities that occur far outside the EU proper but may reach the Union in various ways. Such extended perspective has widened the scope of strategic thinking in EU capitals. As a consequence, the EU has raised its ambition of becoming a more global player in the international security arena.

Moreover, the EU continues to be confronted with a charged agenda of global challenges and key threats. The European institutions establish an ever larger watch-list of demanding cases that require analysis, assessment and action. The most urgent contingencies are treated with care but their root problems cannot be solved, neither quickly nor easily. While these challenges remain on the to-do list and absorb increasing resources, new conflicts emerge and threaten to escalate. If they are not dealt with the EU runs the risk of suffering from an even wider and more complex need to respond.

Earlier action seems to be one of the more efficient ways to cope with such a dynamic security environment. The experience of the EU shows that as long as a conflict remains small the Union is more likely in a position to handle it. Is, therefore, prevention the EU's logical strategic approach to international conflict? Can the concept help the European capitals to adapt to new types of security risks? Can the preventive approach thus be useful in renewing the transatlantic partnership or will it rather strain future European-American security cooperation?

The EU's preventive approach: a strategic asset?

For the EU the benefits of preventive policy are beyond doubt. If one can tackle more of the causes of a conflict early on, there is less of a basis for conflicting parties to justify violence, to prolong disputes, and to reject peace building efforts. Likewise, the earlier a conflict can be defused the less likely it becomes that it will slide into violence, spill over into neighboring regions, and affect European interests. As the European Security Strategy (ESS) suggests, the EU needs to be prepared and act before a crisis occurs: »Conflict prevention and threat prevention cannot start too early.«[2]

---

2 Council of the European Union. »A Secure Europe in a Better World: European Security Strategy.« Brussels. (12 December 2003), 7.

The EU is convinced that prevention is the right focus to master today's risks and threats. The question is, will it be paying for the EU to embark on such a preference? Does it, in fact, help to reduce cases of escalating violence around the world or will it simply serve the Europeans to unite around a commonly acceptable project – good for the record of unification, but without strategic weight? Despite these question marks, the EU seems to mean it: prevention is not just a fashionable trend, it is regarded as serious and fundamental. This impression can be gained from the Union's declaratory policy as well as from the resources attributed to conflict prevention including the operational structures built up and the techniques developed.[3]

1. Declaring prevention a priority

Before the »preventive engagement« appeared as one of the key notions of the ESS in December 2003 two earlier documents had been prepared, one by the European Commission and one by the Council of the European Union. The Commission's April 2001 Communication on Conflict Prevention[4] reviewed main instruments in this field and put forward recommendations for specific actions. The document sets out four main objectives:

- make more systematic and coordinated use of EU instruments to get at the root causes of conflict,
- improve the efficiency of actions targeting specific causes of conflict (the so-called »cross-cutting issues« such as trafficking in drugs or human beings, illicit trade of diamonds and small arms, competition over scarce water resources etc),
- improve EU capacity to react quickly to nascent conflicts,
- promote international co-operation with all partners of the EU (partner countries, NGOs, international organizations such as UN, G8, OSCE, ICRC as well as other regional organizations).

Building on this Communication and on its own experience and views in this field, the Swedish Presidency launched the initiative of developing a Programme for the Prevention of Violent Conflicts[5] endorsed by the June

---

3 For a more extensive analysis of the EU's conflict prevention policy, see Reinhardt Rummel, »Advancing the EU's conflict prevention policy,« in *Conflict Prevention and Human Security: G8, United Nations, and EU Governance*, ed. John J. Kirton and Radoslava N. Stefanova (Aldershot: Ashgate Publishing, 2004).
4 European Commission. »Communication on Conflict Prevention.« Brussels. (April 2001).
5 European Council. »Programme for the Prevention of Violent Conflicts.« Göteborg. (11-12 June 2001).

2001 European Council at Göteborg. The EU Programme has a policy approach very similar to the one of the Commission's Communication. It puts forward a number of guidelines for action in the EU's Common Foreign and Security Policy (CFSP) and the European Security and Defense Policy (ESDP). In particular, it calls for the setting up of clearer political priorities for preventive actions, notably through the identification of priority areas and regions at the outset of each Presidency and the adoption by the General Affairs Council of so-called preventive strategies. It also concentrates on co-operation with and through international organizations.

This EU Programme continues to be the main reference point today because the commitment the heads of state and governments had made was to »pursue conflict prevention as one of the main objectives of the EU's external relations.«[6] Many further documents issued by various European institutions reinvigorated the commitment to prevention. As reflected in the European Consensus on Development[7] adopted by the Council, the European Parliament and the Commission in November 2005, the EU will continue to develop comprehensive plans for countries where there is a significant danger of conflict, which should cover policies that may exacerbate or reduce the risk of conflict. It will maintain its support to conflict prevention and resolution and to peace building by addressing the root-causes of violent conflict, including poverty, degradation, exploitation and unequal distribution and access to land and natural resources, weak governance, human rights abuses and gender inequality. It will also promote dialogue, participation and reconciliation with a view to promoting peace and preventing outbreaks of violence.

By placing prevention at the centre of EU efforts to address violent conflict and other security threats and concerns, the ESS and the various EU conflict prevention programs would appear to be compatible and consistent. The rift among EU member states over the 2003 Iraq war did raise severe doubts about the solidity of this consistency, but other indicators (further enlargement of the EU membership; elaboration of the Constitutional treaty; growing number of EU crisis management operations) seem to have reconfirmed the basic choice for prevention of all EU countries. The preventive approach has even been extended to a wider dimension of security, including the proliferation of weapons of mass destruction (WMD), inter-

---

6 Council of the European Union. »Programme for the Prevention of Violent Conflicts.« Brussels. (June 2001), point 1/paragraph 5.
7 Council of the European Union. »Joint Statement by the Council and the representatives of the Governments of the Member States meeting within the Council, the European Parliament and the Commission on European Union Development Policy: 'The European Consensus'.« Brussels. (22 November 2005). www.dfid.gov.uk/eupresidency2005/eu-consensus-development.pdf (accessed February 18, 2007).

national terrorism, and organized crime as additional challenges. In these fields, prevention may have to get close to pre-emptive moves.

When the EU declares prevention as its primary approach to security, this does not mean that preventive policy is regarded as the only way to deal with violent conflict or with other security concerns. Brussels rather seeks to engage in critical countries and regions of the world early on before disputes there escalate into violence, before crime and war destroys the societies and the basis for living in these countries and before those instabilities risk to spill-over to Europe and impact upon vital European interests. The practical conclusion and the subsequent rationale of this analysis is to contribute to stability elsewhere and, thus, to keep threats away from the Union and to avoid more demanding and more costly European intervention later-on.

Despite its preference for such a proactive policy, the EU does not shy away from late intervention, if prevention has failed and armed conflict has occurred. When it comes to humanitarian aid and to post-war reconstruction, little reluctance seems to exist in Brussels. In fact, most of its short term operations are post-conflict cases designed to avoid a re-ignition of violence. The largest part of the Union's practical emphasis on post-conflict stabilization, though, is motivated by preventive calculations. In these cases, short term intervention is followed by structural long term engagement – each requiring a specific mix of resources.

Resources attributed to preventive activities

The EU originally started its conflict prevention policy in the mid-1990s on the basis and with the instruments of its supranational external relations and development aid. This required – particularly on part of the European Commission – to become more conflict sensitive and, in a sense, more »political« with regard to its seemingly »non-political« economic, financial and other instruments. Dormant as well as hot conflicts in many regions of the world became part of the Commission's conflict prevention agenda. Likewise, European soldiers and armed forces had to learn that their profession consists of more than defending their homeland. It also includes political and other non-military tasks. In fact, most of the operations belong to the field of non-traditional security rather than to traditional defense.

Commission-centered conflict prevention: European Commission officials, grown up with project work in rural development areas, skilled in supporting the creation of small and medium sized enterprises in developing countries and engaged in human rights and democracy building programs, learnt to include concerns of local, intra-state and regional conflict in their work.

Meanwhile, the EU is already heavily engaged in conflict prevention through its traditional means: development co-operation and external assistance, trade policy instruments, social and environmental policies, diplomatic instruments and political dialogue, co-operation with international partners and NGOs, as well as the new instruments in the field of crisis management.[8] Conflict sensitive assistance had also to be learnt by private non-governmental organizations who carry increasing responsibility in those failing states where the government is weak and can hardly act as a counterpart for support offers from outside.

A key question in these cases is, will traditional programs and projects reduce conflict in a given region or will it – unintentionally - stimulate existing disputes and hostilities further? For example: To support the creation of media for all ethnic groups in a country is fine and helps with non-discrimination of minorities, but it may lead to more separation of and animosities among cultural groups instead of mutual respect and cooperation. The European Commission quickly found out that most of its instruments did not allow for assistance in urgent cases. Development aid, even if provided with conflict-sensitivity as a goal, would take too much time to show results. Commission measures could help in the long-term and produce important structural impact, but would not be suitable for the short-term.

Council-centered conflict prevention: The other lesson learnt was that in some cases development measures would not be successful if applied on their own and that, in addition, forceful means were needed. In cases like Rwanda and the armed conflicts in the Western Balkans in the nineteen nineties, military and police forces would have been required early on in order to avoid genocide, mass killings, human rights abuses and turmoil. The UN had been asking for respective resources but the EU at the time was not prepared to respond to this request. This was the moment when the EU member states decided to launch the ESDP project in order to build up additional conflict prevention and crisis management instruments consisting of specific civilian, police and peacekeeping forces:

- Among the civilian forces you find experts of the rule of law and specialists of civil administration as well as emergency experts, altogether some 6000 personnel.
- Among the police forces the EU registers those specializing in internal security, the combat of organized crime or the securing of borders, altogether also some 6000 personnel.

---

8 European Commission. »Civilian instruments for EU crisis management.« Brussels. (April 2003).

- Among the peacekeeping forces one would find experts of security sector reform and small battle groups (thirteen, with some 1500 soldiers each) able to deter or stop local violence.

Thus, taken together, by now the EU has gathered a civilian and military reserve force for conflict prevention and peace support missions that can be launched on a very short notice. The ESS reads that »none of the new threats is purely military; nor can any be tackled by purely military means.«[9] Not only can violence not simply be countered with violence, the comparative advantage of Brussels is its variety of instruments and skills, military and non-military.[10]

The EU keeps saying that it has to use all of its instruments to deal preventively with the large range of concerns. This is the formula to express that civilian and military assets as well as those from the Community and from the member states shall be included. On paper, this is quite an impressive arsenal, in reality and for well-known reasons, the real amounts for operations are substantially smaller. Yet, the resources that have proven to be available are of a relevant size and quality. Only a few of the Union's resources are explicitly reserved for preventive operations, such as the financial Rapid Reaction Mechanism[11] which is managed by the Conflict Prevention Unit of the External Relations Directorate-General of the European Commission. Much more important funds are located with the various geographical and functional cooperation and development programs of the Union. These programs existed before, all of them have been reviewed to serve preventive goals.

The EU itself is not satisfied with the level of resources it so far has attributed to prevention: »While the EU capacity to deal with crisis situations has been strengthened in the past years, there continues to be a need to enhance the capacity to deal with tensions and insecurities as early as possible to prevent the outbreak of violence and address structural causes of conflict as well as ensuring that violent conflicts do not re-emerge in the post-conflict phase.«[12] The EU and particularly the European Commission and the European Parliament admit that its efforts have been suboptimal. There-

---

9 »A Secure Europe in a Better World: European Security Strategy.« 7.
10 European Council. »Action Plan for Civilian Aspects of ESDP: Adopted by the European Council.« (17-18 June 2004). http://ue.eu.int/ueDocs/cms_Data/docs/pressData/en/misc/81344.pdf (accessed February 18, 2007).
11 European Commission. »Rapid Reaction Mechanism (RRM): Overview.« http://ec.europa.eu/comm/external_relations/cfsp/cpcm/rrm/index.htm (accessed November 18, 2006).
12 European Commission. »Conflict Prevention Overview.« http://ec.europa.eu/comm/external_relations/cfsp/cpcm/cp.htm (accessed November 18, 2006).

fore, new and more differentiated programs like the Stability Instrument are launched. [13]

Operational structures for preventive policies

Taking the period since 2001 as a proof, the EU can claim that it has introduced the idea of conflict prevention both on the European and on the national level of the member states. Certainly, due to its institutional deficits, not all of the EU's agencies have been fully engaged in the enterprise. Likewise, some member states have been late in mainstreaming conflict prevention while others have been forerunners. The Scandinavian countries and the Netherlands are among the most advanced groups with the United Kingdom (UK) taking the lead.[14] With its Conflict Prevention Pools London has managed to overcome some of the long-standing structural hurdles and to exploit the synergies of integrating military, developmental and aid related capacities.[15] The EU is grappling with such a holistic approach. With the respective elements of the Constitutional Treaty pending (European Foreign Minister, European External Action Service), the EU has at least started to develop a few substructures that will facilitate a comprehensive conflict prevention policy.

Early warning and analysis competences are indispensable for conflict prevention and they need to be followed up by planning and implementation bodies.[16] All of them have gradually emerged on the EU level even though scattered among the European Commission and the Council. The Commission is pretty strong regarding fact-finding and analysis given its functional and geographic experts both in Brussels and in the field. The Commission's delegations have been included in the network of information gathering and assessment that the EU has built up in parallel with the creation of the

13 »The European Consensus on Development adopted by the Council on 22 November 2005 and welcomed by the European Council on 15-16 December 2005 states that the Community, within the respective competences of its institutions, will develop a comprehensive prevention approach to state fragility, conflict, natural disasters and other types of crises to which goal this Instrument should contribute.« Council of the European Union. »Draft Regulation of the European Parliament and the Council establishing an Instrument for Stability (7443/2/06 Rev2).« Brussels. (3 May 2006), 3.
14 Nicolaus Rockberger, *Scandinavia and ESDP: Are the Nordic States Holding Back?*, *Strategische Analysen* (Wien: Büro für Sicherheitspolitik, November 2005).
15 Greg Austin, *Evaluation of the Conflict Prevention Pools*, DFID EVSUM EV647 (London: Review of the UK Government approach to conflict prevention, 2005).
16 Annika S. Hansen, *Against all Odds: The Evolution of Planning for ESDP Operations*, Study 10/06 of the Center for International Peace Operations (Berlin: September 2006).

ESDP. In 2001, the Commission has established within its Directorate-General for External Relations its own department for conflict prevention including assessment capacities and expert input from outside (Conflict Prevention Network, Conflict Prevention Partners[17]). With its huge EuropeAid agency the EU can draw from a well of experience regarding programs and projects of development policy.

This richness of internal and external expertise coming from the European Commission can be channeled to and merged with the knowledge that is generated and processed within the new set of bodies in the Council that deal with peace support operations and the prevention of conflict. Among them is the Policy Planning and Early Warning Unit, a small but powerful unit, established in 1999, located in the Secretariat of the Council and headed by the EU foreign policy chief, Javier Solana. The task of this unit is to support Solana with analyses, assessments and options for action. There is also support from the Situation and Operation Centre. With the creation of the Political and Security Committee (PSC) the member states in 2001 introduced a new decision making body on questions of conflict prevention and crisis management. The PSC which is a permanent body on political directors level responsible also for the political guidance of ESDP operations is supported by a Military Committee and Staff as well as a Committee for the civilian aspects of security.

This institutional fabric has not yet been fully developed into a homogenous set of bodies dealing in a coordinated way with European foreign and security policy including conflict prevention. Rather it is still burdened with institutional division and competition as well as lack of cooperation and trust. To mention a few problems: the Commission is held at arms length by the Council regarding military affairs; the foreign policy departments in the Council Secretariat are rivaled by the Policy Planning and Early Warning Unit; member states do not fully share their intelligence. These deficiencies and several others reduce the coherence and efficiency of the EU's conflict prevention activities, a disadvantage which can hardly be balanced by the well advanced European set of tools for conflict prevention.

Techniques developed to deal with violent conflict

There is no worldwide accepted textbook (no *Clausewitz*) for the art of conflict prevention. The UN (DPKO, UNDP, Peacebuilding Commission) have

---

17 The Conflict Prevention Network (1997-2001) and the Conflict Prevention Partners (since 2005) have been projects supported by the European Commission to assist the European institutions with analysis and recommendations based on practical and academic expertise from EU member states and beyond.

been conceptual forerunners. Over the last ten years, the EU has devoted some of its energies to developing skills and best practices. From early warning schemes to conflict impact assessment the EU has elaborated a methodology of prevention policy with the list of conflict indicators built into the country strategy papers as well as on a regional level.[18]

Taken together, the tools of EU prevention policy aim at more than just proactive policy. They aim at a sustained, comprehensive and inclusive process of building up failed or failing states. This requires a certain level of stability at any given critical moment during this process and it requires tackling the root causes of violence in a given conflict-prone society.[19] The EU tries to address trigger factors and basic reasons for dispute alike. Consequently, it is trying to mainstream conflict prevention in all of the EU's policies and instruments. As an example, the Country Strategy Papers (CSPs) play an important part in ensuring a coordinated approach to conflict prevention. This means that when CSPs are prepared, risk factors are systematically checked. For that purpose, the European Commission's geographical services are using conflict indicators. Those indicators look at issues such as the balance of political and economic power, the control of security forces, the ethnic composition of the government for ethnically-divided countries, the potential degradation of environmental resources and so forth.

On the basis of this conflict analysis, attention is then drawn to the CSPs and to those underlying causes of conflict that external aid or other EU instruments should target. The Conflict Prevention Guidelines[20] provide useful information on how to integrate a conflict perspective and design new programs for conflict prevention. At the level of the programming of assistance, the Commission is putting emphasis on the strengthening of the rule of law, support to democratic institutions, the development of civil society and the reform of the security sector. This approach is key to supplanting conflict or preventing its re-emergence and is also consistent with the Commission's emphasis on institution building as part of development policy priorities. In post-conflict situations, peace-building initiatives are essential for ensuring lasting peace. When the situation allows, the Commission is gradually engaging in rehabilitation activities as well as demobilization, disarmament and reintegration programs (so-called DDR programs).

---

18 Javier Nino-Pérez, »EU instruments for conflict prevention,« in *Conflict Prevention: Is the European Union Ready?*, ed. Jan Wouters and Vincent Kronenberger (Brussels: 2004).
19 See the Check-list for Root Causes of »Conflict Prevention Overview.« Of the European Commission.
20 See the Conflict Prevention Guidelines in »Conflict Prevention Overview.« of the European Commission.

With all of these new instruments, institutions and concepts the EU has found a fruitful field of action even though the impact is ambivalent. When focusing on the *output* of the EU its record regarding conflict prevention is impressive. The EU has developed a growing machinery for conflict prevention and crisis management that is about to reach a relevant size. If used skillfully, this potential is of strategic weight in international security. The direct *outcome* of preventive policies of the EU is less obvious, except in a few low-profile cases, as repeatedly mentioned by European officials such as the High Representative, Solana, or the Commissioner on External Relations, Ferrero-Waldner. They would mention the former Yugoslav Republic of Macedonia or Montenegro or Ukraine where in the past the EU has helped in critical moments to defuse local inter-ethnic dispute. As more recent cases of successful prevention, they would list the Aceh Monitoring Mission, the Border Assistance Mission to Moldova and Ukraine, and the various missions to the Democratic Republic of Congo.[21] But too many conflicts from the EU's watch-list remain unresolved and require long term stabilization efforts, military intervention, or both.

The EU's preventive policy: a sphere of learning

Since the key documents and action plans on conflict prevention were launched in 2001/2003, all of the EU's institutions have been trying to integrate the concept into their activities. They have all had the same experience: while conflict prevention is a plausible strategy, it seems to be one of the hardest to implement. Despite some achievements on the ground, Brussels continues to operate pretty much in a sphere of learning with only a few convincing practical show cases of success.[22]

Yet, as the annual Presidency report on conflict prevention rightly claims, »substantive progress towards a more effective approach by the EU towards preventing violent conflict« has been made.[23] This is visible in a more active approach to conflict-related issues, in the development of applicable capabilities, in the more effective integration of instruments, and in the way in which the EU is building partnerships with other actors of con-

---

21 Benita Ferrero-Waldner, »Conflict Prevention: looking to the future,« Speech held at the Conflict Prevention Partnership dialogue on 'Five years after Göteborg: the European Union and its conflict prevention potential', Brussels, 12 September 2006.
22 Reinhardt Rummel, »The EU's Involvement in Conflict Prevention: Strategy and Practice,« in *Conflict Prevention: Is the European Union Ready?*, ed. Jan Wouters and Vincent Kronenberger (Brussels: 2004).
23 Committee for Civilian Aspects of Crisis Management. »Draft report to the European Council on EU activities in the framework of prevention, including implementation of the EU Programme for the Prevention of Violent Conflicts (10051/04).« Brussels. (2 June 2004), 13.

flict prevention. On the other hand, the same report admits that many important practical fields remain underdeveloped such as the follow-up to early warning issues, the link between security and development, a comprehensive approach to fragile states, and the strengthening of a rule-based international order.

Since the ESDP has started its operations in January 2003 some twenty missions have been launched. Most of the missions are small (10 to 100 experts) or medium-sized (several thousand), some of them have been completed, others are ongoing and have been enriched by long-term EU programs. All of the missions have a preventive goal, some more explicit than others. In almost all cases the EU is faced with a situation where crisis and abrupt transformation has occurred before. In these cases Brussels applies so-called post-conflict conflict prevention in order to help to make sure that violence does not escalate again. The EU's preventive activities have taken place mainly in its immediate neighborhood, like the Western Balkans, the Caucasus and Africa, but also started to move toward the Middle East and Southeast Asia.

As can be experienced from those activities, successful conflict prevention has to be designed in a timely and tailor-made fashion which requires not only sophisticated instruments but also sensitive orchestration with local as well as international partners. In most cases, prevention is a demanding and costly enterprise. After several years of intervention practice, the EU is still learning, but a few guidelines have emerged which can and should be shared with other conflict prevention actors in the world such as the US and which furthermore can and should be improved together. Four constituting guidelines for prevention are characterized in the following.

Prevention driven by an integrated approach

The EU used to be regarded as a civilian power lacking the will and the potential to use military force in international relations. Surprisingly, there was no collective EU military force worth mentioning until quite recently. This has changed with the build-up of the ESDP since 1999 and its peacekeeping force (including battle groups). The EU has autonomous and specialized forces to offer when asked to assist with a UN stabilization mission, as in the case of the Lebanon peace force, or when called on by a regional organization to support a preventive operation, such as the request from the African Union (AU) to the EU for logistical support in the Darfur peacekeeping case.

The EU has taken over the lead of international low-level military stabilization operations in the Balkans and in Africa (Concordia, Artemis). Combined civilian and military operations are the next phase of the EU's new policy of intervention as realized in the case of Bosnia-Herzegovina (Althea, EUPM). Since 2005 a small civil-military planning cell has been build up in Brussels which allows for more such integrated operations. Integrated planning and autonomous operation of the EU without support from NATO and national headquarters is certainly a learning process for all parties involved.

Some of the EU member states have pioneered this approach, especially the UK with its Africa Prevention Pool and the Netherlands with a respective device have been combining foreign, development and defense policies in an integrated and targeted manner. The civil-military cell is the conceptual nucleus of a broadly based EU security policy. It is a test field and an experiment to learn about an innovative approach to conflict management by overcoming the traditional narrowness of either the military or the non-military instruments and decision-makers. In Brussels, prevention has become part of a civil-military process of assessment and implementation. It is no longer regarded as a civilian domain.[24] There is an inherent tendency to assign a secondary role and status to civilian measures. Experience of the EU shows that this is not justified. The requirement is to look at both the civilian and the military resources and to determine their respective function within a broad approach rather than integrating the civilian assistance strategies into military doctrine.

More importantly, the EU still grapples with the well-known structural problems of integrating short-term and long-term measures within one strategic move. Linking Community instruments with CFSP/ESDP assets remain an institutional and procedural challenge. Applying the full spectrum of instruments for crisis management and conflict prevention, including diplomatic, political, military and civilian, trade and development activities requires more fundamental reforms of the political system of the EU (and, in fact, of the member states) than has been ventured into so far. The emphasis of the EU on holistic strategies for support in post-conflict situations which focuses on meeting both the immediate security needs and the long-term reform of the security sector is in line with the broad civil-military approach which ESDP is designed to represent.

There are still some who feel that civilian operations by the Council are a duplication of work already done by the Commission or – worse – who regard the Council's international policies of lower impact given that it cannot match the weight and expertise of the Commission. Council representatives claim the opposite, namely that their missions are likely to make a greater impact on the ground: »Using manpower directly generated by member states produces – in co-operation with the Commission – a higher degree of commitment and ownership than do the more arms-length pro-

---

24 Agnieszka Nowak, ed., *Civilian crisis management: the EU way*, *Chaillot Paper 90* (Paris: EU Institute for Security Studies, June 2006).

grams that the Commission organizes.«[25] A future European Foreign Minister would be in a position to choose from both sources of expertise and instruments and to launch initiatives either on the Commission or the Council track. The Parliament via its instruments (budget, hearings, reports) may have to play an important part in the process of choosing the option that promises to achieve the best result.

With regard to civilian capabilities, the EU's experience shows that a more substantial process of commitment, preparation and training is required to reach the level of professionalism as achieved within the military component of ESDP.[26] Emphasizing the civilian component of ESDP will allow the EU to make better use of the military in conflict prevention as well as in post-war stabilization efforts. One needs to learn from the rich experience in the Balkans (including the March 2004 riots in Kosovo) that a more tailor-made and differentiated response capability should be organized for escalation situations, for transition situations from war to peace, and for situations of fragile peace, where re-ignition of fighting may occur or where riots may lead to the spread of violence.

A similar case can be made regarding a civilian reserve for the purpose of dealing more specifically with so-called human security. In their report, commissioned by the High Representative for CFSP, Mary Kaldor and her team focus on basic insecurities caused by gross violations of human rights within regional conflicts and failed states.[27] These violations are the source of new global threats including international terrorism, WMD, and organized crime. The report suggests a Human Security Response Force being composed of 15 000 men and women, most of them being civilian. While this force seems to be largely identical to the civilian component of ESDP, it would also contain a Human Security Volunteer Service.

Could one contemplate such a service together with the US? Or is there too much fear that such a connection would reduce the EU's image and confidence which it has built up over time? Is the US able and willing to apply an integrated approach to conflict prevention?

---

25 Nicole Gnesotto, ed., *EU Security and Defense Policy: The first five years (1999-2004)* (Paris: EU Institute for Security Studies, August 2004), 192.
26 See the Civilian Capabilities Commitment Conferences of 22 November 2004 as well as of 13 November 2006 including their Ministerial Declarations.
27 Group on Europe's Security Capabilities Study. »A Human Security Doctrine for Europe: The Barcelona Report of the Study Group on Europe's Security Capabilities.« Barcelona. (September 15, 2004) http://www.lse.ac.uk/Depts/global/Publications/HumanSecurityDoctrine.pdf (accessed February 15, 2007).

Prevention achieved by a sustained effort

A good knowledge of the dynamics of a respective conflict is needed in order to determine the right moment for intervention and to calculate the mixture of instruments to be applied now and later during the evolving conflict cycle. Very often, the international community is waiting far too long before moving from warning to action. Quite often one finds help for the short term, but long-term engagement on a high level with a broad spectrum of instruments is hard to get. The lesson to be learned here is to concentrate on, and include from the start, all stages of a conflict: the escalation phase, the crisis phase and the period of post-war reconstruction and rehabilitation.

For the time being, most resources of the EU's security efforts still flow into the reconstruction phase. Brussels has tried, but did not achieve, to shift the emphasis toward preventing the escalation of international conflicts. Likewise, it has been demanding to think in more comprehensive terms and plan on exit strategies before starting an operation. There is still a tendency in Brussels to »visit« conflicts rather than tackling the root causes and engaging long term. This is even more so with regard to horizontal issues such as terrorism, organized crime and the proliferation of WMD and their root causes. EU officials, like the Irish Foreign Minister, have specified the lesson: »Addressing poverty, exclusion, denial of basic human rights, gender inequalities, discrimination against minorities and the effects of pandemics are fundamental to what we see as a practical strategy aimed at the root causes of conflict.«[28]

Operation Artemis, launched in Ituri Province, Democratic Republic of Congo (DRC), in June 2003, helped to stabilize security conditions and improve the humanitarian situation in support of UNSC Res. 1484 which authorized the deployment of an interim emergency multi-national force until September 2003. The European military force worked in close co-ordination with the UN Mission in DRC (MONUC). In parallel, the use of development instruments has been helping to consolidate security in DRC and to work for good governance and rule of law as essential factors for the peace process. In the meantime, the EU is providing assistance to the setting up of an integrated Police Unit in Kinshasa. This is intended to help to reinforce the internal security apparatus and to ensure the protection of State institutions. Likewise the EU's military mission to temporarily reinforce MONUC from July to November 2006 was following a request of the UN Secretary General. The goal and the hope of these operations were to con-

---

28 Tom Kitt, »Opening Statement ath the European Regional Conference on the Role of Civil Society in the Prevention of Armed Conflict,« Dublin, 31 March 2004, 3. The Irish Foreign Secretary, Tom Kitt, made this statement during Ireland's EU presidency.

tribute to a critical sector at a critical juncture in order to prevent further destabilization of the country and to facilitate general and presidential elections and the building of a democratic government.

Such cases demonstrate the sustained manner in which the EU tries to operate. Does the US place the same emphasis on sustainability of preventive measures? Could the EU and the US agree on complementing and re-inforcing each other in this regard?

Prevention via the multilateral approach

Conflict prevention is too big a task for a single state or organization. Only effective co-ordination with international partners can help achieving that goal. The EU experienced that the multilateral approach delivers the best results. Therefore, all its conflict prevention and crisis management missions are open for other partners to join in. Also, Brussels will not enter another country, not even with civilian experts, if it has not been invited by the government and the conflicting parties concerned, and if the action takes place within a UN mandate.

A lesson that the EU is about to learn in this context regards the need for more reliable international regimes in order to extend sets of international standards as a universal reference for dealing with specific countries or regions of instability. Thus, the EU has been supporting the creation of further international institutions (such as ICC), of regimes (such as in the field of Human Rights), and conventions (such as on small arms or on DDR). As an example, the EU3 (UK, France, Germany) in 2005 and 2006 negotiated with Teheran to try and turn the Iranian leaders away from any plan of developing nuclear weapons. A major reference for those negotiations are the Nuclear Proliferation Treaty (NPT) and the International Atomic Energy Organization (IAEO).

The EU support for peacekeeping operations in Africa which can be made possible through the European Development Fund (EDF) is to be regarded as a growing field of prevention. Bringing the parties together in the Darfur crisis and the North-South Sudan war displays a mediation effort that the EU would not have attempted a few years ago, but it also demonstrates the limitations of influence. In a different approach, the EU can contribute funding to African-led operations such as in Burundi, Liberia and the Ivory Coast aimed at securing stability and implementing peace agreements, but in none of these cases will the outcome of these efforts be under the EU's command as repeated events in Ivory Coast and in Sudan have demonstrated.

Despite those consequences, co-operation with relevant regional and international organizations should move ahead. It makes multilateral engagement more effective. In this regard it is encouraging that the EU finally reached out to the UN, a front runner in matters of conflict prevention. The EU-UN Joint Declaration of September 2003 sets out a framework for closer co-operation in conflict prevention and crisis management, especially in the areas of planning, training, communication and best practices. An EC-Communication on EU/UN-relations aims to consolidate international support behind UN objectives and to develop strategic partnerships with specialized agencies. Such a partnership has already been concluded with UNDP covering conflict prevention. High-level meetings have started and steering committees have been established to co-ordinate joint work. EU officials participate in DPKO assessment missions. European Commission services have launched a desk-to-desk dialogue (including early warning information), with integrated UN teams, on five countries. Many more of these exercises in cross-fertilization are likely to be launched.

There are many international initiatives, in which the European Commission participates actively.[29] For example, over the past few years, the EU has taken a leading role in the Kimberley Process, the international trade regime that aims at eliminating 'conflict diamonds' from the legitimate diamond trade. The EU has been a participant in the Kimberley Process Certification Scheme since its inception (representing all EU member states), and has implemented the Scheme through a Council Regulation applicable in all the member states. The EU has been instrumental in setting up an effective monitoring system within the Scheme, and chairs the Kimberley Process in 2007. The EU has also made some headway on conflict timber and forest governance through the EU Action Plan for Forest Law Enforcement, Governance and Trade (FLEGT), and through specific projects in this area. The Action Plan seeks to reinforce the push for good governance in developing countries and linking this with legal instruments and leverage offered by the EU internal market, including the introduction of a licensing scheme to ensure that only legal timber enters the EU.

This small list of activities is indicative for the type of international regime building that enables effective conflict prevention. For instance, EU policy concerning support for the implementation of the Ottawa Treaty banning landmines and the disposal and control of the flow of small arms and light weapons (SALW) is one of the key elements already identified in the Göteborg Programme for Conflict Prevention. Likewise, the EU Mine Action is an example of an effective and visible instrument in conflict prevention. The multi-annual strategy for 2005-2007 called for a »Zero Victim Target« to fight antipersonnel landmines worldwide. The adoption of the strategy coincided with the first Review Conference of the Mine Ban Treaty

---

29 The record in the next few paragraphs follows the description given by the respective services of the European Commission. The full account is to found under: »Rapid Reaction Mechanism (RRM): Overview.«

in Nairobi and is a clear response to the Nairobi Action Plan which asks for a mapping of the remaining challenges posed by landmines.

In accordance with the commitment of the European Union to promoting an effective multilateral system with the United Nations at its core, the EU has devoted particular attention to the activity of the High Level Panel on Threats, Challenges and Change. The UN High Level Panel can be seen to reinforce the approach to security taken by the EU, which emphasizes the need to prioritize preventive action and to address both new and old threats. It also acknowledges the primary role to be played by the UN on peace and security issues whilst underlining the need for institutional reforms. The European Union supports all efforts which have as an objective the well-organized and coordinated engagement of the international community in addressing conflict situations and post-conflict peacebuilding. Thus, the EU has been actively supporting the establishment of a Peacebuilding Commission as a way of addressing the institutional gap in the transition period between the end of armed conflict and the resumption of sustainable development activities.

The EU continues holding »desk-to-desk« dialogues with integrated UN teams as well as regular contact with the UN Frame Work Team in the area of conflict prevention.[30] The EU's Action Plan on Civilian ESDP adopted in June 2004 particularly identified »conflict prevention and resolution in Africa« as an area with considerable potential for cooperation with the UN.[31] Cooperation has also been started with ASEAN when the EU in 2005 contributed to a peaceful settlement of the dispute between the government of Indonesia and the claims of its Aceh Province. The interesting innovation in this case was that ASEAN countries joined the EU's intervention with civilian experts and military advisers of their own. No crisis management and conflict prevention procedures had been prepared for such a contingency but the EU's initiative triggered some further thinking of both the people in the ASEAN Secretariat as well as the member states. On the side of the EU, new ground was entered as well in this case given that the European Commission and the Council Secretariat developed and implemented an integrated overall intervention strategy.[32]

---

30 United Nations General Assembly. »Progress report on the prevention of armed conflict.« New York. (16 July 2006).
31 »Action Plan for Civilian Aspects of ESDP: Adopted by the European Council.« 2.
32 »The Council noted with satisfaction that the EU successfully mobilized its different instruments in a comprehensive manner to support the peace process in Aceh. The Council will consider how further to strengthen the EU's relations with Indonesia and with the wider ASEAN region.« (Council of the European Union. »Council conclusions on Indonesia/Aceh.« Brussels. (27 February 2006). http://www.consilium.europa.eu/uedocs/cmsUpload/Indonesia-Aceh_6652-EN.pdf (accessed February 18, 2007).

The EU has a general priority for multilateralism and a particular interest in multilateral prevention. The US is more selective in its approach with a strong preference for unilateralism. These European-American differences have caused problems for transatlantic security cooperation and will continue to do so in the future.

Prevention via inclusiveness and ownership

The EU has learnt – also in the case of the Aceh Monitoring Mission - that no external actor is capable of achieving a sustainable success in prevention if parties to the conflict are left out of the process, if regional powers are not included, and if security partners are held aloof from the preventive efforts. Any conflict prevention approach needs to be inclusive and accountable. It need to be kept in mind that external assistance cannot replace internal ownership of the conflict and of its solution. The EU's intervention in local conflicts as well as regional crises will always remain insufficient in the sense that the indigenous parties to the conflict finally need to settle their own disputes. External mediators and conflict prevention specialists can provide crucial assistance but in the end most likely lack the cultural sophistication and the local credibility that are indispensable for overcoming disputes.

Another problem concerns the cultural differences. The EU makes sure that it is not imposing any improvement measures and systemic change against the will of the state in question. Brussels is intervening only by invitation from the representatives of the receiving states and on the basis of a written agreement that specifies the terms for both sides and refers to the respective framework agreement with the UN or the relevant resolution of the Security Council. Yet, the EU's operations do not remain without tension and resistance in the receiving country because the measures taken by EU intervention personnel often ask for a radical change of behavior on the ground with respect to corruption, partisanship, internal order, the rule of law, and the use of force. To strengthen the EU's consistency and credibility Brussels has developed a code of conduct that guides any of its external interventions. As the dispute over the so-called Mohammed caricatures at the beginning of 2006 demonstrated, a specific EU mission may risk opposition and rejection if the people of a conflict region feel humiliated by the behavior of the Union in general (in this case the Danish media).

The EU is also well aware of the fact that its resources and capacities are limited in size. It gradually comes to the understanding that it will have to shift parts of its activity and resources from intervention to assistance in order to help with local capacity building for peaceful conflict resolution. As an example, the EU is supporting the creation and the activities of the new

Peace and Security Commission of the AU particularly regarding prevention with funds from its Peace Facility for Africa.[33] In order to do so, the EU had to break a taboo among its development policy community and allow funds from the EDF to be »diverted« to security tasks including the use of military forces for peace support operations. Additionally, programming activities to support activities of three African regional organizations (ECOWAS, IGAD, ECCAS) were launched in 2004. These programs are aimed at increasing the capabilities of those three sub-continental organizations in areas such as early warning, policy planning, political mediation, cease-fire monitoring and electoral observation.[34]

The ownership approach has become more prominent, not only in the EU's relations with Africa but also with the Middle East. Conflict prevention elements have been mainstreamed into the Barcelona Process and the Euro-Mediterranean Partnership (EMP). They follow the guidelines worked out by the Conflict Prevention Network (CPN): Ownership refers to the process by which the responsibility for peace-building, conflict prevention, management and resolution primarily rests with the people concerned. One need to add that the role of the EU -where it shares people's objectives and aspirations - is to empower people to live up to their responsibility in peace-building and related activities. Thus, from the point of view of the EU, ownership fully applies to conflict prevention. To the extent that conflict prevention is contemplated by the EMP, it is subject to the application of the principles of ownership and co-ownership.[35]

While the advantage of the ownership approach seems to be obvious, one of its downsides is also clear: the EU will have less influence on the launch and the outcome of interventions undertaken by these regional organizations.

When focusing on the output of the EU, its record regarding conflict prevention capacity building is impressive. Capacity building for conflict prevention must be taken as a sign of determination on the European side. As mentioned above there are rich assets but also stunning deficiencies, particularly the lack of institutional coherence. The US does not have those coordination problems but it has more reluctance than the EU to realize inclusiveness and ownership. In this respect, policy guidelines on both sides of

---

33 Council of the European Union. »Use by the Commission of EUR 7,7 million from the Community budget to finance the African Peace Facility.« Brussels. (26 January 2006).
34 Niels von Keyserlingk and Simone Kopfmüller, »Conflict Early Warning Systems: Lessons Learned from Establishing a Conflict Early Warning and Response Mechanism (CEWARN) in the Horn of Africa,« *GTZ Report* (October 2006).
35 Roberto Aliboni et al., *Ownership and Co-ownership in Conflict Prevention in the Framework of the Euro-Mediterranean Partnership, EuroMeSCo* (Lisbon: Swedish Institute of Foreign Affairs (SIIA, Stockholm) & Regional Center on Conflict Prevention Jordan Institute of Diplomacy (RCCP, Amman), October 2006).

the Atlantic will differ to a considerable extent. Washington and Brussels will need to neutralize their discord first before they can contemplate coordinated or even joint preventive missions.

Prevention as a Transatlantic concept: options for renewal

Conflict prevention, conflict solution, crisis management and post-conflict reconstruction are relatively new areas of concern for Brussels. These are subjects where the EU as a political entity is less developed as compared to the trade, economic and monetary sectors but where the Union is becoming more and more active and ambitious since a number of years, particularly since the end of the East-West confrontation in the 1990s and the dangers of international terrorism after 9/11.

Ten years after the inception of CFSP and five years after the launch of the ESDP project the EU is significantly better prepared for coping with external security than before. Relatively speaking, the build up of CFSP/ESDP and its practical achievements are still in the embryonic stages, but, as such, they are a success story and at present it seems that there is more to come. The EU has become a more political and a more serious actor, also when it comes to conflict prevention, not least thanks to the possibility of using force. As Robert Cooper (Council Secretariat) rightly claims: »When a country or an organization contemplates the deployment of forces, the atmosphere changes, ambiguity ceases to be an option, decisions go up to the highest levels; the risks, costs and commitment are of a different order from those involved in other actions – making statements or giving aid.«[36]

On this new level the EU is keen to share international responsibility. This is not to be seen as an altruistic move, it rather represents an enlightened understanding of assuring European interest, economic and otherwise. In the European understanding, the EU has to assist with the solving of international conflict and with the prevention of armed conflict in order to allow for fair competition and cooperative relations which are preconditions of economic and cultural exchange in all corners of the world.

For this purpose European-American security cooperation continues to play a role. But how does the EU's conflict prevention policy fit into the transatlantic relationship? Can transatlantic relations profit from a more forceful European security partner? Will NATO be extended to prevention and would this presuppose a change of the US position on prevention? Finally, will both sides of the Atlantic use the preventive approach to learn how to improve their policy toward violent conflict in the world?

---

36 Gnesotto, ed., *EU Security and Defense Policy: The first five years (1999-2004)*, 192.

Change within the US approach?

Is the US a major partner for the EU's conflict prevention policy or is Brussels simply going it alone? Unlike in the EU, the situation in the US is not characterized by a lack of strategic thinking and a deficit in institutional coherence. The US has the expertise and knowledge of conflict prevention in abundance, but the present Bush Administration is not making use of it. Neoconservative ideology does not allow for mainstreaming conflict prevention into the US strategic approach. The fear being that the US may loose some of its status as the dominant superpower. Washington has been reluctant whenever the UN or the G8 had wanted to go beyond the praising of prevention as an important approach to international security concerns.[37] On the other hand, the US President has endorsed some preventive capacity building (such as in the State Department). The US has been quite active in developing homeland security which helps to prevent attacks on the US, on American citizens, and assets in the world. There is less interest on the US side in dealing with the root causes of such danger. First, because these causes are hard to identify, and second, because it would require a self-criticism that does not seem to be appropriate for a superpower.

Yet, both on the level of public discussion and official policy changes are detectable since 2004 when both major fronts of American engagement in Afghanistan and in Iraq started to raise doubts regarding the approach taken and the results achieved. It may well be, as James Dobbins claims, that the US has a tendency to engage in the biggest and the hardest conflicts as compared to other international actors such as the EU and the UN.[38] But this should not be an excuse for neglecting the lesson that nation-building and democracy is in any case a »process, not an event« (Condoleeza Rice). Experienced US Officials have come to the conclusion that Washington needs to switch from media-oriented quick fixes to long-term engagement even if this is more costly financially and politically: »We are interested in the enduring change ... not rapid change that might provide instant gratification of our hopes but that destabilizes the country and creates more problems than we had before.«[39] The UN and other partners are regarded as essential

---

37 Reinhardt Rummel, »The European Union's politico-diplomatic contribution to the prevention of ethno-national conflict,« in *Preventing conflict in the post-communist world*, ed. Abraham Chayes and Antonia Chayes (Washington DC: Brookings Institution, 1996).
38 James Dobbins, »The UN's Role in Nation building: From Belgian Congo to Iraq,« *Survival* 46, no. 4 (Winter 2004-05).
39 Zalmay Khalilzad, »How to Nation-Build: Ten Lessons from Afghanistan,« *The National Interest*, no. 80 (Summer 2005): 22.

by these experts, because they help with acceptance, credibility, burden sharing and endurance.[40]

The other lesson that some academics and officials in the US have started to address is the question of the right mix and proportion of instruments of intervention: »The stark reality is that the United States today does not possess the right mix of skills and capabilities to stabilize and re-build nations.«[41] Other deplore that this deficit is not just a matter of skillful policy but seems to be a structural problem given that the American soft power is declining.[42] In a first move against »short-termism« and narrowness of approach, in July 2004 Bush had ordered the creation of an Office of the Coordinator for Reconstruction and Stabilization (S/CRS) that not only allows for the mobilization of various civilian instruments of nation-building but also has the task of teaming up with the military in the field. The director of S/CRS, Carlos Pascual, is convinced that with this agency and its $125 million annual budget the Bush Administration has drawn the right conclusion of the past and has improved conflict prevention and peace consolidation in substantial ways.[43]

Thus, prevention is certainly not an unknown category to the US. It seems, however, that the concept is less widely shared and used as it is the case in the EU. A superpower can rely on its military force and political determination to satisfy its security needs at a later stage of the cycle of conflict. Regarding threats deriving from a dangerous combination of risks such as terrorism, weapons of mass destruction, and non-state actors, however, even Washington makes sure to act early on and, in some cases, to prepare for pre-emptive intervention. A pre-emptive strike is not part of the official Brussels strategic doctrine, but, if such a critical situation were to arise, one would most likely see an unorthodox move of some of the affected EU member states, certainly France and the UK. The EU declares it as unlikely that such an extreme situation will emerge soon and, therefore, concentrates on the long list of more likely conflict cases and horizontal security challenges.

For the American government, extreme situations such as weapons of mass destruction in the hands of a dictator, who is determined to launch them on the US or on one of its close allies, are the most likely and the most important cases to prepare for. Washington, therefore, invests in its capacity

---

40 Simon Chesterman, »Bush, the United Nations, and Nation-Building,« *Survival* 47, no. 1 (Spring 2004); Stuart Eizenstat, John Edward Porter, and Jeremy Weinstein, »Rebuilding Weak States,« *Foreign Affairs* 84, no. 1 (January/February 2005).
41 Brent Scowcroft and Samuel R. Berger, »In the Wake of War: Getting Serious about Nation-Building,« *The National Interest*, no. 81 (Fall 2005): 50.
42 Joshua Kurlandtzick, »The Decline of American Soft Power,« *Current History* (December 2005).
43 Stephen D. Krasner and Carlos Pascual, »Adressing State Failure,« *Foreign Affairs* 84, no. 4 (July/August 2005).

to either deter or pre-empt these dangers or to shield against them. Naturally, its investment in military operations is much higher than in civilian aid programs. Civilian aid is still huge in absolute terms – roughly half of the EU's amount. More important than the size is the fact that the American Official Development Aid (ODA) seems to serve preventive imperatives less stringently than is the case in the EU. Most of the substantial EU programs that target regional instability and state failure such as TACIS, MEDA and CARDS are guided by preventive imperatives and goals.[44]

If one connects the recent developments at the two ends of the Atlantic its seems obvious that civilian and military means have been identified and partly also combined for preventive tasks and challenges of systemic change and stabilization regarding failing and failed states as well as war-torn countries. This fact leads to a logic conclusion concerning the reform of the Atlantic Alliance: »There is the general point that both the United States and Europe will have to base their future security cooperation on a mix of hard and soft power instruments. The United States, Canada and the European Allies must bring assets from both categories to the transatlantic cooperation table.«[45] If NATO were to extend toward prevention on the basis of a broad mix of instruments, Washington would have to recognize the civilian assets of the EU.

Recognizing the EU's contribution

In the 1990s, the EU had no real foreign policy involvement, except in trade. Now it has missions all over the world, troops in a few hotspots and its individual members are somewhat more wary of going out on a limb than they used to be – though of course they still act unilaterally when they really want.

CFSP/ESDP is the last field of importance that the Europeans have now dared to include in their union-building process. It has been launched in time before the reunification of Western and Eastern Europe and before reaching the borders of more unstable regions in the Wider Middle East and beyond. It has been regarded as a test for the new member states' dedication to a full-fledged Union. As further EU enlargements are drawing to an end, Brussels makes sure that all ingredients of an international actor are on board and are accepted. The mission of an ever closer union is not completed but is continued with CFSP/ESDP and all of the member states are in principle participating in it. The agenda of transatlantic relations can be

---

44 Gustav Lindstrom, *EU-US burden sharing: who does what?*, Chaillot Paper 82 (Paris: EU Institute for Strategic Studies, September 2005), 61f.
45 Stanley R. Sloan, »Building a New Foundation for Transatlantic Relations,« *Euro-Future* (Summer 2006): 15.

widened: all subjects, except collective defense, can now be treated by the European side. Will the US recognize this fact?

It is true – the EU has a preference for soft power and the mild assertion of influence including modest military forces. What it does not have is an active and coherent global policy - because its members do not want it. As a result, it has only moderate influence in international diplomacy and within transatlantic relations. The US does not regard the EU as a strategic partner for international crisis management and conflict prevention. Washington is rating Brussels' integrated capacities low and not worthwhile to form a relevant part of the American strategic thinking. It also rates the broad European approach to security concerns as little attractive. In other words, the EU's most promising efforts in the security sector are not appreciated – to the extend as they could – within the transatlantic context. Too bad that during a period at the beginning of the century when the EU started to develop some strategic structures of its own it lacked the like-minded (or at least an open-minded) American counterpart.

There are other features of the EU's approach to security which are not recognized as essential within the transatlantic setting. As mentioned in the previous section, for policy-makers in Brussels an efficient approach to conflict prevention requires sustainability to last during all phases of a crisis (from pre-conflict, through intervention to post-conflict phases). The EU also praises the importance of multilateral institutions and regimes and appreciates inclusiveness and ownership. If they cannot achieve cooperation in these fields, Brussels and Washington could at least compare notes on the subject. This could be part of a joint learning process.

That the EU's preventive efforts are less recognized than they could be is also due to a rather poor advertising of the European activities and achievements. Brussels could do more to communicate the European message to the world and particularly to the US. »The Union's voice is, at best, garbled; at worst, it is not heard at all.«[46] It is true that the forum for strong public diplomacy in the security field is practically non-existent given that NATO has been downgraded and appears to be less suitable functionally while the EU-US Dialog has hardly reached beyond the level of mutual information. See the February 2005 suggestion of the former German Chancellor, Schröder, to revive NATO as the place where the core transatlantic discourse on security should take place, a proposal that was reconfirmed by Angelika Merkel in 2006.

Moreover, as a relatively rich and stable region, the Union feels the obligation to contribute its share to worldwide security. It is not the aim to become a military superpower next to the US, but rather to develop as a diversified force of influence with a broad interface regarding the increased

---

46 Dov Lynch, *Communicating Europe to the world: what public diplomacy for the EU?*, *EPC Working Paper 21* (Brussels: 2005).

variety and scope of security tasks. Brussels wants to project its concept of peace, progress and stability on the basis of specific European skills adapted to the nature of today's and tomorrow's security tasks. The EU cannot help that in the American perception the European ambition is either neglected or regarded as competitive.

Joint learning process in prevention policy

Yet, there is hardly any alternative for Europe to try and substantiate its contribution to an effective global conflict prevention and crisis management as well as a balanced transatlantic security partnership. Europe cannot find an alternative to the US as a partner for effective prevention. Neither Russia, India nor even China are like-minded enough to understand the sophistication of prevention and to provide the tools for it.

The EU has discovered early on that intervention for preventive purposes even when mandated by the UN and agreed upon with the conflicting parties usually includes two types of challenges. Over time, the intervention becomes quite burdensome and the receiving parties grow intolerant as the intervention drags on and implies painful changes on their part. The intervention may be a soft and sensitive one but its consequences could, after all, be quite far reaching – including regime change. The EU knows that it could not in all cases carry the physical and political burden of too many interventions at a time and that it also needs to distribute the heat that it may receive from the parties involved.

Its capacity building for conflict prevention can be taken as a sign of determination on the European side which cannot be detected on the same scale in Washington. Europe has impressive assets but it also has stunning deficiencies. Part of the deficiencies is that some of the EU's most promising tools (such as the civilian elements of ESDP) lack the experience to serve within a European operation, let alone in a joint transatlantic mission. Roughly speaking, the EU's comparative advantage continues to be in the richness of its instruments. A major disadvantage is that these instruments are scattered and hard to be coordinated given the institutional and legal set up of the EU. The US approach to international security seems to suffer less under those symptoms. Its main flaw maybe an over-reliance on America's military strength, a tendency toward unilateral action, and a lack of standing power.

Could a wider cooperation between the EU and the US be contemplated with the aim of joint intervention for conflict prevention purposes in critical regions of the world such as the Middle East, Central Asia and Africa? In all of these regions, both the EU and the US have a substantial interest (among others regarding economics). A high degree of stability in those regions is of utmost interest to all of them in order to allow for economic progress, prosperity and, finally, internal stability to be ensured at home. In all of these critical regions Europe and America are increasingly harsh economic competitors. The build-up of mutual trust could be a by-product of their joint conflict prevention activities.

The EU's prevention policy has not been invented to serve transatlantic relations; rather could the potential of transatlantic relations be seen as making conflict prevention work. While Europe's preventive efforts are somewhat recognized by large parts of the international community, this is still not the case in the US. A reassessment could be useful for both, Brussels and Washington.

Conclusion

Can the comprehensive approach to security be made fruitful within transatlantic relations? A few scenarios may help with the answer, because depending on the appreciation of a comprehensive response to security, Washington and Brussels would shape the transatlantic relationship in different ways. They would appear to be either alternative or selective partners and they would lean toward either joint leadership or mutual respect.

Alternative Powers: If the US is not opening up to the broader approach, the EU will be perceived as an alternative power. It may not have the weight of countervailing the US, and such an aim may not be pursued, but it may provide the world with an option. Transatlantic relations would either be downgraded or be badly needed to manage the differences.

Selective Partners: If partnership for security (beyond NATO) is recognized as essential on both sides of the Atlantic, the EU and the US are the preferred choice to cooperate despite their mutual deficiencies. Both, however, do not see the need for such collective action. The EU is about to build up »partnerships« with a large list of candidates starting with the UN and ending with Afghanistan,[47] all of them champions of a comprehensive approach. Russia, Brazil, China and India may be needed for limited cooperation, even if there are concerns regarding their approach to security. The US is clearly inclined to get its friends together (mission determines coalition).

Joint Leadership: US and EU agree on a broad approach to security given that they recognize their relative strength as well as their respective weakness. Together they would lead the battle against international terrorism, organized crime and the proliferation of WMD. They would also shape the response to failed states, conflict, escalation and war.

---

47 Council of the European Union. »EU-Afghanistan Joint Declaration Committing to a New EU-Afghan Partnership.« Strasbourg. (16 November 2005).

Mutual Respect: Knowing that the basic defense cooperation between American and European nations remains within the Atlantic Alliance, the US and the EU would continue to cooperate outside of NATO case by case and subject by subject according to their perceived need. They may establish a list of common projects which ties them closer in some distinctive fields but leaves others open for autonomous engagement.

Of the four scenarios, Joint Leadership is the most unlikely to happen any time soon, while Mutual Respect may well become the prime future. Alternative Powers and Selective Partners seem to dominate the presence as well as the transition to the next stage.

References

Aliboni, Roberto, et al. *Ownership and Co-ownership in Conflict Prevention in the Framework of the Euro-Mediterranean Partnership, EuroMeSCo.* Lisbon: Swedish Institute of Foreign Affairs (SIIA, Stockholm) & Regional Center on Conflict Prevention Jordan Institute of Diplomacy (RCCP, Amman), October 2006.

Austin, Greg. *Evaluation of the Conflict Prevention Pools, DFID EVSUM EV647.* London: Review of the UK Government approach to conflict prevention, 2005.

Cameron, Fraser, and Rosa Balfour. »The European Neighbourhood Policy as a conflict prevention tool.« *EPC Issue Paper*, no. 47 (June 2006).

Chesterman, Simon. »Bush, the United Nations, and Nation-Building.« *Survival* 47, no. 1 (Spring 2004): 101-116.

Committee for Civilian Aspects of Crisis Management. »Draft report to the European Council on EU activities in the framework of prevention, including implementation of the EU Programme for the Prevention of Violent Conflicts (10051/04).« Brussels. (2 June 2004).

Council of the European Union. »Council conclusions on Indonesia/Aceh.« Brussels. (27 February 2006). http://www.consilium.europa.eu/uedocs/cmsUpload/Indonesia-Aceh_6652-EN.pdf (accessed February 18, 2007).

Council of the European Union. »Draft Regulation of the European Parliament and the Council establishing an Instrument for Stability (7443/2/06 Rev2).« Brussels. (3 May 2006).

Council of the European Union. »EU-Afghanistan Joint Declaration Committing to a New EU-Afghan Partnership.« Strasbourg. (16 November 2005).

Council of the European Union. »Joint Statement by the Council and the representatives of the Governments of the Member States meeting within the Council, the European Parliament and the Commission on European Union Development Policy: 'The European Consensus'.« Brussels. (22 November 2005). www.dfid.gov.uk/eupresidency 2005/eu-consensus-development.pdf (accessed February 18, 2007).

Council of the European Union. »Programme for the Prevention of Violent Conflicts.« Brussels. (June 2001).

Council of the European Union. »A Secure Europe in a Better World: European Security Strategy.« Brussels. (12 December 2003).

Council of the European Union. »Use by the Commission of EUR 7,7 million from the Community budget to finance the African Peace Facility.« Brussels. (26 January 2006).

Dobbins, James. »The UN's Role in Nation building: From Belgian Congo to Iraq.« *Survival* 46, no. 4 (Winter 2004-05): 81-102.

Eizenstat, Stuart, John Edward Porter, and Jeremy Weinstein. »Rebuilding Weak States.« *Foreign Affairs* 84, no. 1 (January/February 2005): 134-146.

European Commission. »Civilian instruments for EU crisis management.« Brussels. (April 2003).

European Commission. »Communication on Conflict Prevention.« Brussels. (April 2001).

European Commission. »Conflict Prevention Overview.« http://ec.europa.eu/comm/external_relations/cfsp/cpcm/cp.htm (accessed November 18, 2006).

European Commission. »Rapid Reaction Mechanism (RRM): Overview.« http://ec.europa.eu/comm/external_relations/cfsp/cpcm/rrm/index.htm (accessed November 18, 2006).

European Council. »Action Plan for Civilian Aspects of ESDP: Adopted by the European Council.« (17-18 June 2004). http://ue.eu.int/ueDocs/cms_Data/docs/pressData/en/misc/81344.pdf (accessed February 18, 2007).

European Council. »Programme for the Prevention of Violent Conflicts.« Göteborg. (11-12 June 2001).

Ferrero-Waldner, Benita. »Conflict Prevention: looking to the future.« Speech held at the Conflict Prevention Partnership dialogue on 'Five years after Göteborg: the European Union and its conflict prevention potential'. Brussels, 12 September 2006.

Gnesotto, Nicole, ed. *EU Security and Defense Policy: The first five years (1999-2004)*. Paris: EU Institute for Security Studies, August 2004.

Hansen, Annika S. *Against all Odds: The Evolution of Planning for ESDP Operations, Study 10/06 of the Center for International Peace Operations*. Berlin, September 2006.

Keyserlingk, Niels von, and Simone Kopfmüller. »Conflict Early Warning Systems: Lessons Learned from Establishing a Conflict Early Warning and Response Mechanism (CEWARN) in the Horn of Africa.« *GTZ Report* (October 2006).

Khalilzad, Zalmay. »How to Nation-Build: Ten Lessons from Afghanistan.« *The National Interest*, no. 80 (Summer 2005): 19-27.

Kitt, Tom. »Opening Statement ath the European Regional Conference on the Role of Civil Society in the Prevention of Armed Conflict.« Dublin, 31 March 2004.

Krasner, Stephen D., and Carlos Pascual. »Adressing State Failure.« *Foreign Affairs* 84, no. 4 (July/August 2005): 153-163.

Kurlandtzick, Joshua. »The Decline of American Soft Power.« *Current History* (December 2005): 419-424.

Lindstrom, Gustav. *EU-US burden sharing: who does what?, Chaillot Paper 82*. Paris: EU Institute for Strategic Studies, September 2005.

Lynch, Dov. *Communicating Europe to the world: what public diplomacy for the EU?, EPC Working Paper 21*. Brussels, 2005.

Nino-Pérez, Javier. »EU instruments for conflict prevention.« In *Conflict Prevention: Is the European Union Ready?*, edited by Jan Wouters and Vincent Kronenberger. Brussels, 2004, 93-117.

Nowak, Agnieszka, ed. *Civilian crisis management: the EU way, Chaillot Paper 90*. Paris: EU Institute for Security Studies, June 2006.

Rockberger, Nicolaus. *Scandinavia and ESDP: Are the Nordic States Holding Back?*, *Strategische Analysen*. Wien: Büro für Sicherheitspolitik, November 2005.

Rummel, Reinhardt. »Advancing the EU's conflict prevention policy.« In *Conflict Prevention and Human Security: G8, United Nations, and EU Governance*, edited by John J. Kirton and Radoslava N. Stefanova. Aldershot: Ashgate Publishing, 2004, 113-139.

–. »The EU's Involvement in Conflict Prevention: Strategy and Practice.« In *Conflict Prevention: Is the European Union Ready?*, edited by Jan Wouters and Vincent Kronenberger. Brussels, 2004, 67-92.

–. »The European Union's politico-diplomatic contribution to the prevention of ethnonational conflict.« In *Preventing conflict in the post-communist world*, edited by Abraham Chayes and Antonia Chayes. Washington DC: Brookings Institution, 1996, 197-235.

Scowcroft, Brent, and Samuel R. Berger. »In the Wake of War: Getting Serious about Nation-Building.« *The National Interest*, no. 81 (Fall 2005): 49-53.

Sloan, Stanley R. »Building a New Foundation for Transatlantic Relations.« *EuroFuture* (Summer 2006).

Study, Group on Europe's Security Capabilities. »A Human Security Doctrine for Europe: The Barcelona Report of the Study Group on Europe's Security Capabilities.« Barcelona. (September 15, 2004). http://www.lse.ac.uk/Depts/global/Publications/HumanSecurityDoctrine.pdf (accessed February 15, 2007).

United Nations General Assembly. »Progress report on the prevention of armed conflict.« New York. (16 July 2006).

The United States' Perspective on Conflict Prevention

Alice Ackermann

Introduction

While conflict prevention, also referred to as crisis prevention, constitutes a crucial concept in the consolidation of a common European Foreign and Security policy for addressing violent conflicts, particularly on the inter-ethnic and inter-communal levels, in the United States there is less attention given to conflict prevention as a proactive foreign policy instrument. This is not to say that there is no interest in conflict prevention as a strategy for international conflict management. In fact, there have been a few instances in which the United States, together with its European allies, seriously discussed and even cooperated in preventive action, particularly during the 1990s. However, while Europe has moved more in the direction of developing both its military and civilian capacity for conflict/crisis prevention, in the United States preventive action, in the context of preventing the outbreak of armed confrontations as well as its reoccurrence, has remained largely confined to the rhetorical realm, or has been at best been applied sporadically, on an ad hoc basis, and in a geographically-limited manner.

The failure to prevent the 1994 genocide in Rwanda on the one hand, but Washington's active involvement in preventive action in the former Yugoslav Republic of Macedonia throughout the 1990s on the other hand, best exemplifies this inconsistency in applying the principles of conflict prevention in practice. Moreover, the United States' shares with Europe some of the constraints when it comes to implementing conflict prevention which explains the spotty track record in acting preventively on both sides of the Atlantic. These constraints have been expressed as follows: the persistence of the rhetoric-implementation gap; the lack of political will and of tangible commitments as well as resources to interfere in the early phases of a conflict; the problems associated with the legitimacy and legality of international involvement in the internal affairs of states, even in the face of grave human rights violations; and other intervention-inhibiting factors such as the inherent nature and complexity of violent conflicts, especially on an inter-ethnic/inter-communal level, the dilemma of determining proper exit strategies, the use of limited force to stop extreme violent acts such as ethnic cleansing or genocide, or problems associated with civilian-military co-operation in preventive interventions that have a military component.[1]

Moreover, the Bush administration has done little to further advance the debate on conflict prevention, neither nationally nor on the transatlantic level or to co-operate with its European allies on transforming conflict/crisis prevention into a viable international strategy for conflict management, especially in the aftermath of already substantial policy debates in the UN and other international organizations on the necessity of preventing violent conflicts before they escalate into large-scale armed conflicts. Indeed, the Bush administration initially threw out conflict prevention altogether as it was commonly understood by Europeans and Americans alike – that is, preventing the emergence of conflict in its early phases as well as its reoccurrence – with the adoption of the 2002 National Security Strategy and its focus on pre-emption and preventive war. Although different in definition and substance, pre-emption and prevention came to be viewed as synonymous and interchangeable concepts. This development was neither conducive to moving conflict prevention as a policy tool and policy objective to the forefront of international action nor to the transatlantic relationship in general which in the early years of the Bush administration became increasingly strained over Washington's explicitly-self-proclaimed right of pre-emption and its new doctrine of preventive war which was put into practice with the United States invasion of Iraq.[2]

This chapter will explore the United States' perspective on conflict/crisis prevention in the framework of the above-mentioned parameters. In order to shed some light on where we stand at present in the debate on preventive action, this chapter will first focus on the emergence of conflict prevention as a new idea in the international system during the late 1980s. Largely promoted in the United Nations in the late 1980s and early 1990s, conflict prevention surfaced not only as a powerful idea but has become a newly emergent norm, which still awaits its acceptance and institutionalization by the international community.[3] Second, the chapter will examine U.S. thinking on and engagement in preventive action, particularly during the time frame in which international debates on conflict prevention flourished. Lastly, the chapter will provide an analysis on how the revitalization of the transatlantic discourse on conflict prevention could also benefit the wider U.S.-European relationship.

1 See here also, Alice Ackermann, »The Idea and Practice of Conflict Prevention,« *Journal of Peace Research* 40, no. 3 (2003).
2 See here also, Alice Ackermann, »The Changing Transatlantic Relationship: A Socio-Cultural Approach,« *International Politics* 40, no. 1 (2003).
3 For an in-depth discussion on the emergence of conflict prevention as a new norms, see Alice Ackermann, »The Prevention of Armed Conflicts as an Emerging Norm in International Conflict Management: The OSCE and the UN as Norm Leaders,« *Peace and Conflict Studies* 10, no. 1 (2003).

Thinking And Acting Globally on Conflict Prevention

The manifestation of conflict prevention as a newly emerging norm in the global arena is a rather recent phenomenon. In the early 1990s, the international climate increasingly permitted new thinking on the management and the prevention of violent conflicts which was followed in several cases by concrete actions which also had the support of the United States. Much of this new thinking was essential given the end of the Cold War, the changing political developments, and the need to manage the new security environment. At the forefront of rethinking the international community's approach to conflict prevention and crisis management was first of all the United Nations. It was largely to the credit of the United Nations that we have been witnessing revolutionary changes when it comes to new normative thinking with respect to the responsibility to protect and humanitarian interventions, limited sovereignty in the face of grave human rights violations, and post-conflict peace-building and conflict prevention.

Although the idea that armed conflict should be prevented underlies the Charter of the United Nations, conflict prevention during the Cold War referred primarily to preventing a superpower confrontation by avoiding a spillover of regional or localized conflicts. It was not until the late 1980s that the United Nations introduced a number of official statements and documents that ushered in a decade and more of thinking differently about how to respond systematically to violent conflicts in their early, non-escalatory stage. This was particularly relevant for intra-state conflicts, as they came to be identified as the most dominant pattern of armed conflict in the post-Cold War era.

It is not surprising then that the late 1980s and 1990s saw a flurry of UN-sponsored initiatives, which culminated in a series of forward-looking reports, intended to raise international awareness and advocacy for preventive action. The first of such critical initiatives was the 1992 UN Report, *An Agenda for Peace*, which was disseminated widely in the international public domain. At its core was the notion that conflict prevention needed to entail not only preventive diplomacy but also post-conflict peace-building measures. Thus, peacekeeping was no longer considered sufficient to deal with armed conflicts in the post-Cold War era. What was needed was a more extensive and comprehensive array of instruments and activities that could cover all stages of the conflict cycle. *An Agenda for Peace* suggested wide-ranging preventive practices such as confidence-building measures, fact-finding missions, strengthening early warning networks, and preventive deployment.⁴ The last two preventive tools were rather novel concepts, of which the latter, that is, preventive deployment, was implemented in a European conflict zone, with the active participation of the United States.

While conflict prevention as an international approach to armed conflicts remained a vague and mostly rhetorical concept, the *Agenda for Peace* was crucial as an outline for thinking differently about responses to crises and armed confrontations. Its implementation was first tried when the UN Security Council authorized a preventive deployment mission in the former Yugoslav Republic of Macedonia in December 1992, the first ever in the history of the United Nations.

Under UN Secretary-General Kofi Annan, the discourse on conflict prevention was further fine-tuned with calls for the creation of a culture of prevention rather than a culture of reaction. The 2001 UN Report on the »Prevention of Armed Conflict« was the most comprehensive assessment of the UN's capacity toward preventive action. Since then, the United Nations has remained engaged in the discourse, but has also widened its agenda to include other issue related to conflict prevention, such as the responsibility to protect and intervention for humanitarian reasons, as well as the importance of post-conflict peace-building, as a way toward long-term prevention.⁵ The importance given in particular to preventing the reoccurrence of conflicts also led to the establishment of a UN Peacebuilding Commission in December 2005. More over, there is a general perception that the UN has been crucial for the reduction of violent conflicts, primarily because of its emphasis on preventive diplomacy and peacemaking activities.

Conflict Prevention in Practice: Macedonia yes, Rwanda no.

Despite this new rhetoric on conflict prevention which had found much resonance in the UN forum, neither Europe nor the United States managed to move the debate from rhetoric to concrete preventive action when the first major armed conflict occurred on Europe's soil in the early 1990s. One of the first major crisis which Washington, along with its NATO partners, had to manage in the »new world order« was the breakup of Yugoslavia and the ensuing armed confrontations that engulfed the country in 1991. Often largely seen through the prisms of the reemergence of ancient hatreds, the violent conflicts in Yugoslavia, first in Slovenia, then in Croatia, and also

4 Boutros Boutros-Ghali. »Agenda for Peace: PReventive Diplomacy, Peacemaking and Peacekeeping.« United Nations. Report of the Secretary General, adopted by the Summit Meeting of the Security Council, on 31 January 1992. A/47/277-S/24111. New York – United Nations. (1992).
5 For a detailed analysis on the UN's role in the advocacy of conflict prevention, see Ackermann, »The Prevention of Armed Conflicts,« 8-10.

in Bosnia and Herzegovina, made painfully aware the failure to respond preventively, both on the side of the European Union and the United Nations, but also the United States.

In particular, many of the early warning signs, including the outcome of the 1990 Yugoslav elections, the inability of the republics to adopt a common strategy to resolve the chronic economic crisis, and the failure among the republics' leaders to find a compromise solution, were not given the necessary attention. By the time Europe and the United States became involved diplomatically to prevent large-scale violence, polarization of the conflicting groups had already advanced, making mediation difficult. Although both the EU and the then CSCE participated in conflict mediation, after they failed to prevent the initial outbreak of hostilities, the containment as well as the resolution of the conflict was impeded by transatlantic and intra-European differences about appropriate steps as to how to end the war. Moreover, opportunities for prevention were missed because of a lack of leadership and a strong political and military commitment on the part of the United States in the earlier phases of the conflict.[6]

In particular, the United States did not view its involvement in the early faces as crucial for its national interest and thus maintained that the management of the conflict be best left to its European partners and to European regional institutions. Moreover, because of the widely-held perceptions in Europe and the United States that regional institutions, in particular the EU, had failed to avert the crisis but also because of the unwillingness of the United States to assume a leadership role for containing and settling the war at an early stage, the United Nations was called in to fill the void. As European pressures grew on the United States to take on a more asserted role following the carnage in Bosnia and Herzegovina, the United States resorted to the use of NATO air power to end hostilities. However, by that time, the war in Bosnia and Herzegovina had already changed territorial circumstances on the ground, not to speak of the death toll and refugee situation that the armed conflict had unleashed. Thus, the United States shared with its European counterparts the responsibility for not taken preventive action early enough to avoid the large-scale destruction and human suffering witnessed in many parts of the former Yugoslavia.

The failure of the first Bush Administration to be not more actively, and preventively, involved in the early phases of the conflict in Yugoslavia, however, also eventually resulted in major policy adjustments. In 1992, the United States supported CSCE-initiated preventive action to place observers within areas of Serbia – Sandjak, Vojvodina, and Kosovo, with an integrated office in Belgrade, to monitor the human rights situation. However,

---

6 The literature on the disintegration of the former Yugoslavia is extensive. For a reference, see here for example, Susan L. Woodward, *Balkan Tragedy: Chaos and Dissolution After the Cold War* (Washington, DC: Brookings Institution Press, 1995).

the most pronounced preventive action came also in 1992, when the CSCE participating States, including the United States, agreed to the establishment of a long-term monitor mission in the former Yugoslav Republic of Macedonia, the so-called Spillover Monitor Mission to Skopje. It had its headquarters in Skopje but with additional posts in Tetovo and Kumanovo, both of them close to the border of Serbia. The first head of mission was the United States Ambassador Robert Frowick, who negotiated in September 1992 the »Articles of Understanding,« with the Macedonia authorities which gave the Mission an explicitly »preventive mandate.«

The Clinton Administration, which came to office in 1993, took a more assertive role toward conflict prevention in its foreign policy, although it also maintained the rather ad hoc manner of its predecessor. Nevertheless, crisis prevention formed the centre of the Clinton Administration's first National Security Strategy in 1994 of »engagement and enlargement« which outlined that preventive diplomacy was to be supported by democratization, development assistance, diplomatic mediation, and overseas military presence. The Clinton Administration also made conflict prevention part of its African Crisis Initiative and the Greater Horn of Africa Initiative. Washington's emphasis on conflict prevention also led to the establishment of the Secretary of State's Preventive Action Initiative in 1994, which was intended to be an »integral mechanism to improve political and diplomatic anticipation of violence.«[7]

Already during his confirmation hearings in early 1993, Secretary of State Warren Christopher outlined U.S. foreign policy objectives voicing his opinion that the United States should move in the direction of preventing rather than reacting to conflicts which is what crisis management entails. In his hearings, he stated the following:

We can't afford to careen from crisis to crisis. We must have a new diplomacy that can anticipate and prevent crisis…We cannot foresee every crisis in the world, but I strongly believe that preventive diplomacy can free us to devote more time and effort to facing problems here at home. I would very much like to be known as someone who is involved in preventive diplomacy. Crisis management, of course, is important, and I'm sure there will have to be a lot of crisis management. But I'd rather very much like to be crisis preventer.[8]

This rhetoric was soon put into practice when the administration took the decision to participate in the UN preventive force which had been deployed to the former Yugoslav Republic of Macedonia in January 1993, following a UN Security Council Resolution in December 1992. The United States'

---

7 Carnegie Commission on Preventing Deadly Conflicts, *Preventing Deadly Conflicts: Final Report* (New York: Carnegie Cooperation, 1997), 108.
8 Cited in Alice Ackermann, *Making Peace Prevail: Preventing Violent Conflict in Macedonia* (Syracuse: Syracuse University Press, 2000), 117.

decision to participate in the UN preventive force was announced on 11 June 1993 by Secretary of State Christopher at the North Atlantic Cooperation Council in Athens where concerns over the war in Yugoslavia and its possible spillover potential dominated much of the discussions.

The deployment of U.S. troops to expand the already existing so-called UNPROFOR contingent in Macedonia, later renamed the UN Preventive Deployment Mission (UNPREDEP) was authorized by the Security Council on 18 June 1993. The first U.S. contingent arrived on 12 July to assume duties, and U.S. personnel was increased from 300 to 550 soldiers in April 1994, eventually leading to an entire UN preventive force of nearly 1000 soldiers, with the other half provided by Northern European countries. On 23 December 1994, President Clinton evaluated the importance of U.S. forces to the former Yugoslav Republic of Macedonia in his fourth report to Congress, noting the U.S. commitment toward conflict resolution in the former Yugoslavia. However, at the same time, the President made it also clear that this was only to be a temporary and a limited engagement on the part of the United States, with the objective to »limit the conflict« and to prevent a Balkan-wide spillover.[9]

However, there was no such engagement to preventive action when it came to regions beyond Europe. In the 1994 genocide that took place in Rwanda, the United Nations could neither gather sufficient backing from countries like the United States, nor could it get a mandate to expand existing troops on the ground and to intervene in the protection of civilians when the killings began in April 1994. In fact there was considerable reluctance on the part of the United States to engage militarily, largely because of the killings of U.S- and other peacekeeping troops in Somali in 1993. Because of domestic politics, and in the aftermath of Somalia, the United States lacked the political will to assume a leading role in initiating any collective intervention that could have stopped the genocide. In fact, on 5 May 1994, a Presidential Decision Directive stipulated that any U.S participation in UN peacekeeping forces could only be forthcoming if there was a threat to international peace, that any such threat was in the U.S. interest, that there were acceptable risks, that there was an exit strategy, and that there was an adequate command and control structure. Coming in the aftermath of the Somalia crisis, the directive was certainly intended to keep the United States from getting entangled in conflicts that were geographically removed and not within the sphere of its national interests. Moreover, there was sig-

---

9 For a discussion of U.S participation in UNPREDEP, see Ackermann, *Making Peace Prevail*, 116-118. For a in-depth analysis on UNPREDEP see also, Henry S. Sokalski, *An Ounce of Prevention: Macedonia and the UN Experience in Preventive Diplomacy* (Washington DC: Institute of Peace Press, 2003).

nificant reluctance to assist the UN in bailing out from operations when they proved to be unsuccessful, as had been the case in Somalia.[10]

In 1998, both the UN Secretary General as well as President Clinton acknowledged that they could have acted earlier to prevent the genocide in Rwanda. While the Clinton Administration had as one of its foreign policy objectives to assist Africa in fighting instability, conflicts, and economic degradation, all of which were laid out in subsequent National Security Strategies, it did choose not to get involved when it came to prevention of large-scale mass violence. Moreover, what these two different case studies also demonstrate is that the United States was prepared to participate in preventive action but only to the extent that preventive action could be limited, that the United States would not become engaged in a larger military operation, and that the armed confrontation took place in a geographic region in which the United States had a strategic interest.

From Prevention to Pre-emption

On 11 September 2001, terrorism emerged as the central security concern of the United States which also brought a shift to the country's previous preoccupation with peace-keeping and peace-making in former conflict zones, such as for example in Bosnia and Kosovo. The ensuing »war on terror« which provided the rationale for U.S. engagement in two major armed conflicts—the war in Afghanistan and in Iraq, also interrupted the existing international discourse on conflict prevention of the 1990s, as policy attention, not only in the United States, but also in Europe, shifted toward combating terrorism.

However, while in Europe, the EU pushed ahead since the beginning of 2000 with developing and strengthening its crisis prevention and management capabilities, the United States took a different turn. For one, the Bush administration took a broad view of pre-emption by also including prevention when it adopted its new National Security Strategy in 2002. Building on a concept President Bush had articulated in a speech at West Point in June 2002, pre-emption, defined as the anticipatory use of force in the face of an imminent attack, was broadened to also encompass the use of preventive force.[11]

This policy shift toward the importance of pre-emption and preventive war did much to create a semantic confusion between the two terms – pre-emption and prevention. In the months following the release of the 2002

10 See Ackermann, *Making Peace Prevail*, 37-51.
11 Michael E. O'Hanlon, Susan E. Rice, and James B. Steinberg, »The New National Security Strategy of Preemption,« *The Brookings Institution Policy Brief*, no. 13 (December 2002).

National Security Strategy, international discourse on conflict prevention became rather muted, although it was clear that preventive action as outlined in the context of the National Security Strategy was different from the international discourse on conflict prevention that had preceded the 11 September terrorist attacks.

Second, as a result of the military campaigns against Afghanistan and Iraq, and the ensuing reconstruction efforts in those countries, the United States shifted its policy approach toward assistance in post-war reconstruction. On 5 August 2004, Secretary Powell announced the creation of the Office of the Coordinator for Reconstruction and Stabilization within the Department of State to enhance the United States' institutional capacity to respond to crises involving failing, failed, and post-conflict states and complex emergencies. The core objective of the Coordinator's Office is to co-ordinate but also to institutionalize the United States' civilian capacity to prevent or prepare for post-conflict situations, and to help stabilize and reconstruct societies in transition from conflict or civil strife. The Coordinator' Office has also developed a Post-Conflict Reconstruction Essential Tasks Matrix as a tool describing the full spectrum of tasks that the international community has to perform in a post-conflict environment. The Matrix entails aspects of post-conflict reconstruction such as providing for security, good governance and social-well being, economic reconstruction, and justice and reconciliation.[12]

Conflict Prevention By Other Means

It can thus be argued that the United States' commitment to the prevention of violent conflicts in the Bush administration has not been completely abandoned. In fact, there appears to be a shift in the approach to conflict/crisis prevention, not only in the United States, but even to some extent in Europe and in the United Nations. This shift away from interfering in the early phases of a conflict to one which centers on the prevention of the recurrence of violent conflicts through international assistance in post-war reconstruction is a crucial one. This development is also reflected in the creation of the UN Peacebuilding Commission which was supported by Europe

---

12 Office of the Coordinator for Reconstruction and Stabilization United States Department of State. »Post-Conflict Reconstruction – Essential Tasks.« (April 2005). See also, Office of the Spokesman United States Department of State. »President Issues Directive to Improve the United States' Capacity to Manage Reconstruction and Stabilization Efforts.« (14 December 2005).

and the United States equally, and which came out of the UN 2005 World Summit.[13]

Moreover, the US continues to provide support for conflict prevention activities through its Agency for International Development as well as through its engagement in regional organizations, such as the Organization for Security and Co-operation in Europe (OSCE). For example, in 2001 the U.S. Agency for International Development (USAID) and the Woodrow Wilson International Center for Scholars sponsored a joint conference with the objective to develop a new approach to foreign assistance by developing a long-term strategy which would include conflict prevention and capacity-building in societies. While the USAID has already been involved in conflict prevention through its many activities in economic development and democratization, the conference underlined that »despite numerous initiatives, U.S. Government agencies have been slow to incorporate conflict prevention in their planning process.«[14] Moreover, the conference participants advocated the creation of an early warning system for policymakers.

The OSCE, in which the United States also serves as a participating State, is recognized by its 56 participating States as a primary instrument for early warning, conflict prevention, crisis management, and post-conflict rehabilitation, making it an organization that is involved in all stages of the conflict cycle. In particular, the OSCE's emerging central focus is shifting more and more to preventing the reoccurrence of violent conflicts, primarily through post-conflict rehabilitation activities, but also through the support of reform and transition processes. In this regard, the United States has played a major role, as it has been an active supporter of long-term and sustainable peace-building activities in post-conflict environments, especially with regard to South East Europe.[15] Here, the range of preventive post-conflict and transition activities is substantial, ranging from democratization and good governance to Rule of Law to security sector reform to economic reforms to public administration to education to refugee return and facilitating inter-state co-operation in war crimes proceedings to the protection of human rights as well as rights of persons belonging to national minorities, to fighting organized crime and corruption. The United States has also been supportive of the OSCE's High Commissioner, an institution that was specifically created as an instrument of early warning and conflict preven-

---

13 See here for example, Karin L. Johnston, »The U.S. and Germany in the United Nations: Cooperation Prospects and Conflict Potential,« *AICGS Issue Brief* (July 2006).

14 US-AID. »The Role of Foreign Assistance in Conflict Prevention.« 2001 Conference Report. http://www.usaid.gov/pubs/confprev/jan2001/index.html (accessed February 16, 2007).

15 See here for example, Marc Perrin de Brichambaut, »The OSCE and South Eastern Europe,« *Cross Roads: Macedonian Foreign Policy Journal* 1, no. 1 (December 2006).

tion. Moreover, the United States remains committed to the prevention of the reoccurrence of violence in Kosovo, not only as a member of the Contact Group but also as an OSCE participating State.

Prospects for the Future: Transatlantic Cooperation in Conflict Prevention

The 2006 National Security Strategy offers some hope that the United States is willing to reach out to its European partners again, emphasizing diplomacy and democratization as well as more reliance on multilateral institutions and alliances. While pre-emption remains a part of the document, it downplays preventive war.[16] Thus, this might also be the time to reinitiate a transatlantic discourse on conflict/crisis prevention. This would entail that the United States and Europe develop together a strengthened and sustained commitment to conflict prevention, whether it is in the early phases of a violent conflict or whether it is intended to prevent the reoccurrence of conflict. Moreover, conflict/crisis prevention must become an explicit part of the security agendas of Europe and the United States with discussion being initiated on how to garner the political will and commitments as well as structural capabilities to respond to violent conflicts, especially in their early phases.

Other, more concrete areas for transatlantic cooperation can also be suggested. For one, it would be crucial to establish a transatlantic early warning network for policy makers, a prerequisite for effective preventive action. Moreover, transatlantic cooperation can be facilitated through the establishment of a lessons learned/good practices unit where information can be exchanged between the European Union and the United States on preventive engagements. To understand why some conflict prevention strategies succeed while others fail is vital for future policy guidance and for the assessment of objectives and outcomes. Also, the United States and the EU could cooperate when it comes to the training of civilian staff engaged in crisis prevention.

One can certainly think of many different avenues for transatlantic engagement. The crucial prerequisite though will be that both, Europe and the United States, will think of conflict prevention as a necessity for future international conflict management.

---

16 For a discussion on the 2006 National Security Strategy, see Philip H. Gordon, »The End of the Bush Revolution,« *Foreign Affairs* 85, no. 4 (2006); Joseph S. Nye, »Transformational Leadership and U.S. Grand Strategy,« *Foreign Affairs* 85, no. 4 (2006).

References

Ackermann, Alice. »The Changing Transatlantic Relationship: A Socio-Cultural Approach.« *International Politics* 40, no. 1 (2003): 121-136.
–. »The Idea and Practice of Conflict Prevention.« *Journal of Peace Research* 40, no. 3 (2003): 339-347.
–. *Making Peace Prevail: Preventing Violent Conflict in Macedonia.* Syracuse: Syracuse University Press, 2000.
–. »The Prevention of Armed Conflicts as an Emerging Norm in International Conflict Management: The OSCE and the UN as Norm Leaders.« *Peace and Conflict Studies* 10, no. 1 (2003): 1-13.
Boutros-Ghali, Boutros. »Agenda for Peace: PReventive Diplomacy, Peacemaking and Peacekeeping.« United Nations. Report of the Secretary General, adopted by the Summit Meeting of the Security Council, on 31 January 1992. A/47/277-S/24111. New York – United Nations. (1992).
Conflicts, Carnegie Commission on Preventing Deadly. *Preventing Deadly Conflicts: Final Report.* New York: Carnegie Cooperation, 1997.
Gordon, Philip H. »The End of the Bush Revolution.« *Foreign Affairs* 85, no. 4 (2006): 75-86.
Johnston, Karin L. »The U.S. and Germany in the United Nations: Cooperation Prospects and Conflict Potential.« *AICGS Issue Brief* (July 2006).
Nye, Joseph S. »Transformational Leadership and U.S. Grand Strategy.« *Foreign Affairs* 85, no. 4 (2006): 139-148.
O'Hanlon, Michael E., Susan E. Rice, and James B. Steinberg. »The New National Security Strategy of Preemption.« *The Brookings Institution Policy Brief*, no. 13 (December 2002): 1-8.
Perrin de Brichambaut, Marc. »The OSCE and South Eastern Europe.« *Cross Roads: Macedonian Foreign Policy Journal* 1, no. 1 (December 2006): 105-112.
Sokalski, Henry S. *An Ounce of Prevention: Macedonia and the UN Experience in Preventive Diplomacy.* Washington DC: Institute of Peace Press, 2003.
Office of the Coordinator for Reconstruction and Stabilization United States Department of State. »Post-Conflict Reconstruction - Essential Tasks.« (April 2005).
Office of the Spokesman United States Department of State. »President Issues Directive to Improve the United States' Capacity to Manage Reconstruction and Stabilization Efforts.« (14 December 2005).
US-AID. »The Role of Foreign Assistance in Conflict Prevention.« 2001 Conference Report. http://www.usaid.gov/pubs/confprev/jan2001/index.html (accessed February 16, 2007).
Woodward, Susan L. *Balkan Tragedy: Chaos and Dissolution After the Cold War.* Washington, DC: Brookings Institution Press, 1995.

About the Authors

Alice Ackermann serves as Political Officer at the OSCE's Conflict Prevention Center in Vienna where she is responsible for field operations in South-Eastern Europe. Prior to her posting at the Organization for Security and Cooperation in Europe (OSCE), she held various teaching posts in the United States and Europe, including as a professor of conflict and security studies at the George C. Marshall Center in Garmisch-Partenkirchen, Germany, a German-American governmental institution. She holds a Ph.D. in international relations and international security studies, and is an expert in the field of conflict prevention/conflict analysis. Dr. Ackermann's research has been published widely in journals such as the Journal of Conflict Studies, Security Dialogue, Peace and Change, European Security, and The International Spectator. She is the author of Making Peace Prevail: Preventing Violent Conflict in Macedonia (Syracuse University Press, 2000), and the producer of an award-winning documentary on the prevention of violent conflict, From the Shadow of History (Cinema Guild, 1997).

David Brown is a Senior Lecturer in Defence and International Affairs at the Royal Military Academy Sandhurst. His main research interests are international terrorism, the EU's internal security and policing arrangements and US foreign policy. His recent articles include: 'Defending the Fortress: Assessing the European Union's response to trafficking', European Security (2004) and 'NATO and terrorism', Contemporary Security Policy (2005). Having just completed work on his co-edited book, 'The Security Implications of EU Enlargement: Wider Europe, Weaker Europe?' (MUP, 2007), he is currently finalising his first research monograph, 'Unsteady Foundations? The European Union's counter-terrorist strategy 1991-2006' (MUP, 2008) and will subsequently be researching a co-authored comparison of contemporary US foreign policy, 'Clinton and Bush's Foreign and Security Policies: Clear Blue Water? (Routledge, 2009).

Daniel L. Byman is the Director of Georgetown's Security Studies Program and the Center for Peace and Security Studies as well as an Associate Professor in the School of Foreign Service. He is also a non-resident Senior Fellow with the Saban Center for Middle East Policy at the Brookings Institution. He has served as a Professional Staff Member with the 9/11 Commission and with the Joint 9/11 Inquiry Staff of the House and Senate Intelligence Committees. Before joining the Inquiry Staff he was the Research Director of the Center for Middle East Public Policy at the RAND Corporation. Dr. Byman has also served as an analyst on the Middle East for the U.S. government. He is the author of Deadly Connections: States that Sponsor Terrorism; Keeping the Peace: Lasting Solutions to Ethnic Conflict; and co-author of The Dynamics of Coercion: American Foreign Policy and the Limits of Military Might. He has also written widely on a range of topics related to terrorism, international security, and the Middle East.

Fraser Cameron is Director of the EU-Russia Centre, Adjunct Professor at the Hertie School of Governance, Berlin, and Senior Advisor to the European Policy Centre (EPC). A former academic and diplomat, Dr Cameron was an adviser in the European Commission for more than ten years and was closely involved in the development of the EU's external relations, including enlargement and the common foreign and security policy. He was Political Counsellor at the EU's delegation in Washington DC from 1999 to 2001. Dr Cameron has been a Visiting Professor at Bruges, Florence and Edinburgh, and has lectured widely in Europe, Asia and the US. He is the author of a number of books and articles on European and international affairs. His most recent books include 'The Future of Europe – Integration and Enlargement' (2004), 'US Foreign Policy after the Cold War' (2005) and An Introduction to EU Foreign Policy (2007) all published by Routledge.

Matthias Dembinski, born in 1958, is a senior research associate at Peace Research Institute Frankfurt (PRIF). Since 2001, he has been serving on PRIF's executive board. Before joining PRIF in 1996, Dr. Dembinski has been a research fellow at the Stiftung Wissenschaft und Politik in Ebenhausen. He has published extensively on Europe's foreign and security policy, transatlantic relations, European security issues as well as nuclear disarmament and nonproliferation. He holds a Ph.D. from Frankfurt University.

Franz Eder, born in 1980, is research assistant at the Department of Political Science, University of Innsbruck, and he is founding member of the International Security Research Group (ISRG – www.security.research.at). He was visiting research fellow at Institute for Middle East Studies in winter 2004 and at the German Institute for International and Security Affairs in spring 2005. In his research Franz Eder focuses on conflict and crises

management and the Caucasus. He is currently working on his doctoral thesis »Security in the Caucasus«.
(franz.eder@uibk.ac.at)

Daniel Hamilton is the Richard von Weizsäcker Professor and Director of the Center for Transatlantic Relations at the Paul H. Nitze School of Advanced International Studies (SAIS), Johns Hopkins University; and Executive Director of the American Consortium on EU Studies (ACES). Dr. Hamilton has held a variety of senior positions in the U.S. Department of State, including Deputy Assistant Secretary for European Affairs, responsible for NATO, OSCE and transatlantic security issues, Balkan stabilization, and Northern European issues. Dr. Hamilton has a Ph.D. and M.A. with distinction from the Johns Hopkins School of Advanced International Studies, with a concentration on U.S. Foreign Policy, European Studies and International Economics. He also was awarded a Doctor of Humanities h.c. by Concordia College in May 2002. He received his B.S.F.S magna cum laude at Georgetown University's School of Foreign Service, and studied at the University of Konstanz and at St. Olaf College.

Gerhard Mangott, born in 1966; Studies in Political Science, History, Slavonics and Philosophy at the Universities of Innsbruck and Salzburg.
Current affiliations: Professor for Political Science with the focus on International Relations and East European Affairs at the Department for Political Science at the University of Innsbruck. Senior Research Fellow on Eastern Europe Austrian Institute for International Affairs, Vienna. Lecturer at the Diplomatic Academy in Vienna.
Main research areas: Russia and Ukraine: domestic politics; foreign and security policies; US Foreign Policy; Energy Security; Transatlantic security relations.
(gerhard.mangott@uibk.ac.at)

Reinhardt Rummel, is a Lecturer in European Studies at Ludwig-Maximilians-University of Munich (LMU) and a Senior Scholar at the Centre for Applied Policy Research there. Since 1972, he has been a member of the research staff and head of the EU External Relations Department of the German Institute for International and Security Affairs in Berlin. From 1997 to 2001, he built up and directed the EU project Conflict Prevention Network (CPN) in Brussels. He received scholarships at the Center for International Affairs, Harvard University (1980-81), and at the Woodrow Wilson International Center for Scholars, Washington, D.C. (1989-90). His teaching as-

signments include the School of Advanced International Studies in Bologna (1981-82), Complutense University in Madrid (1999-2003), Canterbury University in Christchurch (2004) and Renmin University in Beijing (2006).
(reinhardt.rummel@lrz.uni-muenchen.de)

Anthony Seaboyer, born in 1975 in Fredericton, New Brunswick, Canada, is Fritz-Thyssen Fellow of the German Institute for International and Security Affairs, Berlin and member of the institutes research unit »European and Atlantic Security«. While studying Political Science, Philosophy and History, he worked for Professors at the University of Bonn and the Free University of Berlin. Between 1999 and 2004, he was a staff member or office manager for members of the German Bundestag. After working in the political section of the Canadian Embassy, Berlin, he joined the institute in 2005. He also teaches International Relations at the University of Greifswald. His research topics include Transatlantic foreign and security policies, proliferation of WMD and missile defence. Currently, he completes his doctoral thesis: »The EU as a player in international non-proliferation policy« in which he analyses the success of European non-proliferation policies towards Iran, within the NPT, and »Global Partnership«. His most recent publication is »What missile proliferation means for Europe» in *Survival* together with Dr. Oliver Thränert.

Martin Senn, born in 1978, is research assistant at the Department of Political Science, University of Innsbruck, and he is founding member of the International Security Research Group (ISRG). Martin Senn studied Political Science as well as English and American studies at the Universities of Innsbruck and Vienna. In spring 2007, he was visiting research fellow at the Peace Research Institute Frankfurt (PRIF/HSFK). In his research Martin Senn focuses on arms control, nuclear non-proliferation and emerging nuclear powers. He is currently working on his doctoral thesis »Arming to Threaten the Peace of the World. A Constructivist Approach towards the Rogue State Phenomenon.«
(martin.senn@uibk.ac.at)

Jeremy Shapiro is the research director of the Center of the United States and Europe (CUSE) at the Brookings Institution and a fellow in foreign policy studies. At CUSE, he is conducting a project on the role of Europe in the war in terrorism, the European experience with counterterrorism at home, and the lessons for the United States. Prior to Brookings, he worked as a policy analyst at RAND in Washington, DC from 1997 to 2002. At RAND, he researched and wrote on a variety of national security issues for the U.S. Army, the U.S. Air Force and the Office of the Secretary of Defense, including information warfare, terrorism, homeland security, and political constraints on the use of force. Mr. Shapiro has also held positions at the National Defense University, at SAIC, and at the Oracle Corporation. He has a B.A. in Computer Science from Harvard University, an M.A. in International Relations and International Economics from the Johns Hopkins School of Advanced International Studies, and is a Ph.D. candidate in Political Science at MIT.

Derek D. Smith, a recent graduate of Yale Law School, received an A.B. in Government from Harvard University and a D.Phil. in International Relations from Oxford University as a Keasbey Scholar. He has written articles on nonproliferation issues for *Security Studies*, the *Yale Journal of International Affairs*, the *Korean Journal of Defense Analysis*, and the *Korea Herald*. Derek has worked at the U.S. State Department, the National Defense University, and the U.S. Department of Justice. He has also taught international security courses at Oxford, Yale, and American University. He currently serves as a law clerk to Judge Randolph on the United States Court of Appeals for the District of Columbia Circuit.

Oliver Thränert, born in 1959 in Braunschweig, is Head of the Research Unit »European and Atlantic Security« at the German Institute for International and Security Affairs in Berlin. Prior to this appointment, Dr. Thränert was a Senior Research Fellow of the Department of Foreign Policy Research, Friedrich Ebert Foundation, in Bonn (1986-1999) and Berlin (1999-2001). From 1990 to 1993 he also served as a lecturer for International Relations at the University of Darmstadt. In spring 2000, Dr. Thränert taught at the Free University of Berlin. In the summer of 1991, Dr. Thränert was a Visiting Research Fellow at the Center of International Relations, Queen's University, Kingston/Ontario. In addition to his numerous scientific publications, Dr. Thränert frequently appears on German TV and radio stations as an expert and provides articles in German newspapers such as *Frankfurter Allgemeine Zeitung, Frankfurter Rundschau, Financial Times Deutschland, Handelsblatt* and *Die Welt*. Main research topics include the proliferation of nuclear, biological and chemical weapons; arms control in general; and missile defenses.